NAVAJO INDIAN

HOPI IND. RES.

Ft. Defiance

RESERVATION

COCONINO

Peach Springs

Williams

SAN FRANCISCO PEAKS

Flagstaff

Winslow

Holbrook

①

APACHE

Colorado River

Little Colorado

Colorado

Jerome

YAVAPAI

Camp Verde

NAVAJO

River

Springerville

Prescott

Date Creek

SKULL VALLEY

LONESOME VALLEY

PEEPLES VALLEY

BRADSHAW MTS.

Bumble Bee

Pine

Payson

MOGOLLONS

WHITE MOUNTAIN

Iliams Fork

UA HALAS

Wickenburg

⑤

Ft. McDowell

Phoenix

Verde R.

MAZATZALS

SIERRA ANCHAS

Cherry Cr.

GILA

APACHE

Ft. Apache

IND. RES.

Black R.

SAN CARLOS

INDIAN

MARICOPA

Salt R.

Salt

⑯

Globe

San Carlos

RES.

Gillette

⑱ ⑰

Miami

Geronimo

GREENLEE

Blue R.

EAGLE TAIL RANGE

Maricopa Wells

⑫ ③

Adamsville

Florence

Gila

San Aravaipa Cr.

⑮ Clifton

River

⑩

iente River

Gila Bend

Maricopa

Coolidge

⑬

San Pedro

GRAHAM

Camp Grant

PAPAGO

PINAL

Santa Cruz

⑭

Ajo

INDIAN

MONTEZUMA HEAD

⑧ PIMA

RES.

Ft. Lowell

Rillito Cr.

CATALINAS

Willcox

DRAGOONS

Bowie

Camp Bowie

San Xavier

Tucson

④

COCHISE

⑦

Ft. Buchanan

SANTA RITAS

SONOITA VALLEY

Ft. Crittenden

⑨

Fairbank

⑪

Tombstone

Turkey Cr.

Arivaca

Tubac

SANTA CRUZ

Calabasas

HUACHUCAS

Camp Wallen

Bisbee

Nogales

# ARIZONA: THE LAST FRONTIER

# ARIZONA.

# THE LAST

# FRONTIER

BY

## JOSEPH MILLER

WITH DRAWINGS BY

## ROSS SANTEE

HASTINGS HOUSE          PUBLISHERS          NEW YORK

COPYRIGHT 1956 BY HASTINGS HOUSE PUBLISHERS, INC.

Library of Congress Catalog Card Number: 56-12351

Published simultaneously in Canada by
S. J. Reginald Saunders, Publishers, Toronto 2B

Printed in the United States of America

# FOREWORD

Arizona: The Last Frontier is offered as a companion piece to The Arizona Story, which was published toward the end of 1952. The first volume apparently served to whet the appetite of many of its readers for more of the early newspaper stories and accounts of Arizona's turbulent formative years; at any rate, there have been quite a number of requests from different quarters for "more of the same." The present collection has been compiled in response to these requests and in the hope that it will, at least in part, satisfy the demand.

In The Arizona Story the chief emphasis was on incidents and characters not too well known to the general public; consequently, the more familiar personalities and happenings were touched upon, if at all, in no great detail. Now, however, it appears that the public is eager to hear more concerning these very subjects about which much has already been written and narrated; people interested in frontier lore want to learn more about these fabulous characters and the sensational happenings in which they played such prominent parts. Accordingly, in this volume, we have included a rather comprehensive coverage of events that were only referred to casually in The Arizona Story—such as the Riverside holdup, perpetrated by the notorious Red Jack gang, as well as legends and newspaper reports anent the Lost Dutchman Mine and the weird Superstition Mountain country. Because we have had access to hitherto untapped sources, we believe that we have been able to throw new light on these subjects.

Also, considerable space is devoted to some of the vendettas between various noted frontier editors. The billingsgate fired back and forth by early journalists was a unique phenomenon. Such vituperation has become a lost art. Even in years when furious electoral campaigns are raging, editors nowadays hold their pens in leash, at least in comparison with the unbridled editors of that early era. Contemporary editorials would have appeared pallid and anemic to both newspapermen and readers of those more robust times. And certainly controversy between editors nowadays does not appear to climax in fusillades from six-shooters. But journalism in Arizona in the frontier era was on a personal basis and bitterly vindictive, and sometimes journalistic feuds climaxed on the field of honor, although they seldom had lethal results. Moreover, it was not unusual for an indignant reader who considered himself the object of editorial insult to allow himself the luxury of a pot shot at the offending editor. The resort was to direct action rather than to tedious legal process. In any case, the readers could not complain of ennui when they read through their newspapers. For the muty files of the early press record those conflicts in eager and meticulous detail.

In addition to these matters, we believe that readers of the present volume will find a considerable amount of new material concerning lesser-known events and frontier activities. They will find a good deal of blood and thunder, too. Indeed, if they didn't, they would surely be disappointed. For what else, in a picture of Arizona's hectic past, would they expect to find? And what else stands out more vividly in the record of those times? The newspapers were full of it; they devoted almost as much space to deeds of violence and mayhem as to the Indian troubles (which, by the way, are not covered in this volume, since they were dealt with pretty exhaustively in the earlier one). With practically nonexistent—or very sketchy—law enforcement; with lawless elements frequently in full control, swaggering along the streets, crowding into saloons; with pistols perpetually cocked for shooting out the lights, at the mildest, and boring holes in innocent bystanders at the worst; in such circumstances, what could you expect but gun fights, stabbings, and wanton killings?

Today this all seems picturesque, romantic, exciting. But to the sober, substantial citizens who came to settle in the Territory, it was necessary for sheer survival to put an end to this lawless chaos. With the coming of the new element of responsible people and the arrival of the railroads, law and order, sometimes by way of vigilante justice, gradually emerged.

Those days are but a memory in the minds of the pioneers who still survive; there are only a few of them left to bear witness to the bloody and tragic drama of that era, and soon they too will have passed away. It would seem fitting, therefore, that some of the lore and color of the old frontier should be preserved so that future generations may realize how great were the trials and tribulations of the men and women who opened up the frontier of Arizona and established civilization there so that we who come after them might prosper and progress.

As in The Arizona Story, the accounts in the following pages are presented almost exactly as they appeared in the early Arizona newspapers; we have made such minor emendations as changing the tense, transposing an occasional paragraph for the sake of clarity, deleting brief passages containing irrelevant material, and correcting a few typographical errors. These accounts have been taken from the more than six thousand volumes of files preserved in the vaults of the Department of Library and Archives in the State Capitol at Phoenix. For access to these files and permission to use them, we offer our thanks to Mulford Winsor, Director, and Alice B. Good, Librarian, of the Department.

We also want to express our gratitude to Ross Santee, who has so greatly added to the interest of these pages with his drawings. Ross Santee has done perhaps more than anyone else, by his drawings and stories, to preserve for posterity the Arizona scene of yesteryear and of our own times as well. We consider it a rare privilege to have had his friendship and wise guidance through the years.

Arizona will always be a land to engage people's interest, not only because of its fantastic past but also because of its ever-enduring scenic beauty and its promise of great things to come. This writer can think of no more fitting conclusion to these remarks than a few lines, signed by "R. H. S.," which appeared in the Arizona Citizen in 1878, in that time printed and published in Florence:

## ARIZONA

Astounding land of weird and mystic scenes,
  Round all thy hopes strange horrors cling unspoken.
In Canyons deep and by thy flashing streams
  Zealous sons sleep the sleep that ne'er is broken.
On in their footsteps let us press unfailing,
  Now is the flood-tide of thy future sea,
And thousands seek a thousand gifts from thee.

JOSEPH MILLER

# CONTENTS

# 1

# THE FORMATIVE YEARS

## ARIZONA: THE LAST FRONTIER

With all the hardships and privations which people have to encounter who lead the van as the star of the empire takes its march across the continent, there is still a charm in frontier life. There is a boundless freedom in the broad expanse of land which man has not yet fenced in and parceled out in metes and bounds, and there is exhilaration in breathing the free, pure air, not yet contaminated by the thousand and one foul vapors that are continually going up from thickly settled regions.

True, the early settlers of any new country are necessarily deprived of many of the luxuries and conveniences to which they were accustomed in their old homes, and we often hear them sigh for those homes and the scenes of their youth.

Discontented friends, you would do no such thing if you lived many years on the frontier. We have known thousands who have talked just the same way, and a number of them did return to their old homes, but none who have lived many years on the frontier, were contented to stay there. All who could, returned to the frontier settlements, and those who could not, pined away and died. Man is never contented, and it is not in the nature of things that he should be. There never was a perfectly contented man or woman on earth, and there never will be. We are always seeking and striving and hoping for something better—and this is the main-spring of all life and progress. If everything that we have aspired and hoped for could be given to us at once, we would be the most miserable creatures imaginable. . . . the human mind is so constituted, that to make life tolerable, there must be something ahead to seek for and hope for and work to obtain.

We are told in history that Alexander the Great had a burning ambition to conquer the whole world. He thought that if he could accomplish that feat he would be supremely happy and contented and have nothing more to desire. Well, he did conquer all that was then known as the world. Was he happy and contented? No. He sat down and cried, because there were no more worlds to conquer!

During our residence in Arizona we have known many men to become disheartened, disgusted and tired of waiting for all drawbacks to be overcome and the Territory to start in a full career of prosperity. We have known some of these men to lose all faith in the ultimate righting of things, and in doleful accents deplore their luck in ever coming to such a country, wish themselves out of it, and that the Territory might sink, and so on. We have known some of this class of men to leave the Territory, and more who would have left, but they were too poor to pay for transportation out, and too lazy to walk, and are to this day eternally growling and cursing the Territory. This class of men never do any good to any country. They are the warts and tubercles of society, and they are about as much use in performing the part of true pioneers in building up civilization in a new country as those effeminate and effete young men who part their hair in the middle.

But there is another class of men, who, while disheartened by the slow progress made in the Territory in consequence of the long protracted Indian war, left the country and returned to the homes of their youth. But they are coming back. Almost every stage and steamer bring some of them. Having once breathed the pure and exhilarating air of Arizona, even the hallowed associations of the home of their childhood cannot hold them, and as a rule, all who have the means to return, do so. We say this is the rule, and we can bring hundreds to testify to the truth of the assertion, and we defy contradiction.

Yes, they come back, and some of them bring young wives with them, and some who had already wives and children at their old homes, bring them with them. This is the foundation of civilization and progress, and without this blessed element there can be no true progress. . . . Take away the influence of virtuous homes; take away the sacred guards that surround the domestic fireside, where husband and wife, brother and sister meet, the only type of Heaven on earth, and where would be civilization? Gone! Hopelessly gone!

Yes, they come back, and they are welcome. May they continue to come back, and bring as many with them as possible, especially of the gentle sex, who will find big hearts and open arms ready to receive them, and help to build up a civilization worthy of our great and rich Territory.

What Arizona needs now is energy. Not merely in one direction nor in two, but in every direction that will tend to develop her resources. Whether it be in mining, mechanical, agricultural, grazing or mercantile pursuits, still the great want is energy.

The Indian war, that great incubus that hung like a pall for so many years, thank God, ceased. For many years men were excusable for an apparent loss of energy, for failing to enter heartily into the various avocations that tend to make a new and wild country habitable, and fit to be a home for civilized man. Because Arizona was a land of blood, and every road and mountain pass was besieged by the savage and bloodthirsty foe. Hundreds of brave and resolute men, who were not to be turned back by any obstacle, paid the penalty of their energy with their lives. And many a home in other states and other lands was made desolate by the death of husband, father or son, at the hands of the Apaches. But happily, that state of things no longer exists.

The Indians are under the control of the military power, and are placed on reservations, where they will be taken care of, and will not be permitted again to roam the country and scatter death and desolation in their path. Only a few renegade savages remain at

large to endanger the lives of isolated parties in remote districts, and those few are being fast hunted down and will soon cease to exist.

However, something must be done to protect our citizens from the murderers and robbers who infest our border. We have a long line of frontier extending from near San Diego, California to Mesilla, New Mexico—a route upon which the United States mails are carried and upon which there are stations at long distances apart. These stations are absolutely necessary for feeding and changing horses of the mail coaches and providing sustenance for the passengers and drivers. Without these stations the mails could not be carried and passengers could not travel, and all life of man and beast would perish for want of water. The life these poor isolated station-keepers lead, is hard enough at best. Often only one man is at a station, because the income will support no more. He sees no one until the stage or some wagon comes along to break, momentarily, the monotony of his miserable solitude. In this manner these stations are kept, until some marauding party, seeing the defenseless situation of the keepers, pounce upon them and rob or murder, and sometimes both, and taking what they can find of money, horses, or other valuables, cut across over the line and are safe.

These things have occurred so often that it seems as though the Government should take some measures to protect our citizens along and near the line. Patrol stations could easily be established, and no great force of men required to protect the whole line.

The soil in the neighborhood of nearly every station between Yuma and Tucson is red with the blood of our peaceful citizens, slain by these hounds from over the border, who sometimes did not spare even women and children, and their robberies are countless. These bandits never attack the mail coaches or travelers on the road, but they watch their opportunity when the station-keepers are alone and unprotected, and then do their work quickly and are off for Sonora. Something must be done to stop this thing, and that speedily, for forbearance has ceased to be a virtue.

The time has come when men should throw off the supineness and lethargy engendered during the years of doubt, perplexity and danger, and put their shoulders to the wheels of progress and advance united until Arizona shall teem with all the blessings of a happy and refined civilization, and "the desert be made bloom like the rose." This happy consummation is within our reach. But we can only gain it by energy. Sloth and inactivity never overcome the difficulties to be encountered in the settlement and development of a new country. Idleness and its handmaid, vice, never accomplished any good. . . .

The people of the frontier, while they should as far as possible feel contented with their lot, have much to look forward to and much to hope for, and they have a great responsibility in shaping the destinies of the future State. This is a responsibility from which we may not shrink, and it is every man's business and duty to enter into it with energy and zeal, that we so improve upon the elements that kind Nature has so profusely spread around us as to make our Territory the home of a virtuous and happy population, contented as far as possible, but remembering that we will always have something higher and better to look forward to and hope for.

Then men of Arizona, awake! Arise! Come out of the slough of despondency! Now is the accepted time. Now is the time for action. By energy we will succeed and have a happy home in Arizona.

—Yuma Sentinel

The foregoing is quite appropriate as a prologue to the drama of the early years of the Territory that is set forth in the present volume. It was compiled from a series of editorials in the Yuma Sentinel, written by that publication's owner and editor, Judge William J. Berry, during the years 1873-76. Judge Berry was renowned as a good lawyer, expert gunsmith, and learned newspaperman; he sometimes practiced his three professions separately, sometimes simultaneously. As a philosopher he had no peer among Arizona's early-day editors. He wrote with fire and enthusiasm and a burning sense of loyalty to this newly settled land, an ardent loyalty which was generously reflected in the issues of his newspaper. He knew his subject matter well, for he had come to Arizona in 1862, a year before the arrival of the party of officials delegated to set up the territorial government, and he traveled over the entire region, then very sparsely populated, from north to south. More of Judge Berry later.

## THE BIRTH OF ARIZONA

A thumbnail sketch of how Arizona came into being should prove interesting to those unfamiliar with its early history. Arizona is a new, yet very old, land. It had been inhabited for hundreds of years prior to the coming of the white man. Throughout its broad expanse are found ruins of prehistoric cities and relics of past cultures which in themselves have a fabulous story. But to come down to the nineteenth century and civil government: The act making Arizona a territory was passed in February of 1863, and the officials of the new territory were appointed by President Lincoln the following month. When the governor's party arrived at Navajo Springs, several miles inside the present boundary line, in December, 1863, it set up camp there. But members of the expedition are said to have been in grave doubt as to whether they were actually within the boundaries of the zone taken from New Mexico for the new Territory. The party hesitated before taking the action, authorized by Congress, that would bring Arizona into existence. Although it was argued that the divide had undoubtedly been crossed the day before, no instruments were available by which the actual metes and bounds could be determined. However, the officials, after scanning the horizon from an elevated point, finally decided that the site was within the limits of what was to be Arizona. They chose Navajo Springs for the inaugural ceremony because there was an abundance of water there for the official party and the few troopers of the New Mexico cavalry who acted as an escort against possible Indian ambush.

Secretary Richard C. McCormick made the following brief remarks, which, in effect, signalized the birth of Arizona on December 29, 1863:

> Gentlemen: As the properly qualified officer it becomes my duty to inaugurate the proceedings of the day. After a long and trying journey, we have arrived within the limits of the Territory of Arizona. These broad plains and hills form a part of the district over which, as the representatives of the United

States, we are to form a civil government. Happily, although claimed by those now in hostility to the Federal arms, we take possession of the territory without resort to military force. The flag which I hoist in token of military authority is no new and untried banner. For nearly a century it has been the honored, the loved emblem of law and liberty. From Canada to Mexico, from the Atlantic to the Pacific, millions of strong arms are raised in its defense, and above the efforts of all foreign or domestic foes it is destined to live untarnished and transcendent.

The flag was raised, cheers given, and prayers offered. Secretary McCormick then administered the oath of office to Chief Justice William F. Turner and Associate Justices Joseph P. Allyn and John T. Howell, and Governor John N. Goodwin took the official oath before the Chief Justice and caused to be read a proclamation in both English and Spanish. The weather was cold, and the last rays of a December sun lingered upon the peaks of San Francisco Mountain when, for the first time, the Stars and Stripes floated in the air of Arizona Territory by virtue of civil authority.

In addition to the new territorial officers, with their three freight wagons and military escort, the party included a score of civilians on horseback, who came to "grow up" with the country.

Two days were devoted to organizing the new Territory and to the customary legal procedures. But the location of the permanent seat of government had yet to be decided upon. Governor Goodwin had originally started for Tucson, then the largest settlement in Arizona, intending to establish the capital there. He was diverted from this course, however, by the commanding general at Fort Union, New Mexico, whose advice to start a new American center in northern Arizona was heeded. The decision was apparently made to avoid any trouble with Confederate sympathizers in southern Arizona.

On the third day after the party's arrival at Navajo Springs the trek westward started, and finally Chino valley, some twenty miles north of the present site of Prescott, was reached. Here the party went into temporary camp in order to start the governmental machinery moving for the future. In the meantime, the party was in doubt as to where it was, officially speaking. Adobe walls had been put up and Fort Whipple [1] established as a protection against attack by Indians, and a camp was crudely built and arrangements made in order to begin business.

Finally from Washington came advices to locate the seat of government of Arizona on Granite Creek, for this site had been reported upon favorably in the survey made several months before. The official order was accordingly issued by Governor Goodwin from his "office" in Chino valley, and early in 1864 the territorial government, along with Fort Whipple, was moved to the new site on Granite Creek, where a little mining community already existed. Here the first contract to be made in Arizona was signed, sealed, and delivered for the erection of the gubernatorial mansion. The site chosen was among the pines amid scenes of great beauty, and a clearing was made and building commenced.

The building was constructed of logs, cut and hewed near the site and sawed entirely by hand. The carpenters were compelled to pursue their labors with one eye on their work and the other keeping a keen lookout for Indians, then known to be lurking near by among the pines. On one occasion all the members of a band of redskins were killed within two hundred yards of the building just as they were preparing to massacre the men at work. The structure to house the official party had eight rooms downstairs, with floors of tamped earth. The big upper story was reached by a ladder and was used as a bedroom by all comers who had blankets or bedrolls to spread on the rough board floor. The old governor's mansion still stands in Prescott, which was the name the citizens selected for the new capital in honor of the American writer and authority on Aztec and Spanish-American history.

Before the gubernatorial party "broke up" in Chino valley, the first newspaper to be published in what was now officially Arizona, the Arizona Miner, was born at that place and was printed on a press brought along by Secretary McCormick. The date of the first issue was March 9, 1864. It was heralded as filling "a long felt want." About three months later, after six issues, the little Ramage

[1] This was the new army post which Major E. B. Willis, of the California Column, was building in Chino valley, some twenty miles north of Prescott, for the safety of the miners who were busily at work in that region.

press and the "handful" of paper and material were packed on a few mules and the outfit moved to Prescott; it was unloaded there on Granite Street and the press was installed in a single-room log hut. It was the official organ of the Territory, published at semi-monthly intervals during its early years at the subscription price of $7.50 per annum, payable in advance. After the first year a number of subscribers fell delinquent and were harshly dealt with in the columns of the newspaper.

A vast amount of business faced the official party of the Territory, and many vexatious matters piled up from all sections for immediate consideration. Arizona was divided into three judicial districts, a census was taken, and an election held for members of a legislative assembly. The first legislature was convened in the fall of 1864 so that a code of laws might be promulgated.

The inrush from the east and west began as soon as the news of territorial organization became generally known, for it was now felt that some element of protection was now available in this mineral-rich region where numerous placer gold deposits had been discovered.

Freighters and businessmen followed the incoming miners as the need for goods and services became apparent, and from a few hundred hardy souls in the beginning, by the end of 1864 the population had increased manyfold and a fairly bustling little town had grown up on the banks of Granite Creek. Prescott, at any rate, got onto the map as the capital of the big domain but lost the honor in 1867 when, through legislative maneuvering, Tucson clipped along the track as a winner and the capital was moved to the southern metropolis. But the tide turned again ten years later and the seat of government came back to Prescott; in 1889 it was shifted again, this time to Phoenix, where it has remained ever since.

It was thus that Arizona came into existence. And then, after almost fifty years, the latter half of which saw a desperate struggle for statehood, she finally became a star on the flag as the last of the old territories of the Union: Arizona, the forty-eighth State, February 14th, 1912.

# 2

# TOWNS OF THE FRONTIER

In the early days of Arizona many camps and towns sprang up here and there, most of them of the overnight variety, with the news of a gold, silver, or copper strike. Most of these were just a huddle of tents, at least in their beginnings. Others came into being as stage stations or ports of call along the Colorado River and, later on, as locations along the newly built railroad lines. Some of these towns boomed and then died when the ore gave out or when the stage line was abandoned, or from some other cause which robbed them of their reason for existing. Other towns prospered and grew, steadily and substantially, while some just managed to keep going. Of various Arizona towns we have selected six of unusual interest which are still with us today and five that have vanished from the face of the desert and mountainside, back into the dust and rocks from whence they were born.

Of the living communities, many of which also figure in later chapters, we have chosen first old Tucson, quoting stories told by some of her earlier pioneers. Tucson is said to be one of the three oldest settlements in the United States. Since its beginning as a walled fort, it has progressed through the years to become Arizona's second largest city, second only to Phoenix, the state capital, a city of metropolitan proportions.

Then there is Tubac, forty-five miles south of Tucson, near the Mexican border, a very old town. We have an interesting story by Charles D. Poston about his experiences there. Tubac was a presidio, garrisoned by the Spanish, in 1752 and a pueblo and mission in 1814. In 1858 the population of the town was about 800, nearly all Mexicans, with a sprinkling of Indians. In 1866, the California Volunteers camped here, and about that time it was headquarters for the Santa Rita Mining Company.

In 1853 J. Ross Browne visited Tubac, and in his Adventures in the Apache Country he mentions that he found the old town almost abandoned, but that the houses were in good shape; his party occupied some of them for a time. When he returned to Tubac ten years later he found it to be a "city of ruin and desolation."

The first Arizona newspaper, The Arizonian, was established here in 1859. The little press was brought in by a mining company which was active in the vicinity at the time.

Charles D. Poston, since called "The Father of Arizona," played an active roll in Arizona's development. He spent the winter of 1854 prospecting the hills above Tubac, and a few years later he was appointed alcalde and placed in complete charge of the town's various governmental functions. In the Arizona State Guide is a passage Poston wrote about the community: "We had no law but love, and no occupation but labor; no government, no taxes, no public debt, no politics. It was a community in a perfect state of nature."

Today Tubac is a cluster of adobe houses, built around a white-plastered church. A few of the old pioneer families still live there, as well as an artist or two. There is an inn, and the place is quite a tourist attraction.

Then there is Bisbee. In the remote year of 1905—remote as Arizona history goes—a Tucson reporter attended a baseball game in what was then a rugged mining camp and duly recorded his impressions of the town. These may not be altogether gratifying to the booster group of today's Bisbee, which has become a great copper-producing center. Nevertheless, they pretty reliably describe what the place was like then, for even a superficial glance through the columns of contemporary newspapers will establish that in most of his account, which we reprint in the following pages, the visiting newspaperman was sticking pretty much to the facts.

The Phoenix Herald carried the following item in 1888: "The town of Bisbee, in Cochise county, some distance below Tombstone, is probably the hardest camp in the southwest. Shooting scrapes occur there every few days."

Kelvin also comes in for a story uncovering one facet of her early days written by the same Tucson reporter, who visited that camp in 1907. His account undoubtedly could have been descriptive of many a frontier settlement in the Southwest. Kelvin was one of the colorful camps in the copper-rich Ray mining district, below Superior in east-central Arizona. Named for Lord Kelvin of England by English capitalists who had just purchased the district, it had its beginning in 1898 when the company built a mill and surveyed a townsite at the junction of Mineral Creek and the Gila River. The millsite was connected with the mine by a seven-mile narrow-gauge railroad.

McClintock's History of Arizona says:

> Old-timers find keen joy in telling the story of Kelvin at its birth. It appears as though all the younger sons of the English stockholders had to be provided with jobs, irrespective of capacity or knowledge. The trails were full of very correctly attired young fellows, riding pad saddles on dock-tailed ponies. Where the material yard and warehouse should have gone at Kelvin, on the only level spot available, were tennis courts. There is authority for the statement that the office force "knocked off" daily for an hour for afternoon tea.

The English company held the property for but a short time, selling out to other interests and leaving the country, probably to the delight of the miners of the district.

A Phoenix Republican reporter visited the Ray-Kelvin district in 1907, and his views were published in the Florence Tribune. He wrote, in part:

There are three saloons now in Kelvin, and three more at Ray. It is understood the company proposes to keep a limit on the saloon business about where it is, especially in the Ray camp. If a man feels that he must get drunk he can go down to Kelvin and buy all he wants, without interfering with those who are working.

When Kelvin became a station on the Southern Pacific railroad line, activities at Ray began to expand and the railroad company changed the name to Ray Junction, although to this day the name of the post office remains Kelvin. The mill was relocated at near-by Hayden some years ago, and today Kelvin, although but a ghost of her former self, is one of a group of small mining communities in the Ray mining district.

Benson, about fifty miles east of Tucson, was an important early shipping point for mines around Tombstone. First called Benson City, it was a stage station where the old Butterfield stages crossed the San Pedro River and later was a railroad center, named for a guest of the president of the Southern Pacific upon the occasion of a visit of inspection to the town's site in 1880.

The Arizona State Guide says of Benson: "Cowboys, miners, and Mexicans still frequent this town that for many years was filled with saloons, tinhorns, rustlers, hustlers, cribs, and crap games." The story on Benson presented in this group was originally printed in a Tucson newspaper in 1906 and highlights the peculiar aspects of the town's architecture.

Modern Benson is in the heart of a fine grazing country. Near by is the extensive Apache Powder Company, manufacturers of high explosives for use in mining operations.

Then there is fair Florence—the early accounts always were kind to Florence, one of the oldest settlements in the state, perhaps because of the charming connotations of its name. In the early days Florence must have been a rather delightful place, but it was also full of the old deviltry, too, so common to many of the frontier settlements.

Today Florence, the seat of Pinal County, unlike Tucson and others of the older towns, still has almost all of its early adobe buildings. The state prison is at Florence.

Of the many vanished towns in Arizona's history, we present accounts of Adamsville, Weaver, Ehrenberg, Galeyville, and Calabasas. It is needless to say anything here by way of introduction to these towns, as the reprinted stories do ample justice to their boom days and offer a few samples of the outlawry and consequent terror that prevailed in many of the frontier settlements during Arizona's past.

## IN OLD TUCSON

"A fine little town you have here," said a Boston man to an Arizona pioneer in the 1880's, "but I'll be blasted if we Eastern fellows know how to pronounce its name. We in Boston have had more heated discussions about how to properly pronounce the word. I called it Tucksin down at the hotel and the whole lobby gave me a laugh; how do you pronounce it, friend?"

"We call it Too-sawn, with the accent on the 'sawn,'" said the old pioneer, lustily, and that's about the way it is.

Henry Morgan, an early-day trader among the Pima Indians, was an authority on their language and was court interpreter for them. He had this to say in the Phoenix Republican in 1891:

> The word Tucson, as we call it, is pronounced by the Pimas, Tchuc-sone. It means black spring or black water. The Pimas have a legend that the devil arose out of the Gila laguna, and that the whole tribe chased him until he disappeared in a water hole of the Santa Cruz River, where Tucson now is.

In connection with the Pima pronunciation of Tucson, it might be said that the Mexicans of the Old Pueblo, as Tucson is often called, and also those below the border, pronounce the word Took-sone, a pronunciation quite similar to that of the Pimas.

There has always been some question as to whether Tucson, St. Augustine, or Santa Fe is the oldest settlement made by Europeans in the United States, but the fact that Tucson is one of them seems, in itself, satisfaction enough without attempting to prove which might be the oldest. It is sufficient to say that four flags have flown over this settlement—the Spanish, Mexican, Confederate, and Union.

In 1873 the Tucson Citizen published an interesting story of early times in the Old Pueblo. In the late 1700's the town provided some measure of protection and security to the inhabitants there against attacks by marauding bands of Apache Indians who infested the area. Following are the words of the reporter:

We met an old lady who is supposed to be over one hundred years old and was born in Tucson. Her name is Mariana Dias, and from her we obtained several historical items relative to old times which were interesting to us. She says as long ago as she can remember Tucson consisted of a military post, surrounded by a corral (wall), and that there were but two or three houses outside of it. The country was covered with horses and cattle and on many of the trails they were so plenty that it was quite inconvenient to get through the immense herds. They were only valued for the hides and tallow, and a good sized steer was only worth three dollars.

This country then belonged to the government of Spain and the troops were paid in silver coin, and on all the coins the name of Ferdinand I was engraved, and money was quite plenty. Goods such as they required were brought from Sonora on pack animals. They had in those days no carts or wagons. The fields in front of and below Tucson were cultivated and considerable grain was also raised on the San Pedro, and with an abundance of beef and the grain they raised, they always had an ample supply.

They had no communication with California, and she never knew there was such a country until she had become an old woman. San Xavier del Bac Mission was built as long ago as she can remember, and the church in the valley in front of town; and there was also a church on Courthouse Square, which has gone to ruin and no trace is left of it.

The priests were generally in good circumstances and were supported by receiving a portion of the annual products, but for marriages, burials, baptisms and other church duties, they did not ask or receive any pay.

On inquiry about the Apaches she spoke with considerable feeling and said that many efforts had been made for peace with them, but every attempt had resulted in failure; that whatever promises they made, but a few days would pass before they proved treacherous and commenced murder and robbery again; that they murdered her husband in the field about two miles below Tucson, and that most of her relatives had gone in the same way, and that she was now left alone.

She relates the circumstances of one peace that was made about ninety years hence. It seems the Apaches got the worst of a fight on the Arivaca ranch. Several were killed and the son of a chief was taken prisoner and brought to Tucson, and the Indians opened negotiations to obtain this boy. The Colonel in command of the Spanish forces agreed with them that on a certain day the Indians should all collect here, and to prevent treachery and being overpowered, he brought in at night and concealed within the walls of the fort all the men he could get from all the towns within 150 miles. On the day appointed the Indians came in vast numbers; all the plains around were black with them. The Colonel then told them if they had come on a mission of peace they must lay down their arms and meet him as friends. They complied with his request and then all the people inside the walls went among them unarmed. The Colonel gave them one hundred head of cattle, and the boy prisoner was brought out and given to his father and they embraced each other and cried, and an era of reconciliation and peace seemed to have arrived. The boy told his father that he liked his captors so well that he desired to live with them, and in spite of all the persuasions of the old man he still insisted on remaining, and the Indians were compelled to return to their mountain home without him. The boy was a great favorite with the people. Some time afterward he went to visit his people, but before leaving he saw every one in the village and bade them goodbye, and promised and did return in fifteen days. A few days subsequent to his return he took the smallpox and died, and very soon afterward the Apaches commenced to murder and rob the same as before.

Our informant then remarked with a good deal of feeling that since her earliest recollection she had heard it frequently said that we were going to have peace with the Apaches, but every hope had been broken and she did not believe we should ever have peace as long as an Apache lived. When she was a girl they made two attempts to take Tucson. The first time the soldiers and males were nearly all away. The Apaches found it out and took advantage of their absence and attacked the town, and would have taken it and murdered every one in it, but for the timely assistance of the Pima and Pagapo Indians who came to the rescue in large numbers, and attacking the Apaches on two sides, killed some of them and drove them off. The next time the sentinel on the hill in front of town discovered them coming and gave the alarm, and after a severe fight the Indians were repulsed. They did not have guns in those days and were armed with spears, bows and arrows.

She referred to the pleasant times they used to have, when their wants were few and easily supplied, and told how they danced and played and enjoyed themselves. We asked her if she thought the people were more happy then than now, but she did not seem inclined to make comparisons, but remarked that if it had not been

for the Apaches they would hardly have known what trouble was; that crime was almost unknown, and she never knew any one to be punished more severely than by being confined in the stocks for a few days; that the laws of the village required all strangers, unless they were of established reputation, to engage in some labor or business within three days after their arrival or leave the town, and to this regulation she attributes their exemption from crime. On inquiry as to whether they had liquor in those days, she said that she never knew a time when there was not plenty of mescal, but that it was only on rare occasions that they drank to excess, and then they acted to each other like brothers.

*The Tucson Citizen related in 1898 that Sam Hughes and nine others first entered Tucson in March, 1858:*

They went into camp at the foot of what is Alameda street. As they had previously heard much of the town they were early astir. Their first greeting however was from an American who entered camp in clothes of fashionable cut, wearing a plug hat and swinging a little cane. He informed the astonished campers that his name was Robinson; that he was a southern gentleman and was traveling for his health. He joined them in a little booze and gave them the news of the country so far as he could.

Camp was made near the spring from which the town drew its water supply and no sooner had day fairly dawned than the maids and matrons of the town began to troop to the spring. On seeing the Americans all involuntarily covered their faces with their *rebozos* [ray-bo'-thos], leaving nothing but their bright eyes visible to the disappointment of the Americans.

The town was at that time confined to what is now known as "Court Plaza." There were three stores in the place; two butcher shops where meat was sold by the *vara*, and two blacksmith shops, but in neither one could a wagon tire be welded and put on.

Several white men were then living there and the day was passed in visiting around and at night the newcomers were entertained with a *baile* [bah'-e-lay]. The whole village was there, men, women, children and Indians. All attending had either to sit on the ground or bring a piece of rawhide or sheepskin with them. The dance was

a pleasant one and was, Mr. Hughes says, as thoroughly enjoyed as
any dance of today.

*Fred G. Hughes, another of Tucson's earlier residents, told of the
Old Pueblo in the Tucson Star of 1904:*

It is just forty-two years ago yesterday (May 20, 1862) that the
California column entered and took possession of Tucson, the Con-
federates evacuating and retreating toward the Rio Grande. There
are not many of the present residents of Tucson who are aware of
the fact that their town at one time formed a part of the Southern
Confederacy. Nevertheless, such is a fact. Early in 1861, Colonel
J. R. Baylor, of the Texas Mounted Rifles, arrived in Southern New
Mexico, and finding all the forts of Arizona and Southern New
Mexico abandoned by the U. S. troops, took possession thereof.
The thirty-fourth parallel of north latitude was made the boundary
between the territory and New Mexico, with the town of Mesilla
on the Rio Grande the seat of government. In December of that
year, General Henry H. Silby of the Confederacy came upon the
scene with his army, consisting of several regiments of Texas troops,
for the conquest of New Mexico, and a Colonel Riley and Captain
Hunter were sent with a detachment of that command to take
possession of Tucson. The Confederates had possession of the
town until the 20th of May, 1862, when they evacuated it upon
the approach of the California column. After the Confederates
abandoned Tucson, and retreated toward the Rio Grande, they
were attacked by Apaches at Dragoon Springs and some forty head
of horses and twenty-five head of mules were taken by the Indians.
Later the Californians got several lessons of the same kind, for the
war in Arizona at that time was a three-cornered affair.

Tucson at that time was a small town of not more than two or
three hundred inhabitants, and a veritable oasis; not a soul living
between Tucson and Yuma on the west and the Rio Grande on
the east, over three hundred miles each way. The town itself was
surrounded by an adobe wall as a protection against the Indians.
People going outside the wall were always expected to go armed
as a protection against the Apaches.

Almost every house had their rock burrs run by burro power to grind their corn and wheat to make their daily tortillas [tor-tee'-ahs]. There was not a saloon nor a church in the town in 1862. Old Sol Warner had a little store in a little shack, but it was like hunting for a needle in a haystack to find his place. However, we did not suffer on that account for we brought a sutler with us where you could buy canned goods for $5 per can, and calicoes at $1 per yard. Sugar was $1 per pound and soap was $1 per bar, other goods being in proportion. As there was no mail route through the country then, it took about forty days to get a letter or paper from San Francisco, the mail generally being brought through by government teams.

Sam H. Drachman came to Tucson in 1867, and of course after the Civil War period the town began to outgrow its old adobe walls. In the Tucson Citizen in 1894 are given Drachman's impressions of the town:

Tucson was a typical frontier town in 1867. Lives were not worth much, money was plenty, prices were high, very high, and the Indians had full sway surrounding. Tucson then had a population of about 1,300—300 Americans and a thousand Mexicans. The sole support of the town was the government supplies. All were engaged in callings more or less tributary to the government. The money came from the government paymasters, and when that was not in use, government vouchers, due on the next arrival of the paymaster, were current. Mexicans got out wood and hay and beef for the army. They would bring in a voucher for $200 or $300 for two or three months' work. This they would take to a merchant, trade some of it out, and get the balance in money. On the next arrival of the paymaster the merchant would get his coin.

The paymaster only arrived every six months. Then such a hurrah as did follow! Everybody had money and plenty of it. Gambling was done in a way that would make 1894 devotees of the Goddess of Fortune open their eyes. Business boomed. The money would last for two or three months, then the era of vouchers would begin again.

Sons of hell the Apaches were. In early days they were treacherous, just as they have been since, and unworthy of trust and without the slightest honor. A man's life was taken in his hand when he went a mile from town, from danger of a lurking fiend, armed to kill from behind some bush. Men have been killed as near as Silver Lake. About Tucson in those days was a succession of bloody horrors at the hands of the Apaches.

Every chance was given the Indians to behave, and they were pressed with threats if they did not cease depredations. They might as well have tried to stop the wind from blowing. Once the Indians gave a smoke signal for peace, and the soldiery went to them. They proposed being on their good behavior, which offer was gladly accepted.

Forthwith good land was turned over to them to work, among it a ranch belonging to Drachman. The Indians were put at cutting hay on a government contract. For a few days those bucks worked and then went off on another killing expedition, leaving the women to work at the hay. When Drachman got back to Tucson he heard great indignation expressed at the devils.

Soon after, the famous Camp Grant massacre occurred in 1871. An armed party of 146 men left town for the Indians, and killed about 100 of them, returning in safety to town. Then followed a "trial." Of course it was a fiasco; no Tucson man would condemn another for killing Apaches. All of these men were tried for murder in one day and all of them cleared.

Freighting was then naturally an important business. Merchandise was sent by water from San Francisco to the mouth of the Colorado; thence it was taken up the river in barges to Yuma. From Yuma it was freighted to Tucson in wagons that were almost like box cars. By the time merchandise had reached Tucson it had enchanced in value 15, 20 or 50 cents a pound, from freight charges.

To the casual visitor [wrote the Phoenix Gazette in 1893], Tucson ever appears quaint. It appears not to be of the times of the nineteenth century, but rather, a reminiscence of the long ago, when the Franciscan friars dispensed the law, when the burro was the accepted mode of transportation, when the harsh speech of the Anglo-Saxon was not known in the Southwest. Leaving the bustling and noisy railroad depot, you step at once into a veritable museum for the antiquarian. On either hand stretch away long lines of low-roofed adobe structures, built for the most part long years ago, alike to each other as two peas in a pod. There are the same thick walls, the same earthen roofs, the same tin gutters and the same thick and heavy pine doors. Were it not for the painted signs at the street corners, all the outlying thoroughfares would be to the stranger destitute of distinguishing marks. There is no regularity to the direction of the streets, wandering around on the cowpath system, all of them narrow, but varying in width from block to block. Sidewalks correspond with the streets, in a few cases where there are sidewalks. Usually the well-sprinkled streets answer all sidewalk purposes. The Cathedral, a noble structure, even if built of the all-pervading adobe, well carries out the medieval impression.

Again, on every hand is to be heard the liquid Spanish accent, at least half of the business of the city being carried on in that language. All among the main streets are signs that proclaim the stores within to be "*tiendas baratas*" (bargain shops), and the mercantile efforts seem especially directed toward securing the trade of the dark-skinned sons of the "*mañana*."

The stores of Tucson are such a feature of the place and are so entirely different from similar establishments in a purely American town, that a short description of their appearance may not be out of place. With one or two exceptions, they are built of adobe, one story in height, and plastered a dull brown or dirty white, on the outside. The doors are generally narrow, while the windows, protected by iron bars, give the buildings a gloomy and repulsive appearance. Less attractive mercantile establishments than these it would be difficult to find in the length and breadth of the Union. No attempt is made to display goods. The interior is narrow and poorly lighted. A common, wooden counter runs around the salesroom, leaving scant space for customers to pass back and forth. But although the barred windows are grimy with dust and ornamented with cobwebs; although the floors are not as clean nor the shelves as tastefully arranged as they might be; some of these unattractive establishments do an immense trade and carry the largest stocks of goods to be found in the Territory. In their roomy warehouses can be found piles of merchandise not exceeded on the Coast, outside of San Francisco and Sacramento. As the trade of Tucson has heretofore been with the border states of Mexico, her mercantile establishments have been conducted with the main object of meeting that trade and supplying the Mexican population of the town. . . .

Out in the "*Barrio Libre*" (free quarter), as the purely Mexican section of the town is termed, one might wander for an hour without noting any evidence that he still was within the confines of the United States. Yet there is one feature of the *Barrio Libre* that surely is not found in Mexico: the bulk of its business appears to be in the hands of the Chinese. On every street corner appears a sign, bearing in Spanish the information that within could be found a store kept by Chung Hoy, or some other son of the Celestial kingdom. American and Mexican merchants have practically abandoned the field, for, as one of those frozen out plaintively remarked: "The average Mexicans like to deal with the Chinese, because with every purchase, however small, they are sure to get a

"*pelon*" (present). It matters not how light the weight is, if the small gift is forthcoming."

There are no street-cars in Tucson, though a grand opportunity would appear to be afforded from the depot down Congress Street and thence out Meyer Street to the left. About all the transportation is done by hacks or open carry-alls, driven by Mexicans. Each have names painted upon their sides, much as was the case with locomotives some years ago. "La Libertad," "El Rayo," "La Union," and "La Estrella," are a few of the names affected.

As the casual visitor desired a bath he was directed "to go 'round on Pennington Street." Arrived there, a long row of bathrooms is noted, big piles of towels and all the needful appurtenances of bathing but, in place of an attendant, the eye rests on a large placard, that reads: "Help yourself and pay in the saloon next door." From this it may be inferred that the populace of Tucson averages well in honesty.

With all good nature and without any personal aversion for the fluids dispensed, what struck the Casual Visitor most strongly was the apparent superabundance of saloons. They appeared to fairly elbow each other on all the principal thoroughfares. It is said there are forty-two of them within the town limits, and, for a town of about five thousand, this number is surely excessive. While the main resorts are evidently well and honestly conducted, there are yet a score or more of "doggeries" that are assuredly a menace to the town. . . .

Getting back to an interesting subject: "What is a *Barrio Libre* anyway?" Tucson has one and we see an account of three persons being shot there one night; and the *Star* says that wife-beating seems to be the most popular amusement out in the *Barrio Libre*.

So queried the Prescott Journal in 1883, to which the Tucson Star replied:

What! Never saw the famous *Barrio Libre*? Young man you are not ready to die, by a jugful. No one should depart to the mystic hence without having first seen the *Barrio Libre*. The *Barrio* has rather an unsavory reputation. Its denizens are not the most orderly and law-abiding to be found in the Territory. It is distinctively a Tucson institution and is of Mexican extraction; Tucson, fortunately for good order, having the only *Barrio Libre* in the United States and perhaps the world. It is a Hades for those who love peace and good order, and a daisy paradise to the reporter who loves to smile at Satan's rage, and at the same time upon a corpse bristling with butcher knives and stilettos of rude manufacture. *Barrio Libre* is a place where the stiff regulations demanded by law are unknown and where the butcher knife, bad Mexicans and worse mescal, diluted with bad Americans, affords the motive power. In Tucson's younger days the *Barrio Libre* was a quarter of the town, in the southern part, where the lower class of Mexicans and the Papago and Yaqui Indians held high or low carnival without being interrupted by officers of the law. When they had a grand *baile*, and put on a guilt-edged finale by killing four or five of the participants, all that was asked of them was to dispose of the carcasses so that the dogs wouldn't be dragging and fighting over human heads, arms and legs in the more respectable quarters of the town. Dogs and children are numerous in this quarter of the old pueblo. The air is musical with the soft strains of the guitar, and very often hazy with the smoothly flowing profanity of some *caballero* from Sonora, who has lost his last *real* at *monte*.

In early times it was a smart juvenile resident of that quarter who knew his father when he met him on the street, and many would have been puzzled if asked to point out their mother—they believed, with "Topsy," that they "just growed." The marriage ceremony was almost unknown in that quarter and was looked upon as a useless custom entirely unworthy of adoption. The man who passed through its streets and came out without having his back as full of butcher knives as a hardware dealer's bulletin board could say that he had performed a miracle, and received the congratulations of the leading citizens.

But that was a long time ago. Tucson is no longer a village, but a city, and civilization then has, hand in hand with progress, trampled over the old order of things and very nearly weeded out the blooming plants of immorality. Many descendants of the old-time residents, however, still reside there, and although the officers keep a close watch they sometimes manage to inaugurate a few of the old customs.

But before you visit this picturesque scene of life across the border, you had better secure a reliable escort. The *Barrio* contains some tough customers, and some as pleasant and polite gentlemen as ever issued a pronunciamento, robbed a church, or cut a throat, can be found within its limits.

*In 1893 the Tucson Star printed the following item:*

Residents in the south part of town—*Barrio Libre*—are bitter in their protests of the condition of affairs at night. Brawling and yelling are altogether too frequent for peace and good will, and the visits of the police there are about as frequent as those of angels.

*And in 1895, the Star carried this notice:*

It has become the custom to speak of South Meyer Street as the *Barrio Libre* though this designation is usually given only when the incidents to be narrated are disreputable. The real *Barrio Libre* comprises an area of considerable extent stretching out on either side of South Meyer and many persons of respectability live within the limits of "free town." They reasonably complain that an injustice is done by generally locating every criminal or disreputable occurrence in *Barrio Libre*. For instance, the woman now in jail for street walking, but originally arrested on suspicion of murder, was said to be a resident of *Barrio Libre* when in fact her home was in *Barrio Tonto* "fool's town." A single district of *Barrio Libre* may teem with disorder, but any other street in the business part of town, where saloons are numerous, may be equally productive of peace disturbances.

# EARLY MATRIMONY IN ARIZONA
## (TUBAC)

Apaches may be very hostile, times very hard, and government very remote; but courting and marrying will go on as long as there is an Adam and Eve upon the earth. After the establishment of Fort Buchanan on the Sonoita, settlers began to come into Arizona from the States. Among them Felix Grundy Aykes, from Tennessee, and his family of race horses, dogs, a hominy block, wife and children. He had started for California in '49, got waterbound in Arkansaw about seven years and stranded on the Rio Grande; but he finally reached Arizona all right.

After the Aykes family got established on the Sonoita, I noticed that a very handsome young Kentuckian we had with us at Tubac, whom the girls called Sugar P. Davis, asked me every Saturday evening for the loan of a horse to go up to Sonoita to spend Sunday. Finally, I said, "Sugar, if you are going to marry Anne Aykes, I should like to give you an infare, now an obsolete custom." Sugar confessed the soft impeachment, and I commissioned him to arrange with his fiance and all the girls on the Sonoita to come down to Tubac and make a day of it,—and so we did—a May day too.

The wedding day was delayed for the arrival of some new-fangled woman's wear expected at the post trader's store in the course of the year; but finally everything was arranged for the first wedding among civilized people on the Sonoita. As Alcalde of Tubac under the Government of New Mexico, I was legally authorized to celebrate the rites of matrimony, baptize children, grant divorces, execute criminals, declare war and perform all the functions of the ancient El Cadi. The records of this primitive period are on file in the Recorder's office of the ancient and honorable pueblo of Tucson.

It required two ambulances to convey the wedding guests from Tubac to the Aykes mansion on the Sonoita, and when we arrived there we camped on the woodpile, and concealed the demijohn of whiskey thereunder. Directly the Tubac contingent was joined by Captain (afterwards General) Ewell, from Fort Buchanan, with a lot of boys in buttons, who camped on the other side of the wood-pile, and concealed their demijohn of whiskey in like manner. There was not any room in the house for the men, and even the back porch had to be used as a dressing room for the bride. Old mother Aykes had purchased a "trousseau" for the bride, consisting of a new-fashioned cinch called a corset, which she was endeavoring to fasten by putting her foot on Anne's torso and throwing her weight on the string.

Bill Aykes, Anne's brother, was a cowboy and mule packer, and I suspect had taken several pulls at the demijohn under the woodpile so when he saw her performance, he shouted out: "That's right marm, cinch her till she sneezes and then trot her out to be married."

When the bride was properly attired the wedding march commenced and the guests on the woodpile filed into the house. Sally Rochester stood up with the bride and John Capron with the groom. The Alcalde was duly sober, for the time of day, and tied the matrimonial knot with a diamond hitch. The wedding supper was superb, gallinas, gusadas, guacollotes estuffa, enchillades, frijoles, chili con carne, dulces and all the sumptuous dishes of the Castilian menu. We reached home somehow or other; by the providence of God.

Tubac became a kind of Gretna Green for runaway couples from Sonora, as the priest there charged them twenty-five dollars, and the Alcalde of Tubac tied the knot gratis, and gave them a treat besides. I had been marrying people and baptizing children at Tubac for a year or two and had a good many God-children named Carlos or Carlotta according to gender, and began to feel quite patriarchal, when Bishop Lamy sent down Father Mashboef (Vicar Apostolic) of New Mexico, to look after the spiritual condition of Arizona people. It required all the sheets and tablecloths of the establishment to fix up a confessional room and we had to wait till noon for the blessing at breakfast; but worse than all that my compadres, who used to embrace me with such affection, went away with their reybosas [sic] over their heads, without even a friendly salutation.

It was muy triste [very gloomy] in Tubac and I began to feel the effects of the ban of the church, when one day after breakfast

Father Mashboef took me by the arm (a man always takes you by the arm when he has anything unpleasant to say) and said:

"My young friend, I appreciate all you have been trying to do for these people, but these marriages you have celebrated are not good in the eyes of God, and these women are all living in a state of adultery, and I have ordered them to suspend connubial relations."

I knew there would be a riot on the Santa Cruz if this ban could not be lifted. The women were sulky and the men commenced cursing, and said they thought they were entitled to all the rights of matrimony. My strong defense was that I had not charged any of them anything and had given them a marriage certificate with a seal on it, made out of a Mexican dollar, and had given a treat and fired off an anvil. Still, although the Pope of Rome was beyond the jurisdiction of even the Alcalde of Tubac, I could not see the way open for a restoration of happiness.

It would never do to let the population of the Territory be stopped in this way, so I arranged with Father Mashboef to give the sanction of the church to the marriages and legitimize the little Carlos's and Carlottas with holy water and it cost the company about $700 to rectify the matrimonial situation on the Santa Cruz.
—CHARLES D. POSTON.

–Phoenix *Herald*, 1891

## BISBEE, 1900-1905

### THE TOWN IN 1900

*George H. Kelly, then State Historian, in reminiscing for the Bisbee Orb in 1928, wrote:*

My earliest recollection of Bisbee goes back to about the first days of December, 1900. . . . Main Street in Bisbee, when I first saw it, was featured, especially, by the number of saloons and gambling houses. Nearly every saloon had, at least, a card room equipped with paraphernalia for playing the American game of poker, and one or two larger saloons were provided with faro tables, crap tables, roulette wheels and other means of separating the miners from the contents of their pay envelopes. Several of these saloons remained open day and night. One distinguishing feature of the gambling saloons in Bisbee was the fact that no women were present, whereas, in Phoenix, Prescott, Tucson and Clifton, all the gambling saloons contained women who engaged in singing, piano playing and consuming wine and other drinks, which they solicited from the saloon patrons, who were also "steered" against the gambling games. An effort was made by "Dad" Walsh, who opened a saloon in Bisbee in 1901, to bring some women "canaries" from Tucson as a new feature in Bisbee, but the public frowned on this innovation to the night life in that town with such force as to cause Walsh and his associates to abandon their efforts.

*The Cochise Review (Bisbee), in an article on Bisbee in 1900, made this statement:*

From a tough, gun-fighting community of two or three hundred souls, it has grown into a city with a population of six thousand. It has experienced ill fortune in its time, but has staunchly ridden the waves of adversity to a port of prosperity and affluence. During its existence its main business street has thrice been razed to the ground by fire, and twice in the days of the camp's infancy did it seem the ore in the mine had been exhausted and that the little town in the Mule Mountains must be abandoned.

### BISBEE, 1905 VINTAGE

*A reporter for the Tucson Citizen visited Bisbee in 1905, accompanying the Tucson baseball club, and he reported his impressions of the town in that newspaper as follows:*

Bisbee, the mining metropolis of the great Southwest, the hustling hamlet on the hillsides, the city of foul odors and sickening smells, the busiest burg in the Territory. That is the way Bisbee, summed up in a nut-shell, looked to a *Citizen* representative Sunday.

No city can be judged finally by a few hours' stay. Impressions received in that time are mainly surface. Yet Bisbee is a city that is long remembered by those who have had occasion to visit it, even though the sojourn be short.

There is much about the city that is to be commended and admired. There is much that might be condemned and censured. It is not a town that would cause the artist to sigh for his brush and his canvas; nor the poet to long for his pen and his paper to make immortal the inspirations received; nor the lover of curio beauty to wax long and loud in his descriptions of beautiful buildings and clean streets and fine sidewalks and well kept lawns. Bisbee . . . . is a burg for the businessman, blunt and pushing, who is looking for the almighty dollar to swell his bank account. . . .

Bisbee is the business town of the Territory. You don't have to remain there long to discover this. It is busy even on Sunday. It is wide open and yet it is run with restrictions. Saloons go about the even tenor of their ways every day in the year. Gamblers find the town a regular gold mine with a steady stream of hard-earned dollars constantly coming over the green cloth into the "kitty." It is likely that Bisbee will ever be thus. Its inhabitants must be amused in some way. Gambling is an amusement that comes high but Bisbee has the wherewithal to pay and kicks not on the price.

Bisbee is good in two respects—it has no wine rooms and women warble not in the saloons. In this respect it is on a par with Tucson. Bisbee claims a population of 12,000. Tucson claims 15,000. Be that as it may, this much is true—you could add Bisbee to Tucson and it would not more than fill the vacant lots within the city limits of the old pueblo. For this enterprising city is not large in area. It is closely built. It is not a city of residences and spacious lawns. Its inhabitants are content to live in shacks built one above the other upon the mountainside. When neighbors quarrel in Bisbee they don't erect "spite fences," for these would do no good. Fact is, when a quarrel arises, the man farthest up the hill has the best of it for he can sit on his front porch and squirt tobacco juice down his neighbor's chimney. Consequently most of the houses have chimney covers which serve the same purpose as a "spite fence" in towns built on the level.

There is every reason why Bisbee should be a bustling burg. It received annually in wages from the bigger copper corporations, millions of dollars per year. The greater part of this enormous sum is spent in the town. Much of it goes to the saloon-keepers and the gamblers who look sleek and fat as they stride about the city in glad raiment and with huge sparklers adorning their fronts.

Bisbee's population is threefold—the working, the loafing, and the sleeping. The day is evenly divided there. The mines work three shifts of eight hours each. While one shift works another sleeps, while the third rests or loafs, for loafing seems to be a favorite occupation with many of the unoccupied miners. You can see the resting squad lined up along the streets, smoking pipes and noting carefully all newcomers who happen to pass along the street.

Two classes make up the population. The one and the larger class is the big-hearted, rough-spoken, horny-handed sons of toil, who take out the rich copper ore from the mountain sides. The other class is the cigarette-smoking, wide-pants, cap-wearing college youth who hails Yale or Harvard or Princeton or Pennsylvania or Michigan or Illinois as his alma mater. The two mix well, for in Bisbee as elsewhere in Arizona, "a man's a man for a' that," and is rated at what he is worth, whether he wears a blue or boiled shirt.

It takes money to live in Bisbee. The "bit" is the small coin there, but what matters it to the residents, who receive salaries ranging from $24.50 per week up. Nothing is cheap in Bisbee. It costs money to get provisions and necessities there. Consequently these are high, but the natives have the wherewith to pay for them and do so without a murmur. The minimum wage for the miner is $3.50 per day of eight hours and many receive $4 and $5, or more, for their time.

Many people in Tucson have difficulty remembering the street names of the old pueblo. It is not so in Bisbee. There are but two streets in the city—Brewery Gulch and Tombstone Canyon. Both are narrow and on both real estate is almost as valuable as though it were lined with gold and silver ore. The best business corner in Tucson with a large building on it rents for $150 per month. A little shack used as a saloon in the heart of Bisbee's business district rents for $250 per month. The leading restaurant pays a monthly rental of $400 and occupies a place which somewhat resembles Rossi's old place. [*Rossi's the famous Tucson establishment known throughout the country as the best café between St. Louis and Los Angeles.*] These are but samples of rentals in the business section of the city.

You can always tell a resident of Bisbee, for they are all high steppers. If they did not step high they would stub their toes as they walk along the street, for there is not a level stretch in the whole city. Brewery Gulch winds and twists and Tombstone Canyon is much the same so that the stranger is dizzy by the time he has inspected the two avenues, from much turning and twisting. And you remember Brewery Gulch. You could not forget it if you wanted to. The street is somewhat frightful from a sanitary standpoint. It is covered with a slime several inches deep and about four feet wide, from which comes a nauseating odor which makes Meyer Street in the old pueblo of Tucson, on the hottest night in summer, smell like cologne. And natives in Tucson frequently hold their noses as they pass along Meyer Street when the weather is hot.

Some day Bisbee may have a sewerage system. Brewery Gulch will be clean and wholesome and will not "smell to heaven." As it is it remains a disgrace to the city. You smell it when you step off the train. Its vile odor is still in the nostrils when you have traveled far from the city out on the cool and refreshing plains where Don Luis and Naco lie in the breezes.

Bisbee has narrow streets and bad sidewalks. Women walk in the street and hold their skirts high else they will trail in the street's slime. Yet Bisbee has charming matrons and beautiful maidens who can hold their own with the fair sex of any city in the Territory.

Bisbee can well be proud of its leading store and leading hotel. The Copper Queen store is a fine place. It does a business not excelled by any store in the Territory. The Copper Queen Hotel is small compared with Tucson's leading hostelry, yet it is fully as modern and up-to-date.

They tell a story about the Copper Queen Hotel and Landlord Rouzer which is vouched for by leading citizens. A gentleman from the East registered at the hotel with his wife. He was assigned to a room on the third floor. He visited the room and in a few minutes came down greatly excited. "I can't keep that room. My wife is nervous and afraid of fire," he said. Landlord Rouzer without changing the expression on his face, remarked in a most matter of fact way, "Oh, my friend, if fire breaks out just raise your window and step out onto the hillside."

They tell another tale. It is about the richest mine of the Copper Queen Company. The mine was lost years ago in a horse race. The owner bet the mine against a mere trifle that his horse could outrun another steed, and lost. The same gentleman today is toiling in the mines as a common miner but happy withal, for he hopes sometime to make a rich strike and become a wealthy man.

[The accepted legend is that George Warren, an old prospector and inebriate, had been grubstaked in 1877 by a busy army scout for whom he staked out some claims in the area. Warren was given a small interest in these claims, one of which later turned out to be the fabulous Copper Queen mine, which brought its subsequent owners millions of dollars. Warren was said to have wagered his share of the claims against a bottle of firewater on his chances of covering a certain distance around a stake in less time than a man on horseback would require to go the same distance. He lost.]

Bisbee has few carriages and fewer automobiles. It boasted an auto once. Mr. Douglas, one of the wealthiest citizens of the town, owned the machine. It bucked on one of the numerous hills and plunged into a ditch. It is still in the ditch and no one has ever since tried automobiling in the mountains.

When one sees the pretty section about Don Luis [two miles south] he wonders why the city was not built there. The ball park is there. The land is level and the surroundings are healthful. There would be no cramping and crowding. There the houses would not need to be built on top of one another. But Bisbee willed it otherwise. Its founders were willing to forego many of the pleasures in their scramble for the dinero.

And the natives in the city in the gulches and on the hillsides are happy. They never complain. True, the dread typhoid is continually stalking about the town, laying victims low here and there, but the death-rate is low, and it is so familiar it is regarded with contempt.

"Why, we wax fat and rich on the odors," one old-timer re-marked. And it may be so.

They do business on a big scale in this settlement. One Pittsburgh company has sunk a million dollars in a prospect and is still putting in money. It has not taken out a dollar's worth of ore. It expects to take out millions shortly. Great is the faith of capitalists in the Bisbee mining country. They don't scruple about expenses. A mine is located. The capitalists come in. Their engineers report. A shaft hundreds of feet deep is ordered sunk. A snug sum, a quarter of a million or so is left behind and the capitalists return to the East to dream of fortunes. Almost without exception their dreams come true.

But after all is summed up, Bisbeeites may be dead stuck on their burg, for this the city must be given due credit, but it seems right good to get back to the old pueblo of Tucson. A comparison of Tucson and Bisbee looms up in this wise: If you wish to make money and live, stay in Tucson; if you wish to make money and merely exist, go to Bisbee. In the old pueblo there is life and pleasure as well as business. In Bisbee there is lots of business and mere existence.

*Although present-day Bisbee is a far cry from the camp as de-scribed by the Tucson correspondent in 1905, it still is a fascinating town and unique in its way. According to the current Arizona State Guide:*

> *Bisbee is the seat of Cochise county, and center of one of the richest copper districts in America, and is the principal town of a large community—the Warren Mining District— built in or near a canyon called Mule Pass Gulch. The Gulch, about six miles long and bordered by high hills, begins above Bisbee on the west and winds downward in an easterly direc-tion, through Bisbee and then Lowell, to the sloping foothills of Warren. Bisbee occupies approximately two miles of the upper and steepest section of this gulch, its houses clinging to the slopes of two long, narrow canyons, terraced tier upon tier. Flights of stone and wooden stairs, dirt trails and casual uneven streets reach the uppermost dwellings.*

The highway through the town is known as West Boulevard; then Tombstone Canyon, with hills and bluffs on both sides high and abrupt, with houses built all over them. Then farther along in the main shopping section, Tombstone Canyon becomes Main Street. Across the street northeast of the plaza—Brewery Gulch and OK Street—at one time the most thickly populated thorough-fare in Arizona—meet Main Street. Brewery Gulch, Bisbee's second important canyon, is about a mile long and joins Mule Pass Gulch at a right angle. Chihuahua Hill rises above it on the east. OK Street is a narrow, paved trail, almost parallel with Brewery Gulch.

It is difficult to describe Bisbee. It is unique in its canyon and hillside setting and must be seen to be appreciated as one of Arizona's peculiarly different cities.

## KELVIN, UNIQUE TOWN

Mountains to the right of them, mountains to the left of them, mountains before them, mountains behind them, echo and re-echo on the people of the big mining camp of Kelvin every time a giant blast of powder tears out of the hills the precious ore which they hold in an almost unyielding grip.

A traveler on the Phoenix & Eastern, the new road recently ac-quired by the Southern Pacific, which extends for a distance of more than one hundred miles to the eastward of Phoenix, asked the question: "What is the largest mining camp in this section?" Immediately the answer came back "Kelvin." And the answer seems justified, as Kelvin is the center for the Ray, Troy and other mining camps of considerable size in this vicinity. It is in this town that the Ray concentrator is located.

The first thing that strikes a stranger in the camp is the unique-ness of the town. There are saloons, eight or ten of them, and they are all bunched up along with the business houses. The camp boasts of but one hotel, that is, only one hostelry of any size. It prides itself on the fact that it has but one officer and he is a constable "elected in the precinct," as one resident put it; "and he has mighty little to do ordinarily, save when one of the bad spells are on," the same genuine booster for his town added. The hotel is quite one of the unique things about the town. The landlord, a pioneer by the name of McGee, is a genial, whole-souled gentleman who goes in for few formalities.

"Do you wish to get a cot or bed?" is the question invariably put to the new arrival. It makes no difference which is selected, for the price is the same. It is the lucky individual, however, who takes the cot on the outside veranda, for the nights are invariably warm and to sleep out-of-doors is the only way to obtain comfort here.

In the morning the sleeper looks for the push button. Perhaps he wishes some water or perhaps he wants to get his bath prepared. He gets neither. He trudges down the stairs and then on the rear porch he is shown the place to perform his morning toilet. There is one large basin and everybody uses it. There is, however, plenty of water and this helps out greatly. But the towel is the great thing. One towel does, as does the basin, for the entire hotel population. "I reckon there is still a square inch of dry place on the towel," the clerk remarks in a matter of fact way, "but if there is not then come inside and I will give you a new one to put up," he adds to the late risers.

But the most unique thing in the camp, after all, is the narrow-gauge railroad. The town can lay distrinction to having probably the narrowest narrow-gauge railroad in the Territory. It travels daily seven miles between Kelvin and Troy, and it looks like a Christmas toy. The biggest thing about the engine is the smokestack, while the cars are large enough only to hold seven or eight men. The road is used almost exclusively in transporting ore from the mines to the mill.

Life is far from monotonous, however, in the camp. Mining men and prospectors are arriving continually and they swap tales about new finds and discoveries all the day long and far into the evening. Then when they have become tongue-weary for the day, the camp becomes quiet, the lights go out and all is peaceful until morning.

—Tucson *Citizen*, 1907

# BENSON

Benson has long been a favorite rounding-up place for cowboys who usually have a month's wages or more in their jeans when they come loping down the main street. Consequently Benson has many thirst emporiums and many places where the fickle Goddess of Fortune can be wooed, but never won. The population figures as high as fifteen hundred. In the same ratio, Tucson should have more than a hundred saloons. Yet there be those among the wet goods dispensers here who objected to higher license on the ground of the number of saloons.

Benson builds saloon buildings and constructs them well. Long experience has made these buildings proof against the raving of the north wind and the behavior of the night. But Benson is branching out. The town is gradually putting on metropolitan airs. It has not been many moons since a company secured franchises for water works and for lighting the town with electricity. Benson is about to line up more strongly on the religious side. The town is building a new church, of the Presbyterian denomination. And this is causing the difficulty and baffling the old-timers who rode the range forty years ago, as well as the budding prospects of the younger generation who have just returned from the Eastern technical schools. Consequently Benson is appealing to Tucson. It wants suggestions and plans and aid in an architectural way. It must not be thought for an instant that Benson is lacking in religious and spiritual culture. Far from it. Benson is as progressive and wide awake as most of the other towns. But, nevertheless, it must be admitted that the church style of architecture is just a little bit new. Where there is an oasis of men in Benson who will tell you how to construct a saloon building, it is a barren desert when it comes to suggestions for church buildings.

It was a brave start, notwithstanding, that the good folk made with the Presbyterian church. It is being constructed of lumber. It assumed proportions and the wet goods men and the ball spinners and card dealers, as well as other folks, stopped on their way down the street to gaze in awe at the religious edifice.

But, alas! The builders failed to reckon with the elements. Benson is situated in a slight depression. From every direction there is a gentle roll down to the town. Benson is also out on the mesa. Consequently the town is frequently wind-swept.

A big wind came up one day last week. It gained force as it rolled down the incline, and when it had passed over the town all that was left of the church building was a pile of twisted and shapeless lumber, bearing no semblance to a house of worship. The eight saloons, however, were standing.

The blow caused dejection and despair. But one wise man thought of Tucson. The appeal will bring results. An architect will draw plans. The church will be rebuilt and it will withstand the blows, even as the eight saloons do.

—Tucson *Citizen*, 1906

## FAIR FLORENCE

*The Prescott* Democrat, *reporting in 1881, on a representative's trip through Southern Arizona, describes the towns of Florence and old Adamsville and relates something of their hectic past:*

Florence is distant from Casa Grande about twenty-eight miles, in a northeasterly direction. It is on the main traveled road to Silver King, Globe and the mining camps of Pinal and Gila Counties. It has a population of about 800, several stores, two hotels, a brewery, saloons, and many handsome private residences. The streets, which are laid off towards the cardinal points of the compass, are broad, and shaded by leafy cottonwoods. Streams of water run on each side of every street, keeping the air delightfully cool and pleasant. The houses are built of sun-dried brick (adobe), with shingle roofs. The adobe is the house for a warm climate; no matter how high the mercury may mount, the interior is always cool.

Florence is the county seat of Pinal County, and does a profitable trade with the mining camps which lie north and east of it, and with the farming settlements scattered up and down the Gila River. Before the building of Pinal City and Globe, Florence was one of the liveliest towns in the Territory; and old settlers, in a convivial and communicative mood, will recall, with a sad sigh of subdued melancholy, the fiscal glories of the burg, "in the brave days of old," when greenbacks were as plentiful as cottonwood leaves; when storekeepers were kept on the run from morn until night; when whiskey flowed like water in the *acequias* [ah-thay'-ke-ahs], and "a man for breakfast" was one of the staple articles on the bill of fare.

[*The saying "a man for breakfast" had its origin in tough frontier towns where, sometimes, as a result of a killing at night, the victim's body was found laid out in the street before breakfast.*]

These were the good old days when the exhilarated exile from Sonora or Chihuahua, or the festive muleskinner from Yuma or Tucson, "made things lively for the boys," when fandangoes and free fights made night hideous and day delirious. The building up of large mercantile establishments at Pinal and Globe has taken away much of the mining trade of Florence, for which she should be the natural center. The opening of new districts immediately to the north and east of the town, however, promises to bring a great deal of this mountain trade again to Florence.

From the feverish excitement, the rush, the roar, the hurly-burly of Tombstone, it is a relief to find a spot like Florence, where people believe there is something else worth living for besides the worship of Mammon; where the struggle for the almighty dollar

—That meanest rage

And latest folly of man's sinking age

does not engross the thoughts of men by day and their dreams by night; where the people believe in the sensible motto, "As you journey through life, live by the way." No town in the Territory, of its size, can show pleasanter homes, a more cultivated, refined and hospitable people. It is an agreeable surprise to meet so delightful an oasis of mental and material fertility in this far-away corner of the Southwest; and there is no one who has sojourned among the Florentines but will always retain the most pleasant memories of its kind and sociable people and of its charming surroundings.

The county court house is a commodious and substantial building, of adobe, and, next to that of Prescott, the finest in Arizona. Of the jail, however, the same cannot be said. It is probably the most insecure prison in the Territory. Built of adobe, the walls are so slight that an energetic prisoner can cut his way out with a jack-knife in an hour. Prisoners charged with capital crimes have to be guarded by a sentinel on the outside. A county like Pinal. which occupies the enviable position of being out of debt, "and money ahead," should certainly do away with the present travesty on a bastille, and erect a secure and substantial edifice in its stead.

## OLD ADAMSVILLE

*From the same account as the foregoing comes this description:*
The old town of Adamsville, about five miles down the river from Florence, is now virtually a deserted village. Its houses are empty and going to ruin; its streets are silent and deserted; the coyote and Gila monster gambol undisturbed through its abandoned stores and lonely gin mills: and Adamsville, or Sanford, as it is sometimes called, is so dead that it will take the sound of Gabriel's trumpet to create any animation in its desolate and deserted highways and byways. Yet Adamsville was a thriving town before Florence had an existence; and it has a history of blood and violence as sanguinary as any place in the Territory. "Cutting and shooting" once held high carnival here, and the grave of many a victim lies thick with desert growth, unknown and unseen by the passer by. Adamsville was, during its brief and bloody existence, as "lively" a frontier town as the most distinguished desperado could wish for. But with the establishment of Florence, its glory departed, and nothing is left to tell of its former greatness save a cluster of tumble-down adobes and an unsavory memory.

It was at this spot in the valley of the Gila, situated between Florence and Sacaton, some five years since, a pioneer named Charles Adams located a piece of ground, erected a shanty and proceeded to divest his property of the offensive shrubbery, preparatory to the sowing of a crop of grain. The location was the center of a large tract of land, and soon a thriving settlement sprang up; the center Adams retained. His position was soon courted by his neighbors as a townsite, and at their solicitations he laid off a town on his property, bestowed lots to whomsoever wished to build, and with one accord the whole community agreed that the town should be named Adamsville. The entire piece of property originally located by Adams was subsequently sold by him, but the town still retained the name Adamsville and all were satisfied, until, early in 1871, Arizona's Delegate to Congress, Richard C. McCormick, to satisfy a personal grudge of a political character against Adams, concluded to have the name changed. With this object

in view he managed to have the name of the post office changed
from Adamsville to Sanford, in honor of George B. Sanford, Captain of First U. S. Cavalry, who was a most successful Indian fighter
in Arizona. His hope and intention was that the town would, for
convenience sake, adopt the name of the post office, when his
purpose would have been accomplished. The object, too, has been
partly secured, but not so firmly rooted that it may not be eradi-
cated. The name of that town is Adamsville; and you pioneers,
who would protect and preserve the memory of one another from
the spoliatory hands of the vandal politician, refer to it as such.
Address your letters, when you have occasion to write thither, to
Sanford P. O., Adamsville, and let outside despoilers see and
understand that they may not manipulate this simple heritage
which you would hand down to posterity.

*An example of the bloody strife which brought death and devasta-
tion in old Adamsville is given in the following account entitled
"Killing on the Gila," published in the Tucson Citizen in 1872
and later certified as to accuracy in the same newspaper:*

On Saturday, March 2, 1872, a party of citizens of American
birth went from Sanford (Adamsville) and Florence to Gandara's
ranch near Blackwater, and became involved in a shooting scrape
in which James Bodel and Pancho Gandara were killed. Whatever
the provocation, Bodel was first mortally shot by Gandara, after
which the latter was shot dead within twenty feet of his own house.
The American party then went to Sanford, determined to kill
Manuel Reyes and probably a few other known desperadoes, if
found; Reyes having a bad reputation and also having sworn that
he would kill four Americans to avenge the death of Gandara.

At an early hour on Sunday morning, Reyes took refuge in a
house of D. C. Thompson, in which were some women. All but
Reyes were allowed to escape, when the house was blown up and,
amid general shooting, Reyes was killed. A few hours previous to
this, a young Mexican named Aguilar was killed—shot from his
horse. An American named Perry was wounded and, according to
reports, two or three Mexicans. One horse was killed, a house destroyed, and probably some other damage done.

Last week we gave an account of the disappearance of William

McFarland; how he left his home at Sacaton, February 15; of his going to Florence and return to Sanford, and then to Gandara's ranch at Blackwater; of his leaving the latter place, February 17, never to get home. McFarland was universally esteemed an upright man and liberal neighbor, and no just cause could be assigned for his murder. It following, in less than two months, the horrid massacre of the harmless and respected Baker family at Bluewater, and the fresh remembrance of several other massacres on the Gila and Santa Cruz, the bona fide citizens about Sanford and Florence took counsel together. They knew of the causeless murder of so many good people, and reasoned as matters were going, some of their number would soon be killed; they likewise had convincing proof that their neighbors were slain by Mexicans; that it had been a practice for years of this bad Mexican element to kill and rob in Arizona and escape punishment; that if some terrible and certain penalties were not visited upon these bandits and murderers, they would be encouraged to bolder and more frequent crimes; in a word, legal patience was exhausted and other modes of redress for, and prevention of, such dire deeds were discussed, adopted and executed.

About $1,200 reward was offered by them for the discovery of the remains of McFarland or information that would discover the murderers. Two weeks had been spent in fruitless search and investigation, except that the deceased was last seen at Gandara's and that no trace of him therefrom could be found, and also that several bad characters were much about there. Owing to conflicting statements being made by parties on the ranch, it was resolved to revisit it and if possible get at the truth but not to kill any one. Our reports seem correct, and we are sure we have one that intended to be impartial, and this one says the party called at the house; inquired if Gandara was in and received an affirmative reply; whereupon James Bodel and another man started to go inside. Just as Bodel entered the door, Gandara appeared with a concealed weapon; said "adios," drew his weapon and killed him, and before getting twenty feet from his door was himself riddled with bullets. This, of course, ended all thought of an investigation. The friends of either party were up in arms, and the scene next day transferred to Sanford where Reyes and Aguilar were killed and before heretofore recited acts transpired. We are assured that from first to last whiskey neither incited nor governed the actors, but that the whole tragedy was marked by remarkable deliberation.

When Gandara and Bodel were killed on Saturday, messengers were at once sent to Ft. McDowell, Tucson and Pinal, for assistance. The one coming here [Tucson] met Governor Safford and Colonel Morrow, and his escort at Picacho Station, and also an escort of twenty-one men under Sergeant Bruckett of Lieutenant Bendire's troop, on their return from McDowell. The messenger had a petition to the Governor for assistance. Colonel Morrow at once volunteered to go via Sanford and remain while needed with his escort of fifteen men, or until other aid arrived; and the Governor induced Sergeant Bruckett and detachment to go with him. The Governor arrived at Sanford before daylight Sunday, and at once endeavored by all his pursuasion and available power to prevent the bloodshed which followed on that day. All his promises to have the bad men arrested were received by those addressed with respectful determination not to be swerved from their purpose to kill Reyes. It seems that less loss of life resulted than if force had been opposed to the killing of Reyes, for when the latter was out of the way, all hands joined in to quiet the people. Of course, common satisfaction did not prevail, but a common disposition was manifested to have peace and law. The Governor again called upon all citizens to obey the law and assist to impartially enforce it against bad men.

Colonel Morrow rendered all possible assistance in allying the troubles and joined heartily in the course of the Governor; and Sergeant Bruckett's conduct was excellent, and both sergeant and men are mentioned in high terms by the Governor and others present.

In cases of this kind, anyone's judgement may be at fault. Different actors and even spectators, witness and judge from different standpoints and feelings; but on one point, none ought to err—that neighborhood wars are often as fatal to the innocent as the guilty, and ought to be resisted and condemned by all. In this instance, it is believed that of four men killed, there was but one very bad one; but suppose there were two or even three, and only one innocent victim, is this not enough to make all good men view the acts with horror which cost a guiltless man his life? If Mexican residents or citizens insist, as many do, that Gandara was innocent, they must bear in mind that the Baker family (father, mother, son and daughter), William McFarland, and others of the well-known slain by their lawless countrymen, were wholly free of guilt and were positively good men to all mankind; also that Gandara, under fear of his own life, as he doubtless was, killed a man who intended no harm to him, just before receiving his own death shots. Let both sides be fairly considered, and let all, whether Mexican or American, and especially those who complain of these frightful killings, do what they can to prevent them.

We beg of both classes not to hold either responsible as a class. Let individuals of each be dealt with according to their acts. Let every man's own conduct build him up or tear him down, and make no one the sufferer for another's crimes. Will our Mexican population, as well as American, bear this in mind and act upon it? They must do their share to prevent innocent Americans from being slaughtered, if they would have their own saved from a like fate.

*In November of the same year the Tucson Citizen reported new killings at Adamsville: the shooting bout between two well-known men, John Rodgers and Captain Henry Kennedy, which resulted in the death of Kennedy and no harm to Rodgers, and the killing of Robert L. Swope by John Willis.*

*Kennedy invited Rodgers into the back yard of a saloon and very shortly shots were heard by those inside. Kennedy was found dead with an empty derringer by his side and a loaded one in his pocket. Rodgers' case was officially examined and he was discharged.*

*At Rodgers' examination, Robert L. Swope and H. Bledsoe both testified before Justice Page and gave it as their belief, based upon what they saw and heard, that the fatal shooting was done in self-defense. Upon that testimony Justice Page discharged Rodgers from custody. The coroner's jury said they found Kennedy came to his death by the shot of a pistol in the hands of John Rodgers while acting in self-defense.*

*The following day Swope, who had testified in the Kennedy killing, was shot and killed by John Willis in the same town and* at the same saloon. An inquest was held at which the testimony was to the effect that Willis shot Swope without provocation and when he was unarmed. The verdict of the coroner's jury was that Swope came to his death by a pistol shot fired by "one Willis." Willis was examined by Justice Page and discharged.

Willis unsuspectingly went to Tucson a few days later and was immediately arrested by Sheriff Ott and lodged in jail upon a warrant ordered by District Court Judge Titus. An account says, "Willis is now resting in our county jail ironed in approved style. He seemed surprised that he could be arrested after a former examination and discharge, and there can be little doubt of his present regret that he killed Swope."

The examination and jailing of Willis gave satisfaction to the people on the Gila, and the Judge emphasized his determination to put a stop to the murdering business in that district.

The Citizen commented:

It will quite likely result in giving time to get rid of all positive evidence against him, and he, too, will be turned loose to execute some of his threats made since imprisonment for the deed. The only comment we need make on these cases is to state that pretty good men are again talking of the necessity of a Vigilance Committee to administer that punishment which the law says shall be (but is not) for the terrible crime of murder. Murder upon murder is committed in Arizona, and yet not one murderer has ever been punished as the law directs.

Late in May Willis was tried. The Citizen reported:

The jury in the case of John Willis on trial for murder, brought in a verdict of guilty as charged in the indictment, last Saturday, and on Tuesday the prisoner was brought before Judge Titus for sentence. The prisoner when asked by the judge if he had anything to say why sentence should not be passed upon him, replied that "he did not think he had had a fair trial," after which the judge ordered that he should be hung, without specifying the date. The counsel for Willis appealed the case to the Supreme Court. A bond of $500 was given for the costs of the appeal, and the case goes over to the Supreme Court, which will meet in Tucson the first of next January. It was the earnest desire of every one that it should hold an adjourned session about the 1st of June to speedily decide just such cases as this, but it was not done, and now the usual delays that have so far resulted in turning loose every murderer in the Territory except one, will have to be submitted to.

In August, 1873, a man and his wife were murdered in Tucson while they slept, and their house was plundered. Three suspects were soon rounded up and jailed. One of the suspects confessed that the three had committed the crime. The Citizen gives an account of what followed:

By ten o'clock on Thursday evening, it was well understood throughout town that the murderers were known and in custody; and the first thing we heard next morning, was an expressed purpose to hang the three (and also John Willis) immediately after the funeral of the murdered man and wife. Stores, saloons and nearly every place of business, big and little, were closed. The funeral was conducted with great solemnity and did not tend to soften the determination to prepare for four more. Immediately afterward, the people to the number of several hundred assembled in front of the jail. Early next morning two posts forked at the top were planted in the ground near the jail door, and upon them was placed a stiff pole about twelve feet in length. To this pole four ropes were fastened with nooses to each, and two wagons were drawn beneath. A Catholic priest desiring to give such consolation as he could to the doomed men, he was given all the time he desired. When through with his ministrations, it was after eleven o'clock. Very soon thereafter, the four men were brought out of jail, with small black bandages over their eyes, put in the wagons, ropes adjusted to their necks, and the wagons drawn out and all four hung side by side. It is thought by some that John Willis was dead or unconscious when placed in the wagon, as he could not stand alone and made no struggle while hanging.

The Citizen concluded its coverage of the affair with a report of the inquest over the bodies of the four men hanged by the people:

We the undersigned, the jurors summoned to appear before Solomon Warner, the Coroner of the County of Pima, at Tucson, on the 8th day of August, 1873, to inquire into the cause of the death of John Willis (and three others); that they came to their deaths in the court house plaza, in the town of Tucson, by hanging; and we further find that the said hanging was committed by the people of Tucson, en masse; and we do further say that in view of the terrible and bloody murders that had been committed by the three, and the tardiness with which justice was being meted out to John Willis, a murderer, that the extreme measures taken by our fellow-citizens this morning in vindication of their lives, their property and the peace and good order of society, while it is to be regretted and deplored that such extreme measures were necessary, seems to the jury to have been the inevitable results of allowing criminals to escape the penalties of their crimes.

*The Phoenix Republican, in 1906, reported:*

Adamsville, situated below Florence on the Gila River, is one of the historic spots in Arizona, it having been one of the first settlements of the whites in the Gila valley. For years it has been nothing but a ruin, and it is stated now that the recent floods in the Gila have washed away the greater part of the ruins, so that in a few years there will be nothing left of Adamsville but the memory of it in the minds of old settlers, and the mention that may be in the official records of the early days.

## WICKED WEAVER

One of the darkest spots in Arizona is the old Mexican adobe town of Weaver. It lays in a gulch between two mountains in the placer gold region of southern Yavapai County, and from the earliest period in the history of the Territory up to the present, everything that has a horror to it in crimes and criminals has been sadly its own. Nothing good has come from it, and as long as the element it harbors and encourages in fiendish lawlessness and cold-blooded murders is permitted, just that long will Weaver thrive in its barbaric life.

The frightful murder of William Segna is not any more startling than the past has to point to. This latest crime recalls the many startling murders within the confines of the peaceful hills surrounding the camp. Scores of human lives have been traced directly to its door and hardly has a year passed but what it has claimed another innocent life. It would seem that time in its civilizing influences cannot wipe from Weaver its annual horror in cold-blooded murder. The murderers of the Barney Martin family, Stanton, Gribble, Verdier and many others; the numerous stage holdups, robbery and a general chapter of criminal lawlessness, has given Weaver a stain that time cannot wipe away.

It is an old saying and as true as it is old, that when a white man goes there, he leaves all hope behind. With only one exception can it be said to the contrary, and that is the instance where a man left before his doom was anticipated, by a few hours only. Worse than all the bloody deeds to stain not only that hamlet, and give to all Arizona a curse from time to time, never can it be said to the credit of the law and order element or of Arizona justice, has a single criminal paid the penalty of his crime. Not a case is there on record in short, where justice has followed a single criminal from that center other than a penitentiary term of slight duration.

Deputy Sheriff Pete Boscha came in to Prescott from Congress on official duties connected with the Segna murder which took place on Sunday night. The news of the murder first reached Congress, and Boscha, after stopping here, hied himself to the scene of the horror. The body had not been disturbed before his arrival at Weaver. The murdered man proved to be an Austrian, named William Segna, who kept a saloon and mercantile establishment at Weaver. The deputy found the body lying on the floor in a pool of its own blood; the head had been almost severed from the body by a stroke of a knife, and the face and body were covered with stab wounds. The room looked like a slaughter pen and the whole presented a horrid and sickening sight. Blood was spattered high upon the side walls of the room, giving evidence of the terrible struggle which had taken place before, the man fighting for his

life and the assassins bent on taking life. The murdered man is highly spoken of as a good citizen and popular man. He worked for the Congress Gold Company for some years; ran a saloon at Congress, and later on started in business at Weaver. He was about 38 years old and a member of the I.O.O.F. [*Independent Order of Odd Fellows*].

Boscha, who had considerable detective ability, went to work to ferret out the perpetrators of this crime. He arrested several Mexicans, and soon brought out enough evidence to fasten the deed upon two brothers named Lucero, two sons of the oldest Mexican family at Weaver. One of the brothers arrested was said to have been seen in Segna's store about the time of the murder. The two brothers were born in the Weaver district and grew up there; their father, blind with age, runs a store there, and to his career as a spectator of a generation of bloody deeds he is known as "The King of Weaver." It was the third and eldest brother of these boys, Pedro, who had been a fugitive from justice for years, and who had been suspected of murdering Gribble and later, Stanton, residents of that district.

—Prescott *Journal-Miner*, 1898


*From the sheriff's office of Yavapai County came a notice, which was published in the Prescott Courier, describing the suspects and revealing that a sack of gold dust valued at about $400 and about $40.00 in silver had been taken from the store of the slain man. The Sheriff stated that he had requested the Governor to issue a proclamation of reward and had ordered all officers to be on the lookout for the suspects.*

*The Governor promptly issued a proclamation, which was also published in the Courier, offering $300 for the arrest and detention in any jail of the Territory and evidence sufficient to convict the person or persons of the crime of killing William Segna.*

*The Courier, a few days later, carried the following information:*

The murder of William Segna is being unraveled slowly and the perpetrators of it are coming to light. Three arrests have been made and the accused are now in jail at Prescott. Deputy Boscha, having them in custody arrived in Prescott from Congress this morning where they had a preliminary hearing yesterday before Judge Francis, who held them to appear before the grand jury. The evidence on which they were committed is said to have been strong, and the accused offered nothing in defense. The names of the three prisoners could not be learned except that two of them are the Lucero brothers and the other is an old time Weaver offender who served a term in the county jail.

When arrested, one of the Luceros was found at Wickenburg, fifteen miles from the scene of the crime, and was taken in by "Susie" Wilson. The others were arrested by Deputy Boscha, near the scene of the killing. Boscha is to be highly commended for his diligent and fearless work in connection with this horrible murder. He has gone among them alone, and it seems from the interest he and others have manifested, a gang of high-handed murderers is to be broken up once and forever, and that section relieved of its annual horror in life taking.

Boscha stated that, since the crime and the apprehension of the suspects, a veritable stampede was on from Weaver, the law-abiding element of that place stating they feared the last tragedy at that place would result as disastrously to the innocent as to the guilty, and as a necessary precaution to save themselves as well as personal property, they would leave the place forever. Old men, women and children were the principal ones to leave.

Besides the ones arrested, it has been definitely learned that a regularly organized gang was maintained, and for the first time, be it said, do the law-abiding Mexicans at that place realize the fate that awaits all, and are willing to give to the officers any clue or knowledge they may have of the deeds which lay at the door of that hotbed of crime.

Three other suspects are being hunted for, and no doubt exists but that the remaining guilty ones will come before what awaits them. That section seems to be thoroughly aroused, and it is about time. If the law is not permitted to take its course, the sentiment of nearly all is that the people who have interests and lives to protect will break up the combination which for over thirty years has held sway in murder, robbery and intimidation.

Toward the end of the year 1898 the Prescott Courier, commenting on the general exodus of the people from Weaver, reported that five more families had left the Weaver district and had moved to Congress because they had assisted officers in obtaining evidence in the Segna murder case and feared that if they stayed there they would be murdered.

In January of 1899, Deputy Sheriff Boscha, of Congress, was in Prescott, and the Journal-Miner quoted him as saying:

"Everything, practically, has moved away from the place. There may be two or three persons there yet, and the buildings still stand, but further than this the settlement is deserted. Some of the Mexicans living there were born and raised in the community, and had never stirred outside; but the moral shakeup the town received over Segna's murder caused them to stir out."

The Phoenix Gazette reprinted the above quote and added this line:

Weaver has had a dark and bloody history, and it is best if it is never settled again.

Of those brought to trial in the District Court of Yavapai County, two of the Lucero brothers were found not guilty and a third brother was found guilty of the murder of Segna and sentenced to life imprisonment.

In connection with the foregoing story, it should be stated that there were two towns named Weaver, the Mexican town and the American settlement which was farther up the mountain and named for Pauline Weaver, noted prospector, scout, and guide who in 1863 had led the Peeples party through this region where a fortune in gold nuggets was picked up on the surface and along the creek beds.

## EHRENBERG POST OFFICE

Ehrenberg, in Yuma County, is now a ghost town. In the early 1870's, when it was at its peak, it was an important place and had a population of about 500. Mail was then routed through Yuma, 125 miles to the south, twice a week over a horseback route. At that time the lower Colorado River was used for steamboat transportation, and this town was the shipping point for freight for Prescott and other mining districts in the interior. After the building of the overland railroads through Arizona Ehrenberg's prosperity began to decline, and before very long it was nothing but a memory.

The following incident occurred around 1893. This account was published as a reminiscence in the Phoenix Republican in 1899, following the appointment of a new postmaster for Ehrenberg:

A late dispatch from Washington announced the appointment
of Gus Livingston, postmaster at Ehrenberg, Arizona Territory.
The mention of a postmaster or post office in connection with
Ehrenberg recalls the funniest thing that ever occurred in the history of the postal system in this country or any other. During Harrison's administration, and possibly for some time before, the
postmaster at Ehrenberg was a man named Daniel. Complaints of
the postmaster's negligence were received at the Department, but
they were vague at first and little attention was paid to them. Even
when Daniel quit sending in quarterly reports it was supposed he
had nothing to report; that there was no business being done at
the Ehrenberg post office.

When Harrison was succeeded by Cleveland a petition was sent
from Ehrenberg for the appointment of a Democrat to be postmaster. In due course the appointment was made and the new
postmaster's commission forwarded to him. After some months,
inquiry was made at the Department on behalf of the new postmaster. His friends wanted to know if he was going to be appointed and suggested, if not, the Department ought by ordinary
courtesy, at least reply to the application and say so. If any further
endorsements of his capability were required they would be cheer-
fully furnished. Thus the attention of the Democratic administration was again called to Ehrenberg post office and the matter was
looked up. It was discovered that no report had been received from
Ehrenberg since Mr. Cleveland's induction into office and it was
also recalled that an appointment of a postmaster had been made.
The whole subject was referred to Inspector Waterbury, whose
headquarters was at Denver.

Mr. Waterbury made a trip to Ehrenberg and found that public
affairs there were in a strange state of neglect. Postmaster Daniel
said he hadn't time to fool with the "damned" post office. He was
engaged in trying to mine. The post office consisted of a candle-
box which was filled with letters, some of which had been posted
and some of which had been received. Many of them were found
to have been there four years. Between the candle-box and the
wall there were several letters, among them some registered letters.
There were several letters from the Department to the postmaster.
Among them was one from Postmaster General Wanamaker to the

postmaster. It was a personal rather than an official communication. Mr. Wanamaker took occasion to effusively thank Mr. Daniel for the signally efficient manner in which he was conducting the Ehrenberg post office. "The efficiency of the Department and the success of the Republicans," wrote Mr. Wanamaker, "depends largely upon the faithfulness and individual efforts of those who have been put into public places."

The commission of Mr. Daniel's successor was found in the candle-box, where it had reposed for several months. There was a letter three years old from an anxious mother in Massachusetts to her son who had come to Arizona for his health. It had been so long since she heard from him, she wrote, that she was almost consumed by anxiety. There were lovers' letters, both going and coming. There were business letters of the utmost importance, many of them, addressed to the postmaster himself. Mr. Waterbury ascertained that for months before his visit Daniel had absolutely discontinued the office. He permitted the mail to be delivered there and received matter for mailing, but the one was never distributed and the other was never forwarded. There had been no cancellation of stamps and no sale. There were, in fact, no stamps on hand and Mr. Daniel was unable to state when the supply ran out, and more, he said he didn't care. If the government didn't like his way of conducting a post office let it hire another postmaster. Mr. Waterbury stayed at Ehrenberg long enough to put Mr. Daniel's successor into the office and get it on its feet again. It was like opening a new post office.

*Thomas J. Goodman was the gentleman appointed postmaster at Ehrenberg to succeed Daniel in 1891. His commission was forwarded to him, and it was found among the letters in the candle box in about 1893 by Inspector Waterbury. Goodman, who was a mining man in the district, apparently hadn't known of his own appointment until the papers were found by the Inspector. Who was postmaster from this time until Gus Livingston's appointment in 1899 is not known.*

In 1894, when Post Office Inspector Waterbury sent his report to the Department concerning the Ehrenberg difficulties, the Yuma Times reported these pertinent points:

In the office were found 158 letters, some of which were post-marked shortly after Postmaster Daniel had assumed charge of the office. Among them were fifty-seven with requests for return on them; several were addressed to Ellisburg, Washington, and had never been forwarded, some of which had been received in 1881; fifty-one were letters addressed to parties in Ehrenberg which the Inspector delivered himself, and seven registered letters. There was in the office, laid to one side, sixty official letters from the Department at Washington addressed to the postmaster, not one of which had been opened. Two full sacks of paper mail lay in a corner, neither of which had been opened.

## GALEYVILLE DIED IN INFANCY

The old mining camp of Galeyville, thirty-five miles north of the Mexican border and fourteen miles west of the New Mexico line, had a hectic and colorful history during its short life, and although the district was revived to a small degree in later years, the real Galeyville of the old West existed for only two short years, 1880-82, and then died when the Texas Mining Company discontinued operations.

Disturnell's Gazetteer, published in 1881, says in part:

Galeyville, sixty miles northeast of Tombstone, is a thriving mining town in the California district of Arizona. It occupies a picturesque site in the midst of shady oaks, on a greensward mesaland, in a cool corner of the Chiricahua Mountains, with the cool and clear waters of Turkey Creek coursing through its streets. The mountains on which the town is situated are noted for the grandeur of their scenery, and will no doubt soon become a favorite resort for tourists. A daily line of stages maintains communication with San Simon, a station on the Southern Pacific railroad, twenty-five miles distant. In the vicinity are numerous mines, which are being energetically developed and yielding high grade ore. Among the number is the Texas, the owners of which have recently put up a smelter and are now shipping bullion.

An article recounting the history of Galeyville appeared in the Tucson Citizen in 1911. The reporter based it on accounts of pioneers who had lived in the district:

The early history of the camp owed its enactment to the operation then of the Texas property. It was in 1880 that operations began. The original locators of this claim made a strike of some rich silver ore, on the strength of which they sold the claims to John H. Galey, of Pennsylvania, who had been attracted to the Chiricahuas by the high price of silver and the reported discovery.

Tombstone was then enjoying her palmiest days, being the nearest large town, but Tucson was then the county seat, this being all Pima County then [later Cochise County]. The Southern Pacific was the only railroad; the nearest point, San Simon. Freighting into this district was done from that point, the charge for hauling the twenty-five miles being $1.50 a hundred.

It is obvious the camp was named for Galey, and after considerable ore had been taken out and a road had been built down to the flat, the smelter was built. The water for the smelter was furnished by a spring situated near the head of one of the washes on the mountainside, being piped down to a tank just above the smelter.

By this time the camp was very lively, the company employing in the neighborhood of a hundred men in mine and smelter. Wages were from $5 to $6 a day; table board $1.50 per day; drinks were 25 cents. And some idea of the cost of mining may be gained from the fact that giant powder brought 40 cents a pound.

The main portion of the town was just above the smelter and was composed mainly of frame buildings and tents although there were a few adobe buildings. Tents and campfires were scattered along each bank of Turkey Creek, and many people had mining locations all over the hills.

[Disturnell's 1881 Gazetteer lists eleven saloons, six merchandise stores, two hotels, two restaurants, two butcher shops, a dairy, two blacksmith and wagon shops, a laundry, three lumber yards, a boot and shoe maker, a jeweler, three lawyers, three notary publics, an assayer, a physician, a sign maker, and a bath house. There was also a post office, newspaper, and Wells-Fargo office.

At about the same period the Phoenix Herald carried an item saying that Galeyville had neither a church nor a school, but was plentifully supplied with saloons.]

On blowing in the smelter it was found that the ore was not self-fluxing and could not be treated; and the camp's future was dimmed. Before long a suitable flux was discovered, however, in the Granite Gap district across the line in New Mexico. By using one part of this ore and two parts of the Texas ore the reduction process was a complete success. So the company bonded the new property and put ten or twelve men at work. The Granite Gap ore was then hauled to Galeyville continuously and for several weeks; so long as the company operated, the smelter then treated the ore successfully.

Shipments delayed, the company rapidly drifted into straightened circumstances, owing the miners large amounts and the merchants suffering in consequence. For a time the merchants did not complain and the miners stayed on; but endurance finally came to an end.

About this time—it was early in 1882—two carloads of bullion were shipped, and Galeyville began to breathe easier, thinking the company would pay up. But all were doomed to disappointment— the "ghost" did not walk again. Manager Galey, who had departed for Tucson in the meantime, sent for his foreman and informed him that the company had decided to shut down. . . .

The miners then conceived the idea of taking hold and operating the property themselves, so as to secure the pay due them; but the other company would not bond them the Granite Gap property, so without fluxing ores they were unable to proceed and Galeyville was a thing of the past.

Those were days of hostile Indians, and Galeyville had more than one scare from roving tribes during which the prospectors in the hills were forced to the comparative safety of the camp. Then there were the cattle rustlers, who would raid down into Mexico and steal cattle and drive them into the Galeyville area, which was one of comparative safety. Along with this there were innumerable specimens of the worst of the bad men. Galeyville was a place for only those who were brave, a place where law and order was impossible, where might and the trigger finger made right—the days of the survival of the "fittest."

In a letter from John J. Gosper, Acting Governor of Arizona, to James G. Blaine, Secretary of State in Washington, in December, 1881, is the following passage, reprinted in the *Tucson Citizen*:

At Galeyville, San Simon and other points isolated from large places, the cowboy element at times very fully predominates, and the officers of the law are at times either unable or unwilling to control this class of outlaws, sometimes being governed by fear; at other times by a hope of reward. At Tombstone, the county seat

of Cochise County, I conferred with the sheriff of said county upon the subject of breaking up these bands of outlaws, and I am sorry to say he gave but little hope of being able, in his department, to cope with the power of the cowboys. He represented to me that the Deputy U. S. Marshal, [Wyatt] Earp, resident of Tombstone, and the city Marshal for the same, and those who aided him, seemed unwilling to heartily cooperate with him [the Sheriff] in capturing and bringing to justice these outlaws. In conversation with Mr. Earp, I found precisely the same spirit of complaint existing against [John] Behan [the Sheriff] and his deputies. And back of this unfortunate fact, rivalry between the civil authorities, or an unwillingness to work together in full accord in keeping the peace, I found two daily newspapers published in the city [of Tombstone], taking sides with the deputy marshal and sheriff, respectively, each paper backing its civil clique and backing the other; and, still back of all this, the unfortunate fact that many of the very best law-abiding and peace-loving citizens have no confidence in the willingness of the civil officers to pursue and bring to justice that element of outlawry so largely disturbing the sense of security, and so often committing highway robbery and smaller thefts.

*In a letter from Galeyville, signed "Clipper," appearing in the Tucson Citizen and directed to the Acting Governor, is this response:*

In reply to your inquiry concerning the "cowboys" who are reported to have been, and still are, raiding along the line of Sonora and Arizona, I will say: The gang who are known as "cowboys" are engaged in stock-raising in the valleys of San Simon and Cloverdale, in the southeastern portion of Arizona, and from good authority I learn that the cattle, horses and sheep now controlled by said cowboys have been stolen from the citizens of Sonora, Arizona and New Mexico. They are reported to have about three hundred head of cattle at or near Granite Gap, in New Mexico, and close to the line of Arizona. It is a well-known fact that they are in the habit of making raids along the border. Until recently it has been the custom to steal horses and cattle in Arizona and drive them into Sonora for sale, and on the return trip steal stock in Sonora and drive them into Arizona and New Mexico for sale; consequently quite a traffic was kept up. This practice has abated somewhat lately, on account of the killing of four cowboys on the Fronteras, in, I think, June last. The circumstances, as near as can be ascertained, are these: Last spring George Turner and M. McAllister, two well-known cowboys, obtained the contract at Fort Bowie for furnishing beef for the command. They and two assistants went to Sonora to either buy or steal beef cattle. They succeeded in driving a large herd as far as Fronteras, where they were attacked by the Mexican citizens. They (the cowboys) were all killed, and one Mexican citizen was killed. Upon the bodies of Turner and McAllister was found the money which it is supposed they ostensibly took to purchase cattle, which amount compared with what they were known to have started from here with proved that the cattle they were driving had not been paid for. This affair has caused bad blood between the cowboys and the citizens of Sonora; each party taking revenge upon the other whenever opportunity occurs; consequently it is unsafe for any person to travel across the border. About a month ago the cowboys went across the border into Sonora, and seeing a good sized pack train in charge of Mexicans, laid in ambush and at the word of command made a dash and succeeded in capturing the whole outfit, consisting of about $1000 in Mexican coin, silver bullion, mescal, horses and cattle. One of the cowboys, in relating to me the circumstances, said it was the damndest lot of truck he ever saw. He showed me a piece of the bullion; I should judge it to be one-half gold. Upon my telling him that trouble would likely arise from this, he replied that it was a smuggling train, and they would not dare say much. There were three Mexicans killed in the affray. A notorious cowboy known as John R. offers to sell all the mutton the town can consume at the rate of $1 per head. No secrecy is observed in this kind of transaction. As regards the local officers of the law, I cannot do better than refer you to the clipping from the Tucson Star, which is hereto attached:

Editor Star:
    Permit me to give you a brief history of a trial before a border Justice of the Peace, known as G. W. Ellingwood.

David Estes was one of two men who robbed a game of about four hundred dollars in cash at the midnight hour in the town of Galeyville, as follows: Estes entered the front door of the saloon in which the game was being played, armed with a Winchester and a six-shooter; his "pal" passing in at the rear of the house, armed in a similar manner. They ordered the players to throw up their hands and surrender all their cash. This accomplished, Estes proceeded to the corral of Babcock & Co. and extracted and confiscated a valuable horse, making the total cleanup about five hundred dollars. Estes was subsequently arrested by Deputy Sheriff Goodman and tried before said Ellingwood, and discharged. His Honor ruled in the examination of the witnesses that they could not testify to the taking of money (ordered by the bandits to be left on the table) unless they of their own knowledge knew to whom a particular parcel of money belonged. This could not be proven, as all the occupants of the room were commanded to decamp instantly, leaving Estes and his pard to take and divide. Thus you see a single pair in Galeyville wins five hundred dollars. Under the ruling of this astute and noble judge no evidence was admitted necessary to conviction. Deputy Sheriff Goodman asked to be sworn to testify that the prisoner offered him five hundred dollars to cast loose his shackles and let him at liberty. This testimony was ruled out by the Court as being irrevelant and not material to the issue. While the trial was in progress the Judge stated to Quartz Johnson that the prisoner could not be convicted, and subsequently that he (the judge) would now stand well with the cowboys.

Another letter from "Clipper" which was printed in the same issue of the Tucson Citizen, followed the above story from the Star:

I will also state another case. "Billy the Kid" [not the "Billy the Kid" of the Lincoln County War], a stripling belonging to the profession, was arrested for stealing horses. Upon his examination the Court ruled that the affidavit upon which he was arrested charged him with the crime of theft, but should have been larceny.

Also the person from whom the horses had been stolen voluntarily stated to the Court that he did not want the boy prosecuted as he agreed to return the horses. The same person told me afterward that if he had prosecuted the boy the other cowboys would steal every head of stock he had, which he, being a poor man, could not afford to stand. The cowboys frequently visit our town [Galeyville] and often salute us with an indiscriminate discharge of firearms, and after indulging in a few drinks at the saloons, practice shooting at the lamps, bottles, glasses, etc., sometimes going to the length of shooting the cigar out of one's mouth. THIS, OF COURSE, PRODUCES A NERVOUS FEELING.*

The situation at this writing is not materially changed from the above. The cowboys, as a class, are not over brave, though there are among them those who have gone through so much difficulty that they have become desperate and take desperate chances.

The Arizona State Guide contains the following:

Among the outlaws who found refuge in Galeyville's isolation and recreation in its many saloons were "Curly Bill" Brocius and his handsome lieutenant, John Ringo. Curly Bill, a bronzed blue-eyed giant with dark, kinky hair, always wore high-heeled, fancy-stitched boots, a wide-brimmed white sombrero, and two criss-crossed gun belts that held his twin forty-fours. He was a discriminating bandit, robbing only the prosperous. Caravans of Mexican smugglers were his special delight; and he showed such a preference in his rustling for Mexican cattle that his name was mentioned prominently in a number of warm-worded diplomatic notes passed between the two governments. Nevertheless he was popular and enjoyed the friendship of many men, including the Deputy Sheriff, Billie Breckenridge, who used the bandit to help him collect taxes. In lawless Cochise County this was one of the sheriff's most difficult and hazardous tasks. But whenever Breckenridge and Curly Bill called the ranchers were eager to pay up, and the Deputy completed his rounds in record time, returning with his saddle pouches bulging with tax dollars.

* The capitalization is the editor's.

*Though killings were frequent, Galeyville was seldom disturbed by the law.*

Curly Bill had, on a previous occasion, shot Tombstone's Marshal White in a ruckus there, the bullet wound eventually causing White's death. Curly Bill was not prosecuted for the deed, as it was decided that the shot that killed White was caused by the accidental discharge of Curly's gun as the marshal grabbed it away from him in an attempt to disarm him. From that time on, it is said, Curly Bill seldom made an appearance in Tombstone, but made his headquarters at Galeyville.

About the middle of 1881, the Tucson Citizen published the following, greatly exaggerated report of Curly's demise:

Curly Bill, a notorious outlaw, was shot and instantly killed at Galeyville by his partner, Jim Wallace. They had both been drinking, and had a few hot words several times during the day. Finally Curly Bill threatened to shoot Wallace "on general principles," but the latter slipped out the door and waited until Bill appeared, and shot him. Wallace was arrested by Deputy Sheriff Breckenridge, and taken before Justice Ellingwood, who discharged the prisoner upon evidence that he committed the deed in self defense. Immediately upon being set free, Wallace left on horseback for parts unknown.

The next week the Citizen published the following bulletin from the Galeyville Bulletin, and although it did not include a retraction, it was quite obvious that the report printed in the Citizen the previous week had been erroneous:

Curly Bill was shot by Jim Wallace, a friend, the ball taking effect in the left side of the neck, three inches below and a little back of the ear, ranging up, the ball making its exit below the right jaw.

The Phoenix Gazette carried a story from the Tucson Journal that said:

From a gentleman who arrived from Galeyville, we learn that Curly Bill is rapidly recovering from the effects of his wound. Curly's escape from death was miraculous, the ball passing between the thorax and jugular vein without touching either. When the doctor examined the wound, Bill asked him what his chances for life were. The doctor replied that the chances were about even. "Then," exclaimed Bill, "I'm going to get well, for whenever I get an even chance I always come out ahead." Curly says his fighting days are over and that he intends to return to Texas to see his old mother as soon as he recovers. He got off a witticism at the expense of his shooter, Wallace. "Boys," said he, "let Wallace go up to Tombstone. They'll turn out to meet him with a brass band!" It is a fact that there isn't much love in Tombstone for Curly, and no doubt Wallace would receive a popular ovation for his service in giving Curly a dose of lead, and thus incapacitating him from mischief for some weeks to come.

## CALABASAS CAPERS

The vanished town of Calabasas, on the Santa Cruz ten miles north of Nogales, has a fascinating history. Long before it became a rip-roaring town in the early 1880s it, like near-by Tumacacori, was an Indian village and a visita of the Jesuits. As early as 1777 mines in the vicinity were being worked by the Spaniards. This site was next to the fine ranch of the Governor of Sonora; later it was a Mexican military post, and in 1856 it was occupied by the United States dragoons as a military base. Later it was farmed by a family named Pennington, after which it was acquired by the Calabasas Mining Company. At the time the railroad was projected in 1880 the place began to boom.

Calabazas is a Spanish word, meaning "pumpkins," and although the town's name was spelled that way in 1866 when a post office was first established there, in 1882 the postal department saw fit to change the spelling to Calabasas. The name supposedly referred to the huge pumpkins which were grown in the area together with *other fine crops. Wild game was also abundant in the surrounding hills, and this combination, together with the prospect of the place becoming a railroad terminal, made for the location of a boom town.*

*The Tucson Citizen described Calabasas as follows in 1882:*

This embryo city, which is laid out mathematically, is divided into squares of three hundred feet face, with intersecting alleys of twenty feet in width. The streets are sixty feet wide and cross each other at right angles. There are two avenues, the Sonoita and the Santa Cruz, each one hundred feet wide, and situated one toward either end of the town. Several blocks have been reserved for park purposes, as also one for the school building, and one for the hotel. Within the town limits there are 2,800 lots of which some 2,500 have been sold, some few for speculative purposes, but mostly to parties who give guarantee to erect suitable buildings within a specified time.

*The Citizen then published a rather facetious item concerning the new town's progress:*

The magic growth of this place is causing much comment. Within the past week five wooden buildings have been put up and others are in course of construction. The principal street is called Buzzards Lane, named so on account of the bad English spoken by two French ladies whose stock in trade consists of a snappish little dog that runs out to bring the unwary in. The upper lights of the town live in brick houses and profit by the style of architecture. . . . The shades of day give place to the glimmer and smell of bad coal oil, when the demi-monde congregate to show their nice dresses and trip the light fantastic. The hug in the dizzy waltz makes one stand amazed amid the whirl until the barkeeper shouts the announcement "promenade your ladies to the bar," and so it goes till some despised railroader calls for a dance when up jumps some noble son of Kansas and gives him the grand bounce.

*In another column, this paper says:*

Calabasas has a population of about one hundred and fifty men, and has sixteen saloons, six gambling tables, two dance houses, two

Chinese gambling houses, one opium den, and five stores, one of which is kept by the Chinese, and but one lodging house, which is a great inconvenience, but the latter is counterbalanced by the comforting presence of an abundance of good whiskey, being sold for a bit of drink; puts good men to bed all over the adjoining mesa. The roundhouse and railroad shops will undoubtedly be built here, and when the work on them commences livelier times may be expected.

*A few months later a letter from Calabasas was published in the Citizen:*

Here we have the finest hotel west of the Rockies and to its attractions are added some ten or a dozen of the best-looking Boston-made girls that the country affords. The Hotel de Santa Ritas, finely situated, as finely built and as finely furnished as any hotel on the coast, barring none. Others may be larger but the wants and comforts of the guests cannot be better attended to. Colonel Sykes, the proprietor, is a man of large means and great capabilities who had in view when building it the comforts of a home, and in it one cannot fail finding them. Colonel Lane is the genial host who together with the Boston girls and the advantages named, makes the hotel one that is exceedingly hard to beat.

*Editor's note: Calabasas was often referred to as "Hell's Hollow" during its boom days, when it was so prominently before the public because of its evil doings as a frontier town. As an example of the lawlessness in the town, some of the incidents within a span of three months in 1882 are given. Some accounts are from the Tombstone Epitaph and others from the Tucson Citizen. All are letters from Calabasas:*

Last Sunday afternoon a saloon keeper from near the Mexico line came to Calabasas and indulged in a shooting fracas, by which two men were slightly wounded, one of them being an innocent bystander. It appears that the saloon keeper and a stranger were having some words in front of Smith & Bain's saloon when a crowd gathered to witness the melee, which ended in the stranger being shot in the arm, the ball penetrating it, and striking another party in the ankle making a very painful wound. After doing the shooting he put spurs to his horse and skipped out; but Deputy Sheriff Vosburg was not long in getting his horse ready, and an exciting race of about four miles was had between the two horsemen, but the Deputy finally took his man and made him drop his guns, two in number, and marched him back to town where he was brought before Justice St. John, and the men whom he had shot not appearing, he was fined to the full extent of the law, which he paid and departed.

Monday morning about seven o'clock, a man came into town from Igo's camp, situated about eight miles from this place, after the Coroner and Deputy Sheriff, asking them to go there immediately. The cause for their presence at that place was the result of a shooting affray in which two Mexicans named Vigil and Gonzales were killed outright and Gordon, a night herder, better known as "Shorty" at the camp, was slightly wounded. The affair happened in a saloon about a quarter of a mile from the camp. It appears that in the afternoon of Sunday, Gordon went up to this saloon, kept by Seabury, and while playing monte, some person removed a new hat from his head and placed thereon an old one. In the evening Shorty again returned to the saloon where the hat matter was brought up, and from words the affair turned to shots. One shot was fired at Shorty by a Mexican but it missed him, when he pulled his revolver, which snapped and he retreated into the street, and as he was doing so was shot in the hip. He dropped and immediately commenced firing among the Mexicans, emptying five chambers of his pistol, when he was assisted to his feet by friends and hurried off to camp. It was near midnight when this occurred, and after lighting lamps in the saloon, which had been extinguished in the fracas, it was found that two Mexicans were killed outright, and one missing, who was wounded, and was last seen entering a dense thicket nearby.

Before the arrival of the Coroner and Deputy Sheriff, the Mexicans, some thirty in number, had assembled and were preparing to make a raid on the camp for the purpose of taking Shorty out and making him dance an air jig at the end of a string of hemp. The men at the camp were well prepared to meet the attacking party, as they were armed with Remington and Sharp's rifles. No doubt but for the timely arrival of the officers, there would have been a few more Mexicans to hold an inquest over. The Deputy Sheriff rode up to the Mexicans and assured them that justice would be meted out to the guilty parties, when the work of holding the inquest was proceeded with. One of the men was shot twice by a pistol or rifle, one of the balls penetrating the heart, and the other about two inches to the left; the other man was undoubtedly shot by a double-barreled shotgun, as a large hole was made in his body near the heart. During the inquest a cranky blacksmith who was present, jerked the Coroner's revolver out of its scabbard and before he could be prevented, shot at a Mexican, just grazing his scalp. The Coroner immediately after the inquest called a court and fined him $100 and three months imprisonment in the county jail; his name is Fred Ball.

During the time of the holding of the inquest, the armed force at the camp kept advancing up a ravine in the canyon, until within several hundred feet of the saloon, when the Deputy Sheriff, who had kept his eyes on them, ordered them to return to camp. Their object in coming up was, that they wished to be on hand in case the Mexicans should attempt to make an attack on the officers and few Americans present, to assist in defending them.

A rumor was circulated in Calabasas that the officers were corralled by the Mexicans and their lives were in danger, when two wagon-loads of well-armed men left that place for the camp, only to meet the Coroner and Deputy Sheriff on their return, all safe and sound.

—Tucson *Citizen*

Calabasas wants to be incorporated. If the inhabitants keep on "removing" each other at the rate they have been doing, there won't be enough left to fill the city offices.

Last Wednesday evening, near Calabasas, some of the laborers employed in that vicinity captured a Mexican in the attempt of smuggling mescal across the line, and representing themselves as custom officials, confiscated the entire cargo. Of course the feat was loudly cheered by their companions and it was moved and seconded that the spoils be "punished" forthwith. This they proceeded to do, but there being several gallons of the contraband it required some little time to get away with it. Jest and merriment abounded and the party was in high glee. The impromptu revenue officers, naturally, were the heroes of the occasion, until one fellow grew jealous of the congratulations showered upon his neighbors, and announced that that feat was nothing compared with something he had done on the San Pedro about a year ago. All asked what it was, and were informed that he "took in" three Mexicans with fifteen gallons of mescal and two bushels of tobacco, with sundry boxes of cigars and baskets of panoche on the San Pedro last summer. The crowd was unanimous in declaring it a fine feat if it occurred, but a number of them doubted.

The hero of the San Pedro said he told the truth, and could whip anyone who thought different and so announced themselves. The fellow who bet on himself, withdrew from the crowd and declared his intention of going to camp for a gun. On the return trip he met one of the "revenue officers" and dared him to a fight. The challenge was accepted, and they commenced to blaze away at each other, being about twenty yards apart. Both had heavy Colt's revolvers, and both advanced as they fired. Two shots from each passed harmlessly, but at the third fire the "revenue officer" fell, mortally wounded. The other fellow, when he saw his antagonist fall, wheeled around and ran towards a mesquite grove and has not since been seen. It is supposed that he made his way to Sonora. The other man, whose name was Bob Scoville, died in about twenty minutes after receiving the wound. Both men were tough characters and Arizona has not lost seriously in being permanently rid of them. A number of men chased the other fellow but were unable to find him. His name was George Ryan.

—Tombstone *Epitaph*

There was a dance at Calabasas last Sunday night. Ordinarily this would be an event of little moment, but on this particular occasion it calls for more than passing mention. It was a mixed gathering, composed principally of American men and Mexican women. There were three white women in the party; recent arrivals from Tucson, and of course they were the pets. The Mexican women danced and enjoyed themselves thoroughly, but among the Americans of the same sex, there was a bitter rivalry.

The cause of the difficulty is unknown but certain it is that it existed, and if one of them wanted to waltz, another was sure to call for a schottische, while the third had her heart set on a quadrille. As may be expected, each of them was escorted by a cavalier, and as a natural consequence the cavalier was a warm partisan of the hobbies and foibles of his lady. Under these circumstances the position of prompter was not an enviable one.

Sally's cavalier would call out "give us a waltz," and Jennie's "bully boy" would reply, "give us a rest; do you want us dancin' waltzes all night? Turn the music loose on a quadrille and see us skip." At this stage Nettie's "fiddler" would chip in "to hell with your waltzes and quadrilles; let us sail through a polka."

When it is remembered that the three most estimable desperadoes in the town were the partners and partisans of the girls, the position of the prompter can be best understood. He finally announced that conceiving it impossible to unite the dancers on any one thing, he take the reins in his own hands, and "run the racket" to suit himself. He therefore announced a quadrille. Scarcely was the word out of his mouth, when Jim Smith, Jennie's "striker," drew his pistol and commenced to pump lead into the prompter. The latter lived for about half a minute and was borne from the room a corpse. His name was Harrington and he was a barkeeper by profession.

Ere the dead body was well out of the room the dance was resumed and continued with unusual vigor. Smith had everything his own way and nobody disputed his authority on the premises. Next morning one of his rivals of the night before made the mention that the prompter did not get a fair deal. The opinion thus expressed was conveyed to Smith and he went in quest of the detractor. A shooting match ensued, in which Smith was again victorious, the other party coming out of the contest with one arm in a dilapidated condition. At last account Smith was a prominent and respected citizen of Calabasas, with nothing to mar his pleasures, sports or pastimes.

–Tombstone Epitaph

Deputy Sheriff Vosburg is a frequent visitor to our town, and would come even oftener but times in Calabasas are a little dull at present. However often he may come he does not come alone as may be seen by the register of our county jail.

Manuel Cota is his latest contribution from a dance house in Calabasas. He carved a fellow dancer for fun, and as that happened to be an infraction of the law he was given board in Tucson and time to explain. On the evening previous to their leaving, a man by the name of Johnson, the keeper of a dance house, was, while calling the figures, shot dead without cause or altercation, which event caused a momentary cessation of the light fantastic; but before the body had been removed or the sound of the death shot had died on the air, a new caller had been substituted and "get your partners for the next quadrille" caused a rush and the fun went on as before. The man who did the shooting mounted his horse and escaped, although closely pursued by the Sheriff and his Deputy, Sutton, the latter firing a double-barrel load of buckshot at the murderer at short range, but without effect, the night being too dark for certain aim. He was, however, followed, but could not be overtaken. In a drunken brawl of several weeks since he had been shot through the arm, and had since that time been carousing about the town, and was generally considered a quiet man. But this killing of Johnson was said to have been without ceremony or excuse.

With reference to the above came a letter to the editor of the Citizen which was printed in that paper two weeks later:

Calabasas, A. T., June 20, 1882

Editor Citizen:

In an extended article in your weekly issue you refer to an occurrence in a dance house here, which resulted in the killing of one Johnson. I wish to correct an erroneous impression which might be obtained from the report as published. This is a border town without municipal organization and is subjected to the experiences of all frontier places. The occurrence referred to was a murder; there was no provocation and the gentleman in charge of the house at the time of the killing fired twice at the assailant before his escape; the Deputy Sheriff was at once on duty and followed his trail —the Acting Coroner was promptly on hand and summoned a jury; a regular physician made an autopsy; an inquest was held and a verdict rendered in accord with the facts presented—the body was taken in charge and prepared for burial before any business was allowed. The rivalry of other villages (now cities) induces the publication of anything derogatory to the health and morale of this locality. I will state for the information of all concerned that any man that is ordinarily active will be exempt from the effects of malaria and if he attends to his own business without being armed he will not be "stood up." To others equally as verdant as your former informant I will state that the steamboats upon the Santa Cruz make their landing at the foot of Sonoita Avenue, discharge their cargo and receive freight as regularly as the tide will permit.

In regard to acts of lawlessness reported to have been committed here and in this vicinity, I will state that they have been perpetrated by "hangers on" of the saloons that follow and stay with every contractor's camp; that the contractors on the line or any community doing a general business without any regular organization should not be held responsible in public opinion for infractions of the law, and I will state further that a municipal organization will soon be perfected and that the room where occupied by tramps, will be occupied by more desirable men.

JOHN HENRY

Reports reached town Thursday night [says the Tombstone Epitaph] of more deviltry at Calabasas, or in the vicinity thereof. That hamlet, situated on the malarial marshes of Pima County, has more blood and thunder to the square inch than any town in the United States. True, it is in an exposed situation, being within a few miles of the Sonora border, where criminals can flee when the legal atmosphere of the United States becomes too warm for them. Besides, the building of the railroad brought together a pack of social outcasts from all parts of the world, to whom abject crime was an amusement, and murder a mere pastime. Sunday evening last, six Italians, who had worked on the construction of the road from the time it left Benson, and had eagerly hoarded their earnings, concluded to depart to pastures new. They had a community of interest and carried a common purse containing $1200. They kept their proposed departure quiet, and left Calabasas without any apparent notice being taken of them, about three o'clock in the afternoon. They went on foot, intending to walk to a station on the road about fifteen miles distant from Calabasas. They had proceeded about half way when they were encountered by seven heavily armed, masked men, who ordered them to throw up their hands.

The Italians had no arms, and hastened to obey the robbers' mandate. Three of the thieves then kept them covered with guns while the rest went through them, robbing the poor devils of every cent they had. They were then ordered to proceed on their journey and the robbers mounted their horses, that were hitched in a neighboring thicket, and rode off in the direction of Sonora.

Soon after, the Italians began discussing the matter and accusations were made that some of the party "tipped" their proposed departure. A row ensued, knives were freely used, and in the course of a few minutes two of the unfortunate men were dead, and the rest fleeing in the direction of Sonora.

About five o'clock the same evening Nelson, a brewer, doing business at Harshaw, and who is in the habit of carting beer to Calabasas, was met by a party of men on the road between Calabasas and Harshaw and robbed of $250. It is supposed that the same men who robbed the Italians also "took in" Nelson. The latter is not certain how many of them there were, but their general appearance is in accord with the heroes of the first robbery. They have not been heard from since.

Two weeks later the Tombstone Epitaph had this story:
They had another shooting scrape at Calabasas Sunday evening. A gentleman who arrived in town Tuesday from that sinful hollow, being approached for news by an Epitaph reporter, gave substantially the following facts:

Sunday evening last some of the tough characters residing in the vicinity were "celebrating" the Sabbath at the camp of a Mexican living near Igo's. The Mexican had some women folks in his family, and the railroaders were making themselves particularly obliging to them. It may be that this was because of a natural spirit of chivalry for the fair sex, and it might have been because they were linguistic students, and anxious to master the soft, tender language of Castile, and then again, it might have been for causes not necessary to mention.

At any rate the señoritas were having a good time. Mescal and whiskey were plenty as water, and everything looked lovely. But mescal and whiskey cannot be drunk all day without its effects being felt, and it is as natural as life that railroaders should fight when their skins are filled with whiskey.

On this occasion four men named James Moroney, Bill Mulcahy, Jack Kingsbury and a fellow named Nevada Jim, were candidates for the smiles of a certain señorita. Angry words came first, to be soon followed by blows. Pistols were then drawn, and Moroney received a ball in the forehead that sent him before his Maker almost instantly. This seemed to sober the others, and knowing that if the friends of the dead man arrived a serious row would ensue, they decamped in the direction of Calabasas.

Arriving at that classic center, they forgot their trouble and entered into the festivities of a dance hall which was in full blast at the time. In the meantime, word of the killing near Igo's was wafted around quickly, and some of the dead man's friends organized a party to pursue the murderers. They followed on to Calabasas, and on inquiry learned that they were in the dance hall. They marched up to the door, revolvers in hand, and seeing the objects of their search waltzing away gayly, turned loose their lead. A scene of dreadful confusion ensued. Not less than fifty shots were fired in half as many seconds. Yelling, cursing, screaming, moaning and the reports of firearms filled the air.

During the melee the three chief criminals escaped by cutting their way through the tent in which the dance was being held. It must not be supposed that the pursuing party had the shooting all to themselves. Far from it. Nearly every man and woman in the room took a hand in it. When the ammunition was exhausted and the smoke cleared off, two men were found dead, and another, a Mexican, has doubtless died since. Four men and three women were wounded more or less seriously, but, as far as could be learned, the three chief criminals escaped without a scratch. Of course their thought was to escape the meshes of the law by crossing into Sonora, and thither they went.

A consultation was held among the survivors at Calabasas and it was decided to start a party on horseback after them. Twelve men armed to the teeth struck out about dusk, resolved to follow the fleeing fugitives into the heart of Mexico, or capture them. Neither the pursued nor the pursuing have been heard from since.

*A few weeks later, in an item in the* Citizen, *was found this startling information:*

News has reached this city, says the Tombstone *Independent*, that the pursuers of the three murderers who made Calabasas howl on Sunday night, a week ago, have returned, having accomplished what they went out for, the capture or death of Mulcahy, Kingsbury and Nevada Jim. In this case it was death to the trio. They were come up with some seventy-five or eighty miles over the border. When the fugitives saw their pursuers coming they took refuge within a bunch of scattered rocks that offered the only shelter on the open plain. Here a severe fight was made, during which the three murderers were killed and two or three of the pursuers were severely wounded. The dead were left on the ground where they fell and the party returned to Calabasas where they were warmly greeted by the citizens of that lively burg.

Sunday evening last, old John Scott, the well known contractor, was packing his outfit preparatory to removing his camp to Silver City, New Mexico, from which place to Deming he had contracted to grade a branch line for the Atchison, Topeka and Santa Fe company. Some of the old employees had made up their minds to go along to the new field of labor, but a number resolved to remain behind and grow up with Calabasas.

This latter party, which was pretty numerous, concluded that a little industry on their part during the excitement consequent on moving camp would be the proper caper. Accordingly several pairs of boots, blankets, overalls and valises were appropriated, and the thieves skipped with their spoil in the direction of Calabasas. When the stolen articles were missed at Igo's camp, a vigorous search was instituted, and suspicion immediately fell where it properly belonged. A chase was agreed upon, and three strong parties, well-armed, went in different directions.

One of these parties struck out toward Calabasas, and, being on foot, it was pretty late in the evening before the city on the Santa Cruz was reached. However, they came up with the robbers in time to prevent the sale of sundry pairs of blankets that were offered for a portion of their value at an impromptu pawn shop. A row ensued, and as the thieves were down to cases and had "soaked" their guns for whiskey some days before, it was a one-sided contest. Nearly all the stolen property was recovered, and the thieves were pounded with pistols until their heads resembled busted tomatoes.

Jimmy McCarty, who was appointed constable of the precinct some weeks ago, with almost unlimited jurisdiction, attempted to quell the row, but in doing so got himself in "hot water" and was soundly kicked. He retired and enrolled a posse to arrest the fighters, and this became the signal for shooting. The railroaders commenced to pump lead in the direction of the constable's party and the latter returned the compliment. Things were decidedly lively for a while, not less than thirty shots being fired in as many seconds. A valuable horse belonging to John McMurray, was shot and killed during the melee, and McMurray himself had a narrow escape.

The citizens rushed around excitedly, and were finally on the point of going to the assistance of the constable, when the railroaders evacuated the town. They departed in the direction of Igo's, and were far from being in good humor. It must not be supposed that it was a violation of confidence on the part of the other fellows that made them feel bad; far from it, that being considered legitimate among them all, when opportunity offered.

As they were contemplating their tough luck, and cussing Calabasas for all it was worth, a horseman hove in sight, and as he was borne by a good-looking horse, the party came to the conclusion that it might be a mistake to let him pass without "holding him up" and investigating his pockets. It was immediately done in the highest style of the profession, and a solid thousand dollars in clean, nice bank notes was abstracted from the traveler's breeches pocket. He was then asked to depart, his horse being also taken, one of the party remarking that as he had no money it would be embarrassing for him to provide fodder for the steed at Calabasas.

The robbers then declared a dividend and divided into squads and have not been heard from since. The man robbed proved to be Deputy Sheriff Fenton of Pima County, who was returning after a cattle-dealing expedition among the lower railroad camps. When he reached the metropolis of the Santa Cruz he immediately gave the alarm, and a squad of determined men under his leadership went in pursuit of the villains. The horse was found near Crittenden, but so far nothing has been heard of the highwaymen.

—Tombstone *Epitaph*

*The following items were printed within a few days of each other in the Tucson Citizen. It was said of Calabasas:*

It is now a prolific source of casualty items and is receiving a baptism of blood. Within its urban precincts the uncertainty of human life is really appalling, and reckless blood-letting follows the most trivial misunderstanding.

Complaints were sworn out before Judge Bragg yesterday for the arrest of several of the most prominent citizens of Calabasas, among them being a Justice of the Peace and several merchants of the town, for having while drunk, burned the tents of some Chinamen in the employ of Colonel White, chopped open their trunks with hatchets and appropriated the money contained and destroyed all else they did not want. Then turning their attention to stoves, lamps and dishes they demolished them beyond repair. It is understood that a portion of them are already sorry for their little game and will eventually be more so before the end is reached. The warrant for their arrest was placed in the hands of Sheriff Paul who promised to have it promptly executed.

It is reported that a certain Justice of the Peace whose precinct includes Calabasas had arrested and tried one of the female members of the flock, and fined her thirty dollars for having wantonly and maliciously fired off her little pistol in the streets of said town. For what reason or at whom deponent saith not, but she, nevertheless, antied up the coin. Now it so happened, as it always does in similar cases, that the lady in question had, to use a Western phrase, a feller, that in a Colt's six-shooter held a full hand, which he with great liberality displayed to the astonished gaze of the dispenser of justice. The Goddess may be blind but her devotee was not; as he saw and exclaimed "a full hand is good by God: remit the fine," and accordingly forked it over to the lucky man who returned it to his weeping dove.

Night before last a couple of rustlers "went through" the inmates of a Calabasas brothel, but failing to sufficiently replenish their wasted fortunes they proceeded to an adjoining saloon and "held up" all hands for their last dollar and then made an attempt to leave town, but Under Sheriff Ward objecting, they consented to remain over, have a hearing today, and then in the interests of the county visit Tucson for a thorough inspection of the jail with a probable view of residing here, for the time being at all events.

*Thus, under the heading of "Calabasas Capers," we have a sampling of about three months of crime and lawlessness in 1882 in the once-lively town of Calabasas, near the Sonoran border, and the half has not been told. Born in 1880, the town declined and died within a few short years because a dream was shattered, and Nogales was made the port of entry on the railroad line, instead of Calabasas, as was originally hoped and planned for.*

# 3

# FRONTIER JOURNALISM

## FRONTIER JOURNALISM

*In a letter appearing in the Yuma Sentinel, reprinted in 1890 from the Los Angeles Times, Harry Brook, an early-day editor of various Arizona newspapers, wrote, under the pen name of "Ancient Mariner":*

Publishing a newspaper in Arizona is quite different from the newspaper business in the Middle and Eastern States. At least it was, and I do not suppose that conditions have changed much during the past fifteen years. Many of the dailies did not publish any dispatches and those that did only took a small amount, generally costing about $30 a week. The population being so scattered—in 1890 the population of the entire Territory of Arizona was just about equal to that of Los Angeles city—it was literally a "long time between drinks" for a newspaper canvasser, and getting subscriptions and advertisements on the outside was an expensive job, especially when, as in my case, one was not on the visiting list of the Southern Pacific Company, although most of the travel had to be done by buckboard or on horseback.

Possible subscribers being so few and far between, prices for subscriptions and advertising had to be correspondingly high. The regular subscription price for a four-page, six-column weekly was $5 a year. None of the papers depended entirely on subscriptions and commercial advertising for support. The "strong holt" of most of them lay in politics, public printing and job work. An election was harvest time for the journals. For the publication of a card announcing the candidacy there was a regular graduated rate, running from $10 for a Coroner, to $250 or so for a Sheriff, and more than that for a Congressman, the price charged including a commensurate amount of "favorable mention."

Then, again, the rates for legal notices were very high, being entirely out of proportion to the ordinary commercial prices. The Sheriff had the giving out of a large number of such notices and these would be given to the one which happened to support him for office, making a very nice perquisite. In some cases, where there was only one paper published in a county, it may be imagined that such a publication had a "pudding." Then, for job printing, rates were charged which would make the eyes of the Los Angeles job printer of 1900 open wide in amazement. Another source of revenue after election, was found in the practice of getting the Legislature, when it convened, to vote an appropriation for a specific number of copies of each Arizona paper for the use of the members during the session, at twenty-five cents per copy. A legislator who failed to vote for such an appropriation was considered something of a freak.

In 1884, I published a somewhat ambitious weekly in Tucson, under the euphonious name of *Sunshine and Silver*. There was a large amount of hard work put into that journal, which contained a number of features then unique in Arizona. It had illustrations and contained no display advertisements or quack medicine literature. Other papers which I either conducted or edited in Arizona were the Pinal *Drill* (1881), the Quijotoa *Prospector* (1884), the Tombstone *Epitaph* (1886) and the Tucson *Tailings* (1885).

The last named was a small four-page afternoon daily but was rather lively and furnished its staid old afternoon contemporary, the Tucson *Citizen*, with a considerable amount of matter for worry and wonder. It received no telegraph dispatches, while the

*Citizen* had a $30 a week Associated Press budget, yet, in spite of this, I succeeded quite frequently in scooping the esteemed contemporary on telegraphic news, so that its subscribers would occasionally ask the editor why he could not compete with such a small and insignificant rival. It happened that the Los Angeles *Herald* arrived in Tucson in the forenoon with a considerable budget of telegraphic news, much of which had not been sent down to Arizona. By picking out the most interesting of this stuff, padding it a little, and giving prominence to anything that was specially interesting to the Territory, a very fair budget of "fresh" telegraph news was obtained.

One of my biggest scoops on the Tucson *Citizen* was when General Grant was dying. The end had been approaching for several days and his demise was expected at any moment. We had a full description of the closing scenes in type, taken from the Los Angeles paper of the previous day, and only awaited the report of his death. The *Citizen* was published in the next building, with an adobe wall between the two back yards. As soon as the first copy of the *Citizen* was off the press it was handed over the wall by a friendly printer. It contained the news of Grant's death, which was quickly hurried into type, and the *Tailings*, with the full report, was on the street before the *Citizen*.

The Quijotoa *Prospector* was as short-lived as the mining camp in which it was published. In order to head off possible competition (as there was always a rush to establish a newspaper in any new boom town), the first few numbers were set up in the office of a small weekly in Tucson, sixty-five miles distant, while awaiting the arrival of a first-class printing outfit that had been ordered from San Francisco. The office in question had scarcely enough material to do its own work, and consequently the early numbers of the Quijotoa *Prospector* consisted of a little six-column, four-page weekly, presenting an astonishing array of type of all shapes and sizes, some of which had been knocking around on the frontier for a quarter of a century. In a canvassing trip for subscribers through the embryo camp before the first number had been issued I took in $315 within a couple of hours, at the rate of $5 a year, of which $30 went for "hospitality," as three-fourths of the "business houses" were saloons. Within nine months after that there were scarcely enough people in that town to load the material on a wagon.

*The Tucson* Citizen *had this to say in 1895 about the high mission of journalism on the frontier in the early days:*

The fun of being a newspaper man went out when the railroad came in. Before that modern innovation tooted its horn across the desert plains of Arizona the editor thought no more of skinning a court with his pencil than he did of scalping an Indian in his sleep. Every threat of personal violence was seen and gone one better. District attorneys and supreme court judges were made to drink of gall and wormwood, together with the common layman, if they betrayed their trust, abused his temporary power or violated the confidence reposed in them. No frowns of the bastile intimidated, and no threats of arrest and prosecution for criminal libel overshadowed, the gall bottle, but the pen was dipped deep, as may be gathered from the following excerpt from the Tucson *Citizen* of 1872. At that time John Wasson was editor and Isham Reavis was judge of the second judicial district court. The latter was arraigned by the *Citizen* for malfeasance in office, and when he threatened retaliatory measures the following appeared:

> Reavis, a few words to you and your court. In common with the mass of the people of the Territory, we hold you and your court in the utmost contempt. We dare you to send along your contemptible warrant for our arrest for contempt of your contemptible self and court; but bear in mind if you do you will not be practicing upon any such as you have done in your district, who will submit through fear of your tyranny and disregard of personal rights and liberty. We dare you again on your contemptible sneak, to send on your contemptible orders for our arrest. We promise the public a history of your tyrannical career in this respect, wherein the timid, poor and ignorant were outraged by your violation of personal rights and liberty. What became of the fines may also be considered. Your actions in the second judicial district justify the belief that you felt as the people did, that your court inspired frequent contempt. Your case will be

continued upon the disagreeable facts as they come to hand and our space will permit. But send the warrant for contempt at any time, and we ask our readers to note your record as we give it space in this paper.

*Said the Tombstone Prospector in 1897:*

Out here in Arizona the life of a newspaper man is by no means smooth sailing, and those who are looking for a soft snap should choose some other vocation. By devoting the same time, talent, enterprise and brawn to raising peanuts or making adobes, each and every one would secure a better living, and an insurance on their lives would not be classed extra hazardous.

*The Phoenix Gazette, sizing up the situation in 1897, said:*

The average editor works eighteen hours a day, sleeps the sleep of the just, pays for his paper in advance, pays his help each week, lives on six bits a week, spaces between meals on paste and roller composition, and lives in constant dread of the inquisitorial grand jury that is composed chiefly of his delinquent subscribers.

But his pay will surely come in the better world because of the good deeds done without remuneration or hope of reward. Who but the editor keeps daily spreading the news of this land of sunshine and mining riches to all the people of the earth? He it is who brings, by truthful writing, all the immigration that yearly comes to buy property and increase the wealth of the Territory. By so doing others are enriched and while the editor plods on in poverty and is stood off year after year, he finally joins the angels with the supreme satisfaction that he has been a benefactor to the human race.

*From the editorials of the Flagstaff Sun-Democrat in 1897 is taken this commentary:*

In the course of human events it becomes necessary for us to announce to the public that we have leased a half interest in this paper, and we shall hereafter assist in furnishing brain food for its many readers.

In this connection we will state that we have had experience as a pencil shover; that we are an adept with the scissors, and as a manufacturer of red hot news, we are without a peer, but the news is of such sensational character that we have often had to seek military protection.

Our style of writing is eccentric, droll and sensational, streaked with originality, or easily distinguished from the writings of the scriptures, owing to our habitual carelessness in handling the truth.

As to our character as a citizen, we can truthfully say that we never loafed around to catch the yellow fever, cholera, and kindred affections; that we never robbed a bank, held up a railroad train, served a term in prison, or worked on the chain gang, or elsewhere. That we always paid our just debts (when we had to), and further the deponent saith not.

In conclusion, and in confidence, we will state in a round-about way, that we are not here altogether for our health; that we will take money, bonds, bills, notes, cast-off clothing, or anything else animate or inanimate in exchange for our newspaper efforts. That we will accept in a professional way, and on easy terms, all invitations, privileges, donations, tips, bonuses and presents; in short everything goes with us.

Aside from the economic hazards of conducting a frontier newspaper, there were often physical hazards as well, in the guise of threats or acts of violence, which were regarded as unavoidable consequences of editorial functioning in those days.

Of incidents of friction of especial interest which might have led to bloodshed, the earliest occurred in 1859 when a clash developed between Sylvester Mowry, candidate for Delegate to Congress, and Editor Edward E. Cross of the Tubac Arizonian. The trouble grew out of certain items of a rather scurrilous nature which had been published in Eastern exchanges.

Some of these items had been written by Mowry, some by Cross. They concerned political differences between the two. Cross was challenged to a duel by Mowry; the challenge was accepted, and Cross and Mowry met near Tubac with their seconds and with Burnside rifles as weapons. Four rounds were fired without effect. At the last round Mowry's rifle did not discharge and it was decided he was entitled to his shot. Cross stood, unarmed, to receive it, but Mowry discharged his rifle into the air, refusing to take advantage of an unarmed man, declaring himself satisfied.

*In the* Arizonian *Cross wrote:*

It is proper to state that at the time of the duel between Mr. Mowry and the editor of this paper a high wind, almost amounting to a gale, was blowing directly across the line of fire, thereby preventing accurate aim. In this case, the proverb "It is an ill wind that blows no good," was aptly illustrated.

*A conflict between Colonel Charles D. Poston (formerly Delegate to Congress and later known as the "Father of Arizona") and the editor of the Tucson* Citizen, *J. A. Whitmore, took place in the Old Pueblo in 1882. The Tucson* Star *reported the affair under the heading "Poston's Bullet":*

To the ordinary observer, the usual scene presented itself at Porter's Hotel. The barroom was deserted except by the mixer of concoctions, the frequenters of that resort having long before enjoyed their morning cocktails. In the dining-room were a few ladies and gentlemen, whose business or social engagements required no earlier hour for breakfast. On the broad and breezy plaza numerous railroad employees or others in search of a cool retreat were lounging in comfortable chairs. Withal, there was an air of security and peace about the place that was in no wise tainted with the complications that so often disturb the moral equanimity of mankind.

Even the entrance of Colonel Poston, shortly afterward, and his partaking of something delicious with Judge Porter at the bar, did not excite any wonder in the minds of the lazy spectators, although his visit to the hotel was a rarity. No one could suspect that his appearance at the hotel had any sanguinary motive, when he naturally and calmly walked out upon the porch in front of the saloon and stood there quietly conversing with his friend for some minutes. He wore no blue shirt; he was not girdled by a cartridge belt; nor was there a pair of six-shooters dangling from his hips. His stylishly cut pantaloons fell languidly over a pair of neatly polished shoes, instead of being tucked in the legs of heavy boots: he did not glance around suspiciously at every passer-by, neither did he expectorate between his closed teeth. In fact it could be readily seen that he was not the dreaded cowboy of Arizona fame. Therefore the people present were greatly surprised when a few minutes later a shot was heard, and the bland and courteous Colonel was noticed standing near the saloon door with a smoking revolver within his grasp.

It had been generally known in this community that a bitter feeling was engendered in the bosom of the Colonel by a derogatory article which appeared in the *Citizen*, and people feared that there would be an unpleasant meeting between him and Mr. Whitmore, the editor of that journal. They were therefore somewhat prepared for the news of the shooting, which spread through the city with lightning rapidity shortly after its occurrence. The story of the encounter, as told by an eye-witness is as follows:

Colonel Poston appeared upon the plaza of Porter's Hotel some minutes after nine o'clock. He was soon joined by Judge Porter, and the two stepped to the bar and took drinks. They then walked out of the saloon door, and were engaged in general conversation a few feet from the entrance, for several minutes. Colonel Poston then walked with the Judge to the southeast corner of the hotel, and parting with him, paced back, passing the saloon door and proceeding several feet beyond. He then retraced his steps until he reached within five feet of the saloon door, and about three feet from the side of the hotel. During these few minutes he showed no symptoms of nervousness or anxiety.

In the meantime Mr. Whitmore had left the dining-room, where he had breakfasted, and proceeding across the barroom, intended passing through the outer door of that apartment. At this place he was brought face to face with Colonel Poston, who upon seeing him, stopped at the spot above designated and quickly, though with some deliberation, drew from the right pocket of his pantaloons, a six-shooter and fired at his enemy. The ball, however, missed its mark, passing through the woodwork to the right of Whitmore and across the barroom, imbedding itself in the wall opposite. Its course was within six inches of the editor's right arm, and on a level with his chest. He abruptly turned and ran across the barroom and into the wash-room, while the Colonel stepped into the doorway watching the retreat of his intended victim. He then passed back to the plaza, after pocketing his revolver, and calmly conversed with some friends for a few minutes before starting down town. . . .

Later, Whitmore appeared before Judge Bragg and swore out a complaint of assault with a deadly weapon, with intent to kill, against Colonel Poston. The latter, appearing, was held in the sum of $500 to appear before the district court.

The reporter first sought Mr. Whitmore, who was readily found in his editorial rooms, attending to the multifarious duties of his business. There were no effects visible of his encounter with Colonel Poston; no nervousness or anxiety.

"Mr. Whitmore, I understand that a personal encounter took place this morning between Colonel Poston and yourself, in which a pistol was used. Have you any objection to detailing the circumstances to me?"

"None in the least. It can hardly be termed an encounter, as it was wholly a one-sided affair. I am not in the habit of engaging in street brawls, and in this I was a negative, rather than a positive, factor. As I was coming out of the east door of the Porter Hotel after breakfast, I was met at the door by Poston, who drew a revolver and without any warning fired at me. I retired through the office and proceeded to the office of Judge Bragg and entered a complaint against Poston for an assault to commit murder."

"What motive prompted Poston to commit the assault?"

"It was undoubtedly on account of an article published in the Citizen, criticizing some of the Colonel's foibles."

"Was this the only means of redress open to Colonel Poston?"

"Had the act been successful, it would have been a cold-blooded murder, as the law gives him proper redress for any fancied grievance, and the proprietors of the Citizen are financially able to meet any damages awarded by the courts."

"Will the matter end here?"

"So far as the Citizen is concerned, the matter, unless some new phases developed, is considered as possessing but little public interest."

The reporter of the *Star* found Colonel Poston in his room shortly after noon. The gentleman was as calm as a summer day, and willingly answered the queries made.

"Colonel, what was the cause of the difficulty this morning in which you are said to have been engaged?"

"An editorial in the *Citizen* impugned my political, moral and social character in a manner not to be overlooked. After it was brought to my notice, I consulted with some of my friends and addressed a letter to the publishers of the *Citizen*, asking for the responsible author, and received a reply. Later, I was passing the *Citizen* office, when Whitmore was sitting in an arm-chair in front, but observing our approach he rapidly retired to the sanctum and when we arrived there he was not there. This morning, having been informed that the editor had gone to breakfast at Porter's Hotel, I thitherward went, and having imbibed a delicate brandy cocktail with Judge Porter at the bar, was fuming an Havana upon the porch when Whitmore appeared at the door, and I therefore leveled and shot, with a very wild range."

"Did you go up to the hotel with the intention of shooting Whitmore?"

"That was my intention."

"Have you had any verbal communication with Mr. Whitmore since the appearance of said article?"

"According to my education and ideas of honor and propriety, such an article forbids subsequent communication, and I have had none except with the pistol."

*Later in the same year, 1882, the Phoenix Gazette came forth with an account of another bloodless affair, this one at Tombstone:*

Arizona has another first-class sensation, and like most blessings of that kind that come to us, the fruitful source is Cochise County. This time it is a resort to the "code of honor," the "court of final resort," and it is two editors that introduce this innovation on our usual methods of settling personal affairs of honor. The affair was the outgrowth of the personal warfare that was being waged by the three rival editors. From this distance it looks as though the two old papers, the *Epitaph* and *Republican*, Dunbar and Purdy, editors, were trying a rather stiff game of bulldozing upon Hamilton, editor of the *Independent*, which is a new venture. Calumny, crimination and recrimination resulted in Hamilton challenging Dunbar to visit *Zona Libre* and settle the matter. The latter politely but positively declined, stating that he did not wish to violate the laws of his country and Territory. Following this Dunbar and Purdy both published cards denouncing Hamilton in the most vile terms. Next day Hamilton came out in his paper, in two cards, in which he respectively branded Purdy and Dunbar as cowards. While Dunbar still held to the law as his protection, this last publication was too much for Purdy, and he immediately sent a challenge to Hamilton, which was, with due formality, accepted. The remainder is told in the dispatches. Purdy and seconds arrived on the ground and found Hamilton and his party waiting—and this doubtless was a matter of surprise. Hamilton's best man produced a pair of new Colt's revolvers. This had a cold steel and deathly appearance, and Purdy's men refused to accept. Purdy's seconds brought forth a pair of old revolvers (but the dispatches neglect to state whether they would work or not), and Hamilton accepted. Purdy then retired from the field and all hands went back to Tombstone. It was a French duel; nobody was hurt, and we suppose the wounded honor of the participants was amply soothed. If this near approach to the passage of arms will have the effect of putting a stop to the scurrilous productions that have been published in our Tombstone exchanges, then, indeed, the people of that section will have reason to be grateful.

The *Tucson Star* contained an item in 1889, concerning S. C. Bagg, of the *Arizona Kicker* of Tombstone, titled "An Energetic Western Editor Who Can't Be Bought Or Run Out":

The last issue of the *Arizona Kicker* contained the following cheerful paragraphs:

Not a Success.—Last Saturday night, soon after eleven o'clock, some gentleman whose identity is unknown to us, fired a charge of buckshot through the side window of our editorial room directly at the spot where our cot is usually placed. Had the cot been there we should have been inquested and buried ere this. But the cot wasn't there. We are not purty, but we are no hayseed. We haven't slept twice in the same spot for the last twelve weeks. We have learned the ways of this community at considerable cost and trouble and we don't propose to plant ourselves as a midnight target. We feel sorry for the gent who wasted his energies and ammunition. He doubtless went away from the window feeling that he was entitled to credit for doing a smart thing. Come again, old chap.

The dictionary defines "billingsgate" as vulgar, abusive language. The word is derived from Billings Gate, one of the gates of London, with its near-by fish market, the latter being noted in bygone days for the abusive language used there.

Most early newspaper editors indulged a penchant for billingsgate; in fact, they reveled in it, especially in their editorials. And this type of editorial, although deplored by more conservative opinion, was nevertheless quite commonly written when the right kind of opening presented itself or when provacation by a rival editor seemed to justify recrimination. It was "personal journalism" in terms of billingsgate, and it reared its ugly head constantly and incontinently in the newspaper columns of those days.

Although this particular style of journalism does not fit into the pattern of the modern newspaper, it should prove interesting to pull back the curtain of the past and present some startling examples of this lost art.

Says the Tombstone Prospector in 1888:

There is no one thing which the public more condemn than personal journalism, and there is not a single reason that can be advanced in its defense, for it is simply defenseless.

The Nogales Reserve, knocks personal journalism into nothingness. It says: One of our strongest dislikes is personal journalism. If, however, men engage in it, and feel that it is incumbent upon them, we believe in going the full length of the tow line. The personal affairs of editors no more belong to the public than the personal affairs of the grocer or mechanic. But when either begin to "feel that way" we believe he should mow a clean swath. If an editor wants to be personal let him ascertain the exact number of sheep his rival has stolen and tell the public. If he has choked two or three mothers-in-law to death, bought silk gowns for fallen creatures, raised a family without ever having gone through the formality of marriage, peopled the town with fatherless progeny, "held out" on his employers and hushed the matter up, or slapped his branding iron on some other fellow's cow, spit it all out—tell the whole business. It may, and no doubt will, make the public deathly sick; but so much the better. The public will feel better than ever when it recovers and be able to kick both combatants out of the community.

President Lincoln, in appointing officials for the new Territory of Arizona in 1863, named Richard C. McCormick of New York as Secretary. Three years later McCormick was appointed Governor and in 1868 was elected Delegate to Congress. In the previous year the capital had been moved from Prescott to Tucson. John H. Marion had acquired the Prescott Miner, which had been launched in 1864 by McCormick. When McCormick ran for re-election to Congress in 1870, Marion fought him bitterly in the Miner, blaming him for Prescott's losing the honor of being the capital. McCormick started another newspaper, the Citizen, in 1870, this time in Tucson, the new capital, with John Wasson as editor, for the primary purpose of furthering his own campaign for re-election. Then the fireworks began.

The following appeared in the Miner:

"Marion, of the Miner, has been more filthy than usual in his present campaign, but as usual he has helped McCormick."

So says the Black Cricket recently imported from Nevada by McCormick & Co., to act as liar, affidavit man, scavenger, scullion and valet de chambre for the outfit. We dare this abominable beggar, who has just been placed on horseback, for his dirty services in the cause of Tom Fitch [Congressman from Nevada], to show where we have been filthy. But, this is a way thieves and blackguards have for drawing attention from their own foul deeds and expressions, and as Wasson has fouled the pages of his own paper with such expressions as "whipper-snapper," "shoo-fly," "superlative bilk," "bummers," "discarded lickspittle," and,

> Toll the bell,
> A crowd of damned souls
> Float down the Stygian river

(meaning the anti-McCormickites), he would like to shift the odium to some decent man's shoulders. Back dog, to your foul kennel!

*John Wasson, in the Citizen, commented on the above:*

After reading the *Miner* of the 17th, we could not refrain from sympathizing with the poor mortal that controls its columns. He feels badly. Something hurts him; his bones always ache; but his feelings are evidently touched now. We wonder what is the matter with the poor sufferer? Is it because a generous people, that have too long stood his abuse, are about to start another paper in Prescott, that will deal fairly and justly with all, and the whole country? Is it because he has used the columns of his sheet to abuse, vilify and misrepresent in the most vulgar manner, every man against whom he has a personal spite, or political difference? Is it because it is generally known that he has no regard for truth or decency in his attacks upon those who oppose him, or against whom he takes a dislike? Is it because he has failed to drive anyone out of the country by calling them carpet-baggers, and stands a good chance of packing his own dirty linen very soon in those much derided circumstances? Is it because his low, vulgar attacks upon newcomers are received as an insult by them, and looked upon as the meanest demagogy by every true friend of the Territory? We ask these few simple questions in order to find out just where the disease is located, and what is the matter. We don't pretend to be a doctor, but we might throw the man into fits perhaps which would evidently be a much happier state of mind than he now enjoys.

*In a letter sent from Prescott, dated January, 1871, appearing in the Citizen, are to be found these choice bits:*

Until the publication of the *Citizen* there has been no paper in Arizona in which any of the misrepresentations of the *Miner* could be replied to or refuted, and while I despise personalities in the newspapers, and believe in the proverbial saying, that "Personal abuse is no argument," I believe it is right and just to state a few truths in reply to the assertions of J. H. Marion, Editor of the *Miner*, rather than by a longer silence to tacitly admit them all to be true.

Marion's course as an editor since he has charge of the *Miner* has been dualistic. As a journalist, he has been remarkably successful in keeping up a good paper well filled with local news, and always giving every encouragement possible to the settlers in the country. . . . The *Miner* is as good a local paper of its size as is published on the Pacific coast.

As a politician, he has pursued the browbeating, over-bearing, bullying line. He is from New Orleans, a Democrat, was a Secessionist, is today an obdurate mourner over the "lost cause" and belongs to the rule or ruin party. He has had the only paper in the county, which has always been Democratic, and having full sweep with no opposition, has had no toleration for those opposed to him in political sentiment. . . . He has often apparently exhausted the vocabulary of epithets in his denunciations of the class referred to, yet in his next issue a fresh batch has invariably appeared, and where words have failed him he has manufactured phrases to express his utter hatred and contempt to all who differ with him in opinion, until he is generally admitted to be the most degraded, foul-tongued, malevolent, uncharitable, political editor on the Pacific coast.

Defeat teaches him nothing; he rallies from the ruins and pitches in again with most detestable and unendurable rancor. To read his writings one might suppose Marion to be a raving, bombastic, loud-mouthed bullying man personally, one whom those McCormickites would dislike to meet in the arena of words or blows. On the contrary he is as mild a mannered man as need be—quiet in speech and behavior, drunk or sober, unless when excited by both political talk and ardent spirits, and even then is not considered dangerous.

He will write about a man in the *Miner* in such pointed terms that the public has no difficulty in understanding who he refers to, calling him liar, thief, and other pet names, and the next day will call on the party at his place of business and when remonstrated with for such action, will take it all back as square as could be asked for, and hide himself under "glittering generalities," as "nothing personal intended," and as he is a weak, sickly, rotten specimen of mortality, he has got off so far in that way. His sufferings from Yumatism [*Marion lived in the Yuma area when he first came to*

*Arizona*] has ruined his bodily health and doubtless affected his mind to such an extent, that he takes a morbid view of matters and things and does not consider that he should be held responsible for anything written by him while under the influence of drugs and potions which he informed the readers of the *Miner* sometime since constitute a large portion of his living.—(Signed) H.

*John H. Marion did not go to the trouble of replying to the above remarks; at any rate, nothing was found in the* Miner *until the fall of 1871, when the following appeared:*

The whiffet of the Carpet Bagger's organ at Tucson appears to be spoiling for a newspaper fight with the *Miner*, but the *Miner* cannot lower its dignity and character, or neglect the interests of its supporters, by noticing so contemptible a blockhead, dog-robber, liar, and slanderer, as we have, time and again, proven the conductor of the *Citizen* to be. The *Miner* deals with principals; never with paid hirelings, cowardly calumniators or unmannerly understrappers who live by doing dirty work for third-rate politicians and their tools: and the only way the brevet bull-whacker in question will hereafter obtain a notice by us will be by placing his foul person in too close proximity to our olfactories. No time or space have we to bandy words with a cur who fills his paper with vile slanders, unchaste phrases and vulgar epithets which he has borne from his father's hearth, and which should never be heard by decent ears. Back, dog, to your kennel!

*In the same issue Marion, in a blast entitled "To the Blockhead of the Tucson Citizen and all others whom it may concern," wrote:*

We had about made up our mind to let the slanderous official organ at Tucson go with the notice we gave it and its conductor on the fourth page of this paper, and would have done so had not the number for August 19th reached us, Monday last, with assertions which, although they would not be believed by those who know us, might be taken for granted by those not acquainted with us. Mr. Wasson, the reputed editor and publisher, claimed to have received a letter from some person in Prescott, which opened with the choice quotation, "Hell's afloat and the river's a raisin'" and which goes on to say, after having alluded to the recent Apache murders and robberies near Camp Verde, and the criminal conduct of General Grover in not having sent out troops to chastise the Apaches: "The Miner chief knows everything, but dare not talk." This letter was, no doubt, written before we had time to talk out, in the Miner, and the eaves-dropping, political hanger-on who wrote it must have learned soon after he had penned his malicious slander about us, that the Miner chief, as he was pleased to call us, did talk out in very plain language; did condemn the course General Grover had taken. . . . "Dare not talk," indeed! Lying wretch, we dare speak, at all times and upon all occasions; not like you, however, from behind a mask, but openly and above board. Furthermore, we wish to inform you that you are a cowardly political bummer, sneaking liar and tell-tale eaves-dropper, without force, character, or standing. So much for this toady, who "bends the supple hinges of his knees, that thrift may follow fawning."

And, now, for Wasson, the menial of carpet-baggers; the boorish fellow who came to the Territory to take an office [Surveyor-General] whose duties he can no more fill than he could those of an honest man and citizen. This adder; this loafer; this Gubernatorial bootblack and scullion, who bummed his living from the military and citizens of this Territory, until he got installed in office, tries to fool people into the belief that he—an abject, cringing slave—is a chivalrous gentleman, and that we of the Miner are "debauched and debased cowards and slanderers." Mercy! has it come to this? Must we, for once, forget our manhood and come down to the level of this human brute? If so, we, the senior editor of this paper, unhesitatingly fling those words back into the teeth of this bluffing dog, and dare him to meet us at any place he may name, and, forever, settle this little matter of cowardice.

The most famous journalistic rencontre of the 1870's took place between the indomitably bellicose Marion of the Arizona Miner, at Prescott, and the equally belligerent but more poetically gifted Judge William J. Berry, a lawyer and gunsmith as well as a newspaperman. Berry became editor, late in 1873, of the Yuma Sentinel. He imparted to Arizona journalism a new and startlingly vigorous tone which at times verged on the fantastically hifalutin' and at others descended into broad Rabelaisianisms. Yet in whatever vein the Judge chose to write, he managed to be entertaining.

In his Salutatory he declared:

In assuming the editorial chair, we are free to say that we have some doubts and misgivings. First, our well-known modesty is somewhat shocked at our own temerity, in this rushing into the editorial arena; into a profession honored by a host of the greatest and best men who have ever trod the earth, and into a contest where many have fallen, and few comparatively have been victorious.

Secondly: We have serious misgivings as to whether our enterprise will be sustained by the people, without whose support any newspaper must fail. The ghosts of a multitude of editors now crowd around us as we write, pointing to their own miserable experience; how they toiled and suffered and hoped; how their efforts were not appreciated by the "dear public"; how they lived on the meanest of fare with sometimes only one shirt in the world, and how they had to lie in bed while the faithful and suffering wife washed the garment; how the poor cusses lived miserably and miserably died! But avaunt, ye diabolical shades! Kind friends have advised us to enter this field; we are in for it now, and here goes—"sink or swim, survive or perish."

Well, gentlemen of the editorial fraternity, we ask your kind indulgence, and while you treat us with courtesy, we will always fully reciprocate, but should any of you treat us with disrespect or abuse, you will run against a snag.

To the public we will say that we will do our best to publish a good paper; one that will be acceptable to the merchant, the miner, the farmer, the navigator, the mechanic, the gentleman of leisure, and the family circle. Nothing of an immoral or scurrilous nature shall ever have a place in its columns.

We will devote our energies to promoting the interests of the Territory and its people, and particularly of Yuma County. We will give the latest and most reliable news by mail and telegraph, and devote a portion of our space to choice miscellaneous reading. Our paper shall not be controlled by any clique or party. Our motto is "Independent in all things; neutral in nothing." But,

Pledged to Truth, to Liberty, and Law.

No gold can buy us, and no threats can awe.

We will endeavor to uphold good order, and drown down crime, vice and rowdyism in every shape. We will ever be found on the side of Justice, Mercy and Truth; the firm friend of the Right, and the uncompromising enemy of wrong.

Friends, countrymen, everybody, we respectfully solicit your patronage. And thus, with a heart full of hope and good-will, "with charity for all, and malice toward none," we launch our little bark upon the great ocean of journalism, trusting that by your favor it may be wafted to a pleasant port.

WM. J. BERRY

*A few weeks after Judge Berry acquired the Yuma Sentinel, and upon the completion of the telegraph from Yuma to Prescott, he came forth on the wings of song with the following:*

"Glory to God in the highest! Peace on earth, and Good Will toward men!"

Thus the Angels sang when this fair world first rounded into view! And thus everything that is good, and pure, and true, throbs with unspeakable joy and exultation at any new and grand achievement in the course of infinite progression. Let everything that lives and breathes burst forth in songs of joy and gladness!

Let even inanimate nature join in the loud acclaim: Come down ye everlasting mountains! and shake hands with the little hills, and let the sounding sea roar its satisfaction! For another link in the great chain of civilization has been welded. Time and space are again annihilated. People separated three hundred miles, who heretofore, in business or social intercourse, required from fifteen to twenty days to communicate with each other, can now talk as it were face to face, in an instant, by playing with "the lightning's fiery wing!" Grand consummation! Glorious achievement!

This is one of the greatest triumphs of Peace. The Telegraph is probably the greatest instrument in the cause of universal peace—in hastening on that happy period when "swords shall be beaten into plowshares, and spears into pruning hooks, and the Nations shall war no more."

The first citizen telegram from Yuma, which we were allowed to send by the kindness of Colonel Rockwell, A. Q. M., and Super-intendent Haines, temporary operator, was as follows:

Yuma, Nov. 11, 1873

To JOHN H. MARION,
    Editor Arizona *Miner*.
Yuma to Prescott, Greeting:
    ALL HAIL! WE SHAKE HANDS BY "THE LIGHTNING'S FIERY WING!"

*In the same issue of the* Sentinel *was printed, in an adjoining column:*

We hope we will not be accused of self-laudation in copying the following very flattering notice from that best of frontier papers ever published, written by its editor, that prince of good fellows, John H. Marion, our old friend and companion through the dark days of Arizona, and with whom we hope to witness a portion of the brightness and prosperity and glory to which our Territory is inevitably tending. Thank you, old friend.

"Judge Berry is well known and held in high esteem by the citizens of this section, having resided in Prescott for several years. He is known as an earnest, forcible writer, and will, we know, instil new life into the *Sentinel*, and cause it to be welcomed throughout the Territory. The Judge has our best wishes for success in his new venture, and we hope he may secure fortune and fame as the defender of the interests of the great State of Arizona that is to be."
—Arizona *Miner*.

*The end of this journalistic honeymoon hove in sight, however, when in the following issue of the* Sentinel *Judge Berry, under the heading "Editorial Meanness," wrote:*

We were never more puzzled in our life than we are now to account for the conduct of that cuss of the Arizona *Miner*. We have been badly, yes, most shamefully treated by him. "To prove this let facts be submitted to a candid world."

On the completion of the line of Telegraph connecting Yuma with Prescott, we, by the kind permission of Colonel Rockwell, A. Q. M., and Commodore Haines, Superintendent, sent a congratulatory dispatch to the editor of the *Miner*, announcing the joyful event. Everybody knows that this is a military telegraph, but as above stated, we were permitted to send that, the first citizen telegram that ever passed over the wires. We esteemed this a high privilege, and expected, and had a right to expect, that it would be gladly received and courteously responded to. Was this done? No; no response ever came. We waited several days, and Commodore Haines repeatedly telegraphed to John H. Marion, the said cuss who presides over the *Miner*, asking him to send some response to our greeting. On the day of our going to press, last week, we particularly desired some recognition of our aforesaid telegram, that we might publish it, and Commodore Haines again telegraphed to the editor of the *Miner* asking him to send some response immediately. But none came! Nor has any come yet.

Now we ask all our editorial brothers and all right-thinking men: "What do you think of such conduct as this?" Can anything be more uncivil or discourteous? We cannot account for it, particularly as the relations between the editor of the *Miner* and ourself have always been of the most cordial and friendly character. We fear that our worst apprehensions are realized, and that Marion's glory has departed. It may be that he is sick. If so, we take this all back. If not, we mean it all, and more too. We had our fears. Take a rusty old bachelor-editor and raise him to the summit of connubial felicity, and in nine cases out of ten it is more than he can stand. His brain reels, reason totters; he is a goner.

Alas, poor Marion! we ne'er shall look upon his like again! We write this more in sorrow than in anger. Adios amigo. "Sic transit gloria mundi."

*In the next issue of the* Sentinel, *in November, 1873, Judge Berry was in a more cheerful mood and printed this note:*

Have had our first party in Yuma. . . . We had been afflicted with low spirits, blues, or whatever they are called, consequent on the low state of our finances, bills overdue, and current expenses of employees to pay, and other things. Ruin seemed to stare us in the face! and suspension seemed inevitable. But we mustered our remaining vitality, put on our go-to-meeting clothes, and went where, amidst the smiles of fair women and the society of pleasant gentlemen, sweet music and generous wine, our earthly troubles were forgotten, and we were transported to the seventh heaven. And now the memory of that fair young widow haunts us still— banishes all else except the desire to see her again, and we are happy. Our frail form can hardly contain all our joy in the musty precincts of a printing office.

Oh, that we might be transported with such a divinity, to the famed bowers of the Lotus-eaters! "and dream, and dream our life away in everlasting bliss!" But no matter; we are happy; and that's enough.

But the following week Marion, of the Miner put Berry back into a fighting mood when he wrote:

The editor of the Yuma Sentinel, Judge Berry, weighs a little over two hundred pounds, and is a dead shot, with rifle, pistol or bowie knife; his foreman, Mr. J. C. Bacon, expresses himself in several languages, and the "devil" of the institution is named "Jesus"; so that editors who may feel like pitching into the institution had better defer doing so, and thank us for the information.

To which Berry, from his Yuma watchtower, reported:

Why didn't you qualify that a little, John? While you noticed our proficiency in the use of arms, why didn't you tell the people of our pacific disposition, which you know so well?—how that we are mild as a suckling dove, etc. In the description of us that you have given to the world, a stranger would infer that we are a dangerous character, which is far from the mark, as our bosom overflows with the milk of human kindness. Look out, old fellow; or we'll give a description of you one of these days.

The irrepressible conflict was building up.

William H. Hardy, a pioneer businessman and politician of Mohave County, provided Judge Berry with a new target when an item was printed in the Prescott Miner regarding Hardy's chances of being elected were he to run for Delegate to Congress. Thereupon the Sentinel erupted:

That miserable old politician, Hardy, is out in the Miner, in a dirty, low, black-guardly letter; just such a one as any man knowing him would expect from that foul and loathsome source.

We only regret that we condescended to notice the old nincompoop at all. . . . We should have left him to the people of Mohave County, who know what a curse the old growling scalliwag has been to them, and know how to appreciate his insane and filthy ravings. This denial of "trying to create sectional feeling," is simply one of his accustomed lies. These are his words in the *Miner:*

> As to our next Delegate in Congress, it is useless to try to elect a man from the northern part of the Territory, as there is material in and about Tucson and Yuma; that a fraudulent vote would be cast to defeat any other but their own choice.

Now, will any sensible man say that there could possibly be a stronger effort to create a sectional feeling than that embraced in those libelous words? But we dismiss the unworthy subject, and beg pardon of our readers for ever having condescended to notice the foul creature in our columns. Wonder if he has washed that shirt yet. Better lay it on an ant hill. S'CAT!

*Late in June, 1874, Judge Berry printed this item:*
By the Tucson *Citizen* of last Saturday we are informed that William H. Hardy, of Mohave County, has "concluded to submit his name to the people as a candidate for Delegate to Congress." *Submit* is good. The old played-out fossil of political ambition can prepare to "submit" to a glorious defeat. Nobody who knows him, except William H. Hardy, thinks that he has any qualifications whatever for the position except ignorance, impudence, assurance, stupidity and sore-headedness. The people don't want his services. And in the *Miner* we find a card from this political absurdity, in which he whines with his usual filth and billingsgate, over a letter signed H. A. B., which we published in the *Sentinel.* Now, we know H. A. B., and know him to be a gentleman and a scholar, while Hardy is just the reverse, and it would take more than Hardy's word to make us believe what he says about H. A. B.'s drunkenness in Mohave County.

Hardy has a great deal to say about men drinking whiskey, but according to the testimony of his neighbors, no man is more fond of it than this same Hardy. True, no man ever accuses him of buying whiskey, but it is notorious that he can drink any given quantity.

As to Hardy characterizing the *Sentinel* as a "dirty, unpopular sheet," nobody will be surprised when they consider the source it comes from. The only dirty thing ever admitted into the columns of the *Sentinel* since it has been under our charge, is that same Hardy. We admit that it is a dirty subject, and our only excuse for ever naming the creature is that last fall he committed an unprovoked and lying assault upon the people of the southern counties of the Territory through the columns of the *Miner*. He was even then figuring upon his chances for the Delegacy, and knowing his unpopularity, particularly in the southern counties, he grossly insulted the people of those counties, thus characterizing the voters of these counties as a set of political scoundrels. We therefore considered it our duty to show up this pusillanimous indivdual in his true light—and we did it. That is our excuse for ever befouling our columns with any reference to him. . . .

Hardy at different times has had much to say about our drinking whiskey. Now, we do not deny that we drink whenever we feel that it is proper for us to do so. A long life of observation has taught us that there are few who are of any account in the world, who do not use stimulating drink of some kind, either openly or covertly. But we have always held that true temperance is moderation, not total abstinence. We have never converted the means of refreshment into temperance or excess. We have a pretty large acquaintance in Arizona, and all along the Pacific Slope and we challenge any man to say that they ever saw us so under the influence of liquor that we lost our propriety, or behaved in an ungentlemanly or rowdy manner, or used ungentlemanly language or were incapable of attending to our business. Whoever asserts or thinks to the contrary, is a liar and a scoundrel.

Hardy may as well hang up his fiddle about going to Congress. All his vituperation and slang will not help him.

*In another letter from "H. A. B." to Judge Berry, printed in the* Sentinel, *were these lines:*

I apologized for my carelessness in the *Miner* to Hardy, and my object in writing to you now, is to apologize to you for sending you an epistle which has been the means of causing you to catch it so strong from Hardy. . . . I hope under this affliction you will bear up with Christian fiftytude, remembering that those who endure to the end are sure of their reward.

Many sympathizers have called on me and urged me to keep a stiff upper lip, and take my regular rations, etc. Tom Hodge says that I had better go out to Minnehaha Flat, and rusticate with Charley Taylor and sober up, but says he can't think of any cool place near Yuma, for you to go to. Hardy's card says I get drunk, but that you can't find whiskey enough to get full on—which indicates one of two facts, either that you now get better liquor than the rot that Hardy used to keep in the old Quartz Rock Saloon in Prescott, or that you can hold more than you used to. As an indication that my feelings are really substantial in your behalf, and touch the spirit, I enclose an order on Wm. B. Hooper & Co., for a bottle of their best to help you fill up.

*In an item entitled "Our Fighting Editor," Judge Berry wrote, in the fall of 1874:*

As the time for holding the general election is near at hand, it is reasonable to expect that the political caldron will soon begin to boil. Now, with the multifarious duties that we have to perform as editor, reporter, canvasser, collector, disburser and sometimes devil, we will not have time to devote to the fighting department, without neglecting some of those before-mentioned duties, so we have after prayerful consideration for the good of our patrons, concluded to attach to our office a fighting editor. We have selected a gentleman who possesses fine accomplishments in that line and can whip anything that walks on two legs. He is not quarrelsome and by no means a rough, but if any person should feel aggrieved and get mad at any little innocent remark that we may make in the Sentinel during the canvass, he has but to call upon the said fighting editor, who will give him ample satisfaction. By this arrangement we will have time to attend to our legitimate duties without having to nurse black eyes.

*And now the conflict really explodes in a rain of verbal shrapnel. In the November 7, 1874, issue of the Sentinel, Judge Berry wrote, in an article entitled "The Arizona Miner," this gentle tirade:*

In the daily issue of this scurrilous sheet, of October 27th, we find an article in reference to ourself, which is altogether characteristic of the dirty nincompoop who edits that journal. We shall not attempt to reply *seriatim* to the charges brought against us in said article, but will simply say that it is a batch of infernal falsehoods from beginning to end. The infernal wretch who edits the *Miner*, and who wrote that article, well knows, as every man in Arizona knows who ever saw him, that he is nothing if not a blackguard. He accuses us of being a gunsmith. We are proud of that, as many a man in Arizona knows that we are a good one. At the same time we are a better editor and a better and more respectable man than he is, which fact is also well known. He charges us with demanding high prices for our gunsmith work. To that we have now to say, that we never got as much as our work was worth, and lost fifteen hundred dollars by trusting certain infernal scoundrels in Prescott and vicinity.

The miserable liar also says that he let us write a communication for the *Miner*, years ago. Why the miserable cuss used to beg us to write for his dirty abortion, and since we quit writing for it, many Arizonans say that the *Miner* is not worth a damn, and that is our opinion too, although we never expressed it publicly before.

But we have not room or inclination to follow up this mendacious writer further. We will simply say that every assertion that he has made in reference to us is a lie. The *Miner* is becoming celebrated for its mendacity. Its editor has been writing the most unblushing falsehoods about better men than we are, and how could we expect to escape his foul pen?

In regard to our being a "judge of whiskey," we will simply say that no man ever saw Wm. J. Berry laid out under its influence; while we had the extreme mortification of seeing the editor of the *Miner*, in a party given by Colonel Baker in Prescott, laid out in the refreshment room, dead drunk, with candles placed at his head and his feet, and a regular "wake" held over him. It was then for the first time that we discovered Darwin's connecting link between the fish and the quadruped. As he lay, with his drunken slobber issuing from his immense mouth, which extends from ear to ear, and his ears reaching up so high, everyone present was forcibly impressed with the fact that there was a connecting link between the catfish and the jackass.

What we have here faintly described is the truth, to attest which there are plenty of living witnesses. Now dry up, or we will come out with some more reminiscences.

*In the next issue of the* Miner, *under the heading "Elephant Berry," was this reply in kind:*

We had intended to let the mammoth ape whose name appears as editor of the Yuma *Sentinel* severely alone, until a day or two ago when a citizen of Prescott requested us to inform our readers that Berry uttered a gratuitous falsehood when he stated in the *Sentinel* that he (Berry) lost fifteen hundred dollars by trusting certain infernal scoundrels in Prescott and vicinity. This being a reasonable and legitimate request, we now assert that Berry lied when he said so, and that it would take more than that sum to pay for the whiskey which Berry "bummed" during his long sojourn in Prescott, not to speak of that which he guzzled in our sister county of Mohave, previous to the day upon which he found himself debarred from the privilege of swallowing free whiskey in the town of Cerbat, in that county.

Again, we have been asked our reasons for not giving the lie to certain assertions of his, regarding ourself. Well, one reason is: Berry is a natural and artificial liar, whom nobody was ever known to believe. Then, he did tell one truth about us, that is, that drink once got the better of us, at a social party given by Colonel Baker. We were drunk that night, and have never yet attempted to deny it. But Berry drank ten times to our once, and the only reason that he did not fall down and crawl on all fours, like the beast that he is, was, there was not sufficient liquor in the house to fill his hogshead.

He has said, in the *Sentinel*, that no man ever saw Wm. J. Berry drunk. In answer to this, we say that Wm. J. Berry lied when he said so. When he lived in Prescott, his first great care was to fill himself with whiskey, after which it was his custom to walk, like the swine that he is, on all fours to his den. Again, he cannot have forgotten his visit to Lynx Creek, in the summer of 1864, when he rolled over a pine log, dead drunk, and served a useful purpose for a jocose man, who is still a resident of this section of Arizona. Yes, Judge, we own up to that little drink of ours; unlike you, we were not pointed out and derided as a regular whiskey bloat; nor did any person ever attempt to use us for a water-closet, as you were used that day, on Lynx Creek.

As to your being a better editor than the writer of this, it is for the public to judge; not for you to assert, although you have asserted it. You have called us a blackguard, regardless of the old story about the pot and kettle.

Hoping that these few lines will find you drunk and obedient to your masters, as usual, we say, in your own "classic" language, "uncork and be damned."

*Judge Berry came right back with a piece entitled "Jackass Marion" in the next issue of the* Sentinel:

We had not intended to make any reply to, or have any controversy with that miserable "what is it?" whose name appears as editor of the Prescott *Miner*. Such dirty, low creatures are beneath the notice of respectable journals. Were he responsible, in a pecuniary sense, we might easily seek and find our remedy at law, in an action for libel and malicious defamation of character. But the result would be in accordance with the old adage, to wit: "Sue a beggar and get a louse."

It is unnecessary for us to say that the tirade of that miserable nincompoop against us is a tissue of lies, concocted by the addled brain of its author, and that not a word of truth is contained in his charges against us. We resided in Prescott for nine years, and have the pleasure of knowing we have a host of friends there and in that vicinity, and that our friends are numbered among the very best people. Marion cannot hurt us by his lies among them. His mendacious character is well known. Among strangers, he might make a temporary impression against us, but the old settlers, who know both him and us well, would soon set the matter right.

We are sorry to have to dirty our columns by any reference to this abandoned creature, and would not have done it, had not a professional chemist sent us an analysis of the constituent parts of this interesting subject. Here is the analysis:

| | |
|---|---:|
| Constitutional liar | 200 |
| Jackass ability | 200 |
| Lunar Caustic | 200 |
| Iodide of Potassa | 200 |
| Sweet Spirits Nitre | 200 |
| | 1,000 |

But we dismiss the disgusting subject. We would remark, however, by way of explanation to our readers, that the publication of the above analysis has caused the peculiar color of our paper this week.

*The journalistic battle ended when, in the January 29, 1875, issue of the* Miner, *John H. Marion published his valedictory:*

Having disposed of the Arizona Miner, my connection with the paper, as editor, proprietor, etc., ceases with the present issue; and before proceeding further, I hereby tender my most grateful thanks to all who have, in any way, assisted myself and the Miner during the seven years and three months or more, that have intervened since I purchased the paper from Mr. McCormick, who founded it in March, 1864. . . .

Believing that I have fought a good fight for my Territory and fellow-citizens; knowing I have always upheld Right and fought Wrong; that I have never attacked private character in the Miner; never taken part in the wrangles of businessmen and contractors; never attempted to blackmail anybody; never wronged an employe or other creditor of mine out of the value of a cent, I now, for the last time, perhaps, use these columns to thank my God, and the friends who have stood by me. . . .

*In the meantime, Judge Berry carried on with the Sentinel, with regrets, perhaps, that his battle of words with John H. Marion, as editor of the Miner, had come to an end. His thoughts turned to more pacific overtures and in May, 1875, he headed an article "Brown Paper":*

Variety is said to be the spice of life, and it is the same with colors as anything else. If nature was clothed in only one color the eye would soon tire of gazing at the monotonous scene. If the flowers were all of the same hue they would cease to call forth admiration. We have therefore thought, in accordance with "the eternal fitness of things," and particularly as the steamer [on the Colorado River] has not arrived with our supply of paper, that we would make a virtue of necessity, and change the color of the Sentinel this week. How is that for an apology?

In the following issue he wrote:

Last week, by way of variety, we treated our readers to beautiful brown paper. We had intended to return to the original white, this week, but reflecting upon the injury that sometimes results from too sudden transitions, we concluded to let our readers down gradually, and as the connecting steamer has not arrived yet with our supply of paper, we have at great expense procured this beautiful buff, or rich cream-colored paper, which is so soothing to the eye. We hope our readers will duly appreciate our efforts to please them.

Then came summer and this bit of elegant prose by the learned Judge:

The nights are glorious for sleep just now. The angels enfold us in their star-dimpled arms and waft us to the bright shores of immortal glory, where we revel in unspeakable delight until the time for waking comes, when we must return to earth. That is what comes of having a clear conscience. Sometimes we'll go to those bright shores to stay, and return to this dull earth no more. The sooner the better.

About two months later, Judge Berry wrote this:

Wanted! A nice, plump, healthy, good-natured, good-looking, domestic and affectionate lady to correspond with. Object—matrimony. She must be between 22 and 35 years of age. She must be a believer in God and immortality, but no sectarian. She must not be a gad-about or given to scandal, but must be one who will be a help-mate and companion, and who will endeavor to make home happy. Such a lady can find a correspondent by addressing the editor of this paper. Photographs exchanged!

If anybody don't like our way of going about this interesting business, we don't care. It's none of their funeral.

*Judge Berry continued with the* Sentinel *through 1876. His vale-dictory read, in part:*

Friends, patrons, readers of the *Sentinel*, hail and farewell! On this occasion, in taking leave of those with whom I have long held intercourse through these columns, it seems to me proper to drop the plural pronoun, the editorial we, and use the simple personal pronoun, I. In fact, I have never properly been we, since I have been running this journal, as I have had no companion to share the sanctum with me, not even a cat, or dog, or pig or chicken, except sometimes when a neighbor's hen would come in and lay an egg in a box behind the press. (Note,—that hen laid six eggs the first week and two on Sunday, and the next week she laid six during the week days and three on Sunday, and she never would cackle, so that her owners didn't know where she deposited her treasure, but on the beginning of the third week she wanted to set on the nest egg, and I kicked her out, and then she made an awful noise and the old woman who owned her knew her voice of lamen-tation and came running, followed by her progeny, but the old critter didn't find any eggs, cause why? They had gone to in-vigorate our body corporate; and since the loss of that hen I haven't felt like we.) Excuse this digression, for I never would have had a chance to relate that episode had I not stuck it in this valedictory, for my successor, who is very sedate, precise and primlike, wouldn't allow any such foolishness unless he perpetrated it himself. . . .

I tender my sincere thanks for the generous support that has been extended to me during the three years and three months that I have conducted the *Sentinel*, and also for the many kind ex-pressions of approbation from those whose good opinion is worth having, which have cheered me along. Farewell!

WM. J. BERRY

# 4

# LAWLESSNESS AND VIGILANTES

## LAWLESSNESS AND VIGILANTES

Precious metal was the prime magnet which brought an influx of early settlers to the Indian-infested territory that is now Arizona. As news of rich discoveries of placer gold in the creek beds and the mountainsides reached the outside world, mining camps mushroomed overnight, and along with the prospectors, miners, speculators, tinhorn gamblers, and the usual ne'er-do-well followers of the golden trail there was always that little army of respectable citizens who form the backbone of any community, large or small.

From the very beginning of the first mining camps respectable citizens were sorely tried and sometimes placed in the most imminent danger from the rampant spirit of lawlessness which invaded these new towns, acknowledging no authority and fearing no man. As a general rule the decent people were forced to combine and give sanction for a time to the stern rulings of "Judge Lynch" until the government assumed the function properly belonging to it. This seemed harsh, no doubt, especially to the public back in the

"States," which could little realize the recklessness of frontier desperadoes. These latter disregarded all law until it placed a noose about their necks or shot them full of holes, and even then they died defiant, crossing over into the beyond bravely, with their boots on.

A few incidents of the general reign of terror and lawlessness and the desperation brought about by the outlaw element are highlighted in the following newspaper items from almost every section of Arizona.

The first is taken from a charge by Judge Backus, sitting in the First District Court of Arizona, published in the Prescott Miner in 1866:

Gentlemen—I am informed that at your present session there will be brought before you a case of murder, one of those unfortunate cases of too frequent occurrence of the too common and promiscuous use of firearms, at once dangerous to the community, as it is discreditable and wicked in the individual. Of the criminal I would say nothing, for it would not be proper for me, at this time, to do so; but of the crime I would emphatically say, it is your imperative duty, in every way in your power, to discountenance and put a stop to this dastardly and barbarous practice of shooting, this perversion of firearms, an invention intended by kind heaven for our safety and protection, to the purposes of the slaughter of our citizens. . . .

Convince our brethren of the older States that we are a law-abiding and law-loving people; that Arizona is not a sanctuary of assassins, or an asylum of crime, and capital and population by an easy and natural course of things will flow in upon us, transforming a feeble and remote Territory into a sovereign State of the Union, making the wilderness and desolate places to bud and blossom as the rose.

From the Prescott Miner in 1870, with crime and lawlessness ever on the increase, we take this admonition in an editorial:

Well may we exclaim, whither are we drifting when, in addition to the horrid, cruel, cold-blooded murders that are almost daily committed by savage Indians, within the confines of this new Territory, civilized (?) men—Americans and Mexicans—quarrel over frivolous matters, and without stopping to allow their tiger passions to subside, hastily resort to deadly weapons to settle their disputes, and kill or maim each other. In saying this we do not wish to be understood as alleging or insinuating that all citizens of Arizona who have misunderstandings act thus desperately, fiendishly, wantonly and unlawfully. Far from it. The great majority of our people are remarkably quiet, cool and law-abiding. But, there is no denying the fact that the Territory has among its population very many bad, passionate men, who are but too ready to stain her annals with crime—bring reproach upon her, and earn for themselves the ignominious name of murderers . . . unless the laws are strictly enforced, unless criminals are punished, crime and lawlessness will increase; armed bullies will terrorize over law-abiding citizens; patience will cease to be a virtue, and the virtuous, honest, law-abiding portion of the community will arise in their might, and swing the last murderous villain into eternity, there to atone for crimes committed upon this Earth. Of course there are instances upon record—and such instances may again occur—where men have been impelled, yes, compelled, to take the lives of others in order to save their own, but, such cases have been of rare occurrence, and it is our earnest prayer that, in the future, they will be less frequent. In moralizing thus, we must not overlook the fact that the almost universal custom in vogue among our people of carrying deadly weapons has been one great motive for the numerous blood-letting scrapes that have disgraced and blackened the fair fame of our Territory, and we hope that the time is near at hand when the cause that compels this general arming will be done away with. Were there no hostile Indians in the Territory, citizens would not be under the necessity of "fortifying" themselves, with deadly weapons, and could go around with those only which God has given them—their arms and tongues—weapons which, although capable of inflicting considerable injury, scarcely ever destroy life.

The foregoing remarks are a necessary corollary to the numerous crimes that have recently been committed by civilized (?) people in this Territory—crimes, at whose mention peaceable citizens shudder. Some of these are, the recent murder of Bradley, in a saloon in this town; the shooting of Garcia, at Florence; the murderous attack upon Mr. Duffield, at Tucson, and the desperate fandango affray at the same place, a short time ago. It matters not that some of the persons killed and mained in these desperate encounters had the name of being bad men. That does not, cannot justify the onslaughts made upon them. . . .

*According to the Tucson Citizen, at a meeting of the citizens of Gila River, held at Florence on February 17, 1873, the following resolutions were passed:*

Resolved, That whereas life, security and lawful and rightful possession of property have been for years past and still continue to be insecure in this immediate vicinity, and in fact throughout the whole of the upper valley of the Gila; and whereas, such insecurity is caused by the wanton and unlawful acts of certain bad men and desperadoes who neither fear nor regard the laws of God or man, and have set both at defiance; and whereas, the tardy administration of justice, not only in Pima County, but throughout the whole Territory of Arizona, seems to have emboldened certain lawless men in the commission of violent acts in our midst; be it

Resolved by the law-abiding citizens of the upper Gila valley, that we have this day met and considered calmly and dispassionately our feelings and disagreeable situation and the bad name that it necessarily brings upon the whole community, we have resolved that we will by our mild strength aid and assist all officers of the law in the faithful and fearless discharge of their duties; and failing to secure this protection to which we are entitled, we are determined to put a stop in a summary manner to any more lawless acts in our midst, and further wish to give notice to all lawless characters that we have borne with their acts until further forbearance on our part would seem to encourage these parties, and that in the future we are determined to put an effectual stop to the further commission of such violent acts as have for the last four years disgraced our settlement.

*The Prescott Democrat, in 1880, reprinted from the Globe Silver Belt of May 29, the following warning, signed by the mystic "601":*
To whom it may concern:

The citizens of the town of Globe and vicinity, recognizing the

importance of establishing an organization in their midst, having
for its purpose the suppression of unlawfulness in all its forms, and
the establishment of peace and justice, announce that such an
organization has been formed, officers elected, constitution and
by-laws adopted, and they have solemnly pledged themselves, their
fortunes and sacred honors to stand by each other in the main-
tenance of justice in our local court, the suppression of all unlawful and uncivilized acts, and in order that wrong-doers may have
warning, and guard against the practice of promiscuously using and
discharging of fire-arms upon our streets and within the town limits,
the using of obscene language within the hearing of ladies, giving
or selling liquor to Indians and the playing of cards in our streets
with them, or the reckless riding of horses through our town, the
jumping of town lots, encroachments upon our streets by building,
or otherwise obstructing the same, the protection of mines and
mine owners in their rights, and in fact any and all unlawful acts:
for these, this publication is made; and while it is regarded that it
is necessary that such a step should be taken, yet believing it to be
a necessity, they hereby counsel all who may be maliciously inclined, to take due notice, and thereby save any action that may be
necessary in the premises.

"601"

*The Phoenix Herald carried this letter from Graham County:*
Fort Grant, April 11, 1881

A band of robbers, known as cowboys, or more recently "rustlers," infest southeastern Arizona and rob the stockraisers of their
property. At another time they turn desperadoes and rob stages
and murder persons. Their headquarters are at San Simon Mead-
ows, where they are fortified in adobe buildings. They have a system of telegraphing known only to themselves, and use the wires
to inform their comrades of danger. The band consists of Americans and Mexicans. Some Mexicans of this band have met an un-
timely death at the hands of a vigilance committee. Will not some
power, either civil or military, put a quietus on this business and
protect the lives and property of our people, against the most
formidable band of robbers ever known in the history of our
Territory?

*Says the Prescott* Democrat, *in 1881:*

Cochise County has two evils, the so-called rustlers and the stage robbers. It would be well for the good people of Tombstone to get together and hang the whole outfit. The lives of the law-abiding citizens should not be allowed to be put in jeopardy because a few cut-throats and stage robbers by their presence demand it shall be so. Hemp, gentlemen, hemp; that is what you need in Tombstone.

*From northwestern Arizona, Mohave County, the Mineral Park* Alta, *in 1882, had this notice:*

"Judge Lynch" has opened court in Mohave County. While the decisions of the "Judge" are not always founded on the strict letter of the law, no complaint is ever laid at his door for dilly-dallying with the accused. If a man commits a willful murder, or other offense worthy of death, and is arraigned before him "the books" and the "quiddits and quillets" of lawyers are not invoked in his behalf. Plain, common sense, usually takes command and not infrequently leads the villain to a limb or the beam of a blacksmith shop and halter in short order, without even a reference to the "statutes in such cases made and provided." The doctrine that "every man is entitled to a fair and impartial trial by a jury of his peers," is correct and indisputable, in communities where society is well organized, where jails are good, and especially where there is the least doubt as to the guilt or innocence of the accused. No body of men, however large and respectable, have a right to take a human life except by due process of law, if there is any doubt as to whether the accused committed a crime for which his life should be taken. But if a villain slays his fellow in cold blood, the proof whereof is abundant and undoubted—as in the case in the dreadful tragedy at Hackberry last Monday—he forfeits his life and the sooner it is taken by the outraged community, and his vile carcass remanded to the dull clod from whence it came, the sooner will go up from all law-abiding citizens the common verdict, "served him right."

*In Tombstone, following the Earp-Clanton feud shootings and numerous other killings which are covered in another chapter in this volume, the Governor of Arizona was appealed to. After a personal inspection tour of the area, he advised the President of the lawlessness and the apparent inability of the peace officers to curb or suppress crime in the Territory. President Chester A. Arthur then issued a proclamation, published in the Tucson Citizen early in 1882, which acknowledged the prevalance of lawlessness in the Territory and the apparent inability of law-enforcement agencies to cope with the situation. He admonished the good citizens of Arizona against aiding, countenancing, abetting, or taking part in any unlawful acts. The President also warned all persons engaged in or connected with the obstruction of laws to dispense and retire peaceably to their respective abodes on or before May 15, 1882, or suffer the consequences of government intervention.*

*When Tombstone had barely cleaned the blood from her streets, the Epitaph, commenting on the President's proclamation and the fact that the citizens of Charleston, her neighboring camp, were to hold an indignation meeting as a result of that proclamation, had this to say:*

If any place in the Territory is entitled to indignate, Charleston is that place. It is there that the cowboys have broken whiskey glasses just as they were raised to the lips by terror-stricken citizens, broken the tops of beer bottles and snuffed out candles with their revolvers. It is in Charleston that clergymen have been compelled to dance and sing in the midst of religious services, to gratify the grim humor of Curley Bill and crowd. It is here that merchants have been compelled to open their safes and turn over their ready cash to the festive cowboys. It is here that the Clantons and McLowrys tied up and disarmed a peace officer for attempting to arrest one of them for disturbing the peace. It is here that Peel and a half dozen others have been murdered in cold blood within the past few months. We would suggest that they (the citizens of Charleston) would embrace these facts in the preamble to the resolutions they will be called upon to pass. . . .

*But despite this appeal to Charleston, the Epitaph just as quickly came to the defense of her neighbor town in its next issue, denouncing some of the newspapers for calling Charleston "the haunt of robbers and cut-throats or cowboys." It stated: "This* town has suffered enough at the hands of villains of every description, and has but one desire—to get rid of them, the quicker the better."

The town of Ash Fork had her vigilantes, too. Here is a letter to the editor, printed in the Prescott Journal in 1884:

Dear Sir:

As we have not an officer of the law with us to enforce law and order, and as we have been in a measure over-ridden with murderers, cut-throats, bunco men, tin-horn gamblers, loafers and worthless characters generally, with one Harlan, alias "Off Wheeler," and his "pal" as the leaders,—yesterday, in the interest of "law and order," it became necessary for the good people of Ash Fork to organize a "committee of safety," and a committee of 101, with free power to act promptly and efficiently, were duly organized, and a notice to leave within fifteen minutes duly served upon the "gang" which was promptly obeyed, and by their leaving we are rid of three of the scoundrels. The town was well guarded last night, and patrolled by the law-abiding citizens, assisted in a great measure by the freighters now in camp. Some of the so-called good citizens of Ash Fork who furnished "bed and board" to the characters mentioned in this letter had better be more careful in the future as to whom they assist, as the committee is determined that loafers, thieves, and the like, shall give this town a wide berth. The promiscuous shooting of revolvers and guns on the streets at all hours of the day and night must and shall be stopped; also "gun plays," as the laws of our Territory will be enforced in a rather prompt, efficient and summary manner. By order of

COMMITTEE OF 101

In 1887, the St. Johns Herald, in Apache County, reported:

Peace again reigns in Springerville. Shotguns, Winchesters and cheese-knives have all been superceded by order. A man there can now go out in his back yard at night without being held up and made to dance a jig on a fence post. Whether there will be any increase in the demand for undertakers and coroners in the next six months remains to be determined.

# 5

# THE TOMBSTONE SAGA

## THE TOMBSTONE SAGA

The town of Tombstone, Arizona, has had a fabulous history. Many of the early-day mining camps have survived to this day; many became ghost towns and turned to dust when the ore gave out. But Tombstone, the most famous of the bonanza towns, is still very much on the map.

The early mining camps always attracted, along with the better class of citizenry, many of the lawless element: gamblers, tinhorn and otherwise; highwaymen, cutthroats, and "soiled doves" of the half-world. As the immense riches of the locality became known, men of all professions flocked in. They came by stagecoach, by burro, on muleback, and afoot to cash in on the great new silver discoveries.

The town of Tombstone was laid out in 1879, and by the end of the year there were some forty houses, cabins, and tents in the camp, and the population was about a hundred permanent residents plus the thousand or more miners who camped outside the town. And as the fame of Tombstone spread, the population increased rapidly during the following few years to some six thousand.

A correspondent for the Tucson Star described the embryo camp in the latter part of 1879 in this manner:

Arriving in this fast mountain city a short time since, I was struck with the great activity manifested in every branch of business. The saloon-keepers are always active, polite and accommodating. The restaurants are models of neatness, and supplied bounteously with the choicest meats and such other dainties as the market affords. Mechanics are employed in erecting buildings in various parts of the town. The lawyers already have more business than they can attend to, simply because they have to carry their offices around in their pockets or hats. I have in mind one notable instance—Lawyer Street is gathering up business today and is lamenting because he cannot find a room, even a shelter from the sun, under which to transact such business as comes to him, and is compelled to do it on the sidewalk. So much for this soon-to-be largest mining town in the Territory.

And speaking of the lack of facilities, here is an item from the Tucson Citizen, 1880:

They had a fair or festival at Tombstone the other night for the benefit of a church, and the only building in town which afforded

sufficient room was the Variety Theater. Ordinarily the bare association of such a place with church charity, would cause the clasps on all the prayer books in the district to rattle with indignation, but the managers of the fair believing in the old motto "Honi soit qui mal y pense" [Fr.—*Shamed be he who thinks evil of it*], proceeded to make the necessary arrangements. That the affair was socially, and more particularly, a financial success, was in a great measure, due to the fact that the objectionable hall was selected, for the reason that immediately in the rear of the building was a dance house which furnished all the music without any charge, there being but a thin partition between the two establishments.

Everything went smoothly enough until the inmates of the dance house began to get warmed up, when the staid members of the church were horrified by such calls as "hoof it to the left," "hug the gals on the corner," "hoop 'em down the middle," "mule punchers to the right," and the never-failing injunction "all hands chase to the bar, and don't you forget it." The next church fair will not take place in the Variety hall.

Cochise County was created out of a part of Pima County in 1881, and Tombstone was the county seat until the latter was removed to Bisbee in 1931. The camp began to decline about ten years after its birth when underground water sounded its death knell as a prosperous mining community. But Tombstone did not die, and the phrase coined many years ago, "the town too tough to die," still holds good today, although the toughness is not in the lawless element of its never-to-be-forgotten past but in the good people, the pioneers, who stuck with Tombstone, reared their families there, and, along with many newcomers fascinated by the place, made it their home.

It is estimated that perhaps a hundred million dollars in mineral wealth has been taken from the Tombstone mines, much of it was during the fabulous first ten years of their existence, although some mining on a moderate scale has been going on ever since that time.

The lawlessness of the early eighties gave Tombstone an unsavory reputation which newspapers throughout the country were quick to exploit with sensational stories and editorials disapproving the apparent cheapness of life and utter disregard of all law and *order in the bonanza town. The following is a sample of this sort of report; it is taken from a New York exchange of 1882, published after the O.K. Corral episode of the notorious Earp-Clanton feud.*

Tombstone, Arizona, is well named. Few people there die in their beds. Between the cowboys and other desperadoes, the uncertainty of life is constantly exemplified. A man with good luck and extraordinary vitality may manage to keep out of the tomb long enough to become a citizen, but such instances are rare. Not long since Deputy United States Marshal Earp was found with nineteen bullets in his body and he is alive yet. He seems to be the right sort of a man for the place.

*Snorted the Tucson* Star, *when its editor read this lurid account:*

Pshaw, this is not half nor a twentieth part. The Marshal had fifty-seven bullets extracted and it is believed there is about a peck yet in his body. Only a short time ago a cowboy had a Henry rifle rammed down his throat and then broken off; he spit the gun barrel out with the loss of only a tooth. It is stated as a fact that more than four-fifths of the inhabitants of the district carry one or more bullets in their bodies. One instance is of record where birth was given to an infant who came forth armed with two bowie knives, and a cannon strapped on his back. Everybody goes armed, men, women and children. Every house has port holes from which the cowboys are shot down. It is a great place for suicides; if a fellow wants to die with his boots on, he just steps out on the street and yells out "you're another," and immediately he is plumped through from all sides with a shower of bullets. Sports play at cards with a knife in the left hand and a six-shooter in the right. It is no uncommon occurrence to see twenty men dumped out of a card room in the morning, and pitched down some mining shaft where the ore has petered out. This is but a faint picture of the situation. Our New York exchanges had better try and get the facts.— Tucson *Star*

—Phoenix *Gazette*, 1882

# THE STORY OF TOMBSTONE'S EARLY DAYS

## WHO DISCOVERED TOMBSTONE?

*A letter to the Tucson Star from a special correspondent follows:*
Mule Pass, A. T., July 10, 1879

In a recent issue of your paper you raise the question in regard to the discovery of the Tombstone mines, and ask for definite information on the subject of who was the actual discoverer of this district. The important part these rich and valuable mines are destined to play in swelling the bullion product of Arizona gives interest to your request, and we will attempt to give the facts as they really are.

Some prior events are connected with this district that give it a historic interest, and may most properly preface its recent history. We refer to about twenty years ago, when the white man, even while traveling the highways of Arizona, took his rifle in his hands, and a tramp into her wild hills was attended with almost certain fatality from the hostile Apaches. There was, however, one bold spirit, who was so devoted to the mining profession, Fred Brunckow, Prussian-born, of rare culture, and high attainments in mineralogy, who possessed the pluck and energy to venture out alone into the upper regions of the San Pedro, where the implacable Cochise held indisputable and bloody sway.

Strange to say, this fearless and devoted explorer passed and repassed unmolested among Cochise's savage bands, which resulted in the discovery of a rich silver mine that bears his name. It is on the east side of the San Pedro, about a mile from the spot now occupied by the Tombstone Company's mill, and about seven miles from the present discoveries, in a small broken range of hills that crosses the river above the mouth of the Babocomari Creek.

Here, under the very stronghold of Cochise, he commenced operating his mine, under the greatest of disadvantages, but with satisfactory results, managing to conciliate the murderous savages; but just as he was getting his operations under way he fell a victim to the hands of his Mexican operatives, who murdered him and robbed his camp of the first run of bullion and all the stock, and escaped into Sonora. The mine lay unoccupied until Milton Duffield, ex-United States Marshal, relocated it about the year 1873, when he commenced opening up the mine. But he was cowardly assassinated by another pretended claimant. The mine was subsequently located by one Rodgers, of Sulphur Springs, and others who commenced prosecuting work upon it. Rodgers was a few months afterwards murdered by the Apaches. Thus three of its consecutive owners have filled bloody graves—a strange fatality— yet the old mine has served its purpose. It stood with its bloody history, and with talismanic influence beckoning the intrepid, enterprising prospector to enter its sad precincts, and look up the secret treasures of this little belt of seemingly forbidden hills.

In the month of July, 1877, chance led Ed Schieffelin, an energetic and intelligent man, to this historic spot. After persistently tramping over many a mountain, hill, and ravine, from Oregon to Arizona, for many a weary day, without a pay streak, alone, poor, and sore-footed, at the tail of his burro—a pick, shovel and a scant outfit of grub constituting all his earthly effects, he reached these fatal, death-stricken hills.

On disclosing his object of prospecting the Brunckow hills to some miners, they, more timid than he, advised him of the sad fate of the former prospectors of the ill-fated district, and further admonished him, that the first prospecting he did over these "had better be for a tombstone, and that when the country became more civilized they would pass by the graveyard and write his epitaph." Hence these sad associations afterwards suggested to him the future name of the district—"TOMBSTONE."

[In his own story, Schieffelin wrote that often in reply to inquiries by soldiers in the area, if he had found anything, he replied that he would eventually. To this the soldiers said, "Yes, you'll find your tombstone," and repeating that several times, the word lingered in his mind; he gave the name to the first location he made, and on the organization of the district, it was called Tombstone from that location.]

A few days prospecting led him to the discovery of a ledge of rich silver- and gold-bearing quartz, which in consequence of the gloomy surroundings he christened "The Graveyard," and two or three other promising looking ledges, among which was the "Lucky Cuss." He kept up the prospect for a few weeks, when the last bean in the pot was spooned out. He then repaired to Tucson, unconsciously rich in mines, but poor in pocket, to try to raise a "grubstake," and get an assay on his rock. Then he sought a modest credit at one of the leading mercantile firms for a sack of flour and a side of bacon, and was cooly refused. He also sought aid by exhibiting to them specimens from his rich find, but was curtly informed that rock was no collateral. Not even could he induce them to advance the assayer's fees to satisfy them of the value of the discovery.

He being of a modest and independent turn of mind, did not seek further to press the importance of his discovery on these doubting Thomases. Little did they think that those pocket specimens exhibited by this truthful, earnest, weather-beaten prospector would soon represent the millions of hidden treasure buried in his then scarcely monumented claims at Tombstone. Did those same over-cautious merchants, who refused poor Ed Schieffelin credit for a sack of flour on the occasion referred to, reflect when they joined the hosannas in that triumphant procession, a few weeks ago, that bore in grand display the first $20,000 run from those same mines, through the streets of Tucson, that the then poor Ed Schieffelin, whose name they spurned from their books of credit, was the Mr. Schieffelin of today, or "Colonel" Schieffelin, if you please, if his modest nature would brook the title?

How true the lines—

> When you are up,
> They all sing out your praise;
> But when you are down,
> They really don't fancy your ways.

Yes, money makes the mare go, and fools and wise men alike often bet on the wrong horse.

Schieffelin then went up to the Signal mill, Mohave County, in the month of December, where he met his brother Al, and Richard Gird, the latter being a fine mineralogist and practical miner. The ore specimens were submitted to him, and on assay, he pronounced the prospect one of high merit, and advised the discoverer to at once look after and secure it. The three at once formed a partnership, secured an outfit, and quietly set out and reached the discovery about the 14th of February following, and entered on an earnest exploration of the district, which in a few weeks resulted in the discovery and location of the "Tough Nut" and other valuable claims.

About the 1st of March, Oliver Boyer and Hank Williams were out hunting stray burros, and happened upon their camp. They became interested and remained, and after a few days' prospecting discovered the "Grand Central" and "Contention." The latter they gave to Gird, on the condition that he did their assaying for them. This prospect was sold to White and Parsons, of San Francisco, a few weeks later, for $10,000, who a short time since refused a round million cash for the same. What a change! Sold a few months ago for the consideration of a few assayer's fees; today, $3,000,000 in sight!

In the month of May following, Colonel Lewis and others entered the district, and a number of other valuable mines were located. The richness of the discoveries soon became noised abroad, and prospectors came in great numbers, and in a short time the district was thoroughly prospected and many valuable locations made.

In this hasty sketch we have essayed to give a bed-rock statement of the facts, for the purpose above mentioned; and in doing so we "nothing extenuate nor aught set down in malice."

D. B. REA

### TOMBSTONE, 1881

*The following letter was published in the Prescott Democrat in 1881:*

On a level ridge among the rolling hills and undulating plains, extending from the Dragoon range on the north to the Mule Mountains on the south, and about nine miles east of the San Pedro River, is the city of Tombstone, the liveliest mining camp on the Pacific Coast. To the north, sixteen miles away, the Dragoon

Mountains—the former stronghold of the Apache Chief Cochise—rear their rocky and rugged outlines, while the low range of the Whetstones on the west and the massive chain of the Huachucas on the south afford a pleasant relief from the base and barren hills and sun-scorched plains which make up the foreground of the picture and encircle this city of silver-bearing renown all round about. Approaching the place from the east or the west the stranger's attention is first attracted to the number of diminutive, one-story frame shanties, which stand like so many sentry boxes on the outskirts of the town, and whose unadorned ugliness and tiresome sameness are the least attractive features of the city with the solemnly suggestive name. A few minutes' ride through these scraggy suburbs and we are in the heart of the city, surrounded by a living tide of moving humanity: a surging sea of hurrying, crowding, jostling human beings who line the sidewalks and fill the streets at all hours of the day.

Life in Tombstone is a whirl of excitement, a moving panorama of existence in a frontier mining camp; a picturesque and never-ending round of active energetic western life in its different moods and various phases. Mammon has here set up his altar, and thousands daily and nightly worship assiduously at his shrine. The "Almighty Dollar" seems to be the goal of every man's ambition. It is a grand lottery where many have staked their all, willing to stand the hazard of the die; a stage whereon speculation, avarice, enterprise and energy play the leading roles. In the fierce race for wealth all men are on an equal footing, and the ragged prospector who hasn't a "quarter" in his pocket, jostles with airy independence, the "solid" man from Boston or New York who can count his wealth by millions. And why not? Although "broke" today, the honest miner may tomorrow be the possessor of a bonanza equal to all the wealth of the Eastern capitalist. Men who entered this camp two years ago, following faithfully in the tracks of the patient burro, now patronize "two bit" bars and smoke genuine Havanas—from Connecticut. Against the few who are basking in fortune's smiles, however, there are many who arrived here on the ragged edge of impecuniosity and are in that distressing condition still. Like every other lottery, the prizes are few while the blanks are many. The "Citizen of the World" would feel at home in Tombstone, for it is purely a cosmopolitan town. Every civilized nation on the globe is represented in the hurrying crowds that throng its streets at all hours of the day and most of the night. . . .

The professionals are well represented. There are said to be sixty-four lawyers in the camp—with several outside precincts to hear from. How they all manage to live is one of the mysteries of the place which even the oldest inhabitant confesses himself power-less to elucidate. That there is a fine *Field* here for attorneys, and that it promises to yield some fat pickings, is almost certain; but the legal line, like many others, is overdone, and many a briefless barrister, who now sits behind his modest shingle, waiting for a client, is likely to remain so.

Notwithstanding the unsettled condition of titles, property is high in Tombstone. Desirable lots in the center of the town are rated at $100 per front foot; rents are correspondingly high. Men who were fortunate enough to secure corner lots at an early day, are now well fixed, financially. Building is going on steadily, and several fine two-story adobe houses are now in course of erection. The theater and public hall, which is being built by the Schieffelin Brothers, will be an ornament to the town and the largest in the Territory.

No one who has not visited the place can form an adequate idea of the marvelous growth of this camp during the past year. A little more than two years ago, when the first house was erected, the present site of the city of Tombstone was a desert waste; today it is a thriving camp of six thousand inhabitants, containing some fine buildings, and commodious mercantile establishments, with a large and steady growing trade. . . .

On the streets and in the hotels investors from all parts of the East and from California, talk mines from morning until late at night, and eagerly watch every opportunity to "get a hold" of some-thing good. Every other man you meet on the street has a pocket full of specimens, and assures you in the strictest confidence that he has "the biggest thing in the District." In the hotels, in the stores, in the saloons, in the restaurants, nothing is talked of but mines and mining. New strikes are being made daily and the owner of a prospect who can show any ore, can readily dispose of it.

The main street, upon which nearly all the business is transacted, is almost a mile in length. The houses in the center of the town are built generally of adobe—many of them being two stories in height, and when plastered on the outside present quite a creditable appearance. Saloons and restaurants seem to be the most lucrative branches of business, and the Tombstoners show their appreciation of refreshment and sustenance for the inner man by liberally patronizing these establishments.

Tombstone is not a pleasant place to live in. The ground on which the town is built is almost exclusively a lime formation, and the heavy ore and freight wagons which are continually passing over it, have ground the surface into a fine powder, which every passing gale raises into clouds of blinding, penetrating dust. This terrible dust, which finds its way into every house, gets into your eyes and ears, insinuates down the back of your neck, and thoroughly impregnates your garments, is the greatest discomfort to life in Tombstone. Old residents do not seem to mind it, but to those not native here, it is a fearful ordeal. The city's water is brought in pipes from the Dragoon Mountains. The quantity is limited, and the quality is not of the best, but of this fact old Tombstoners are in blissful ignorance, their acquaintance with the aqueous element being confined to an occasional slight ablution. Of its qualities as a beverage, they do not entertain a very exalted opinion—preferring something more cheering, and also something more inebriating.

The residents of the bonanza camp are agitated over the matter of titles to town lots. This has been a vexed question with the people of this town ever since its settlement, and late events have further complicated the legal tangle into which property-holders have found themselves drawn. . . . As one phase of the affair it may be stated that several mining claims were located on what is now the City of Tombstone. Among others, one known as the "Gilded Age," takes in a large portion of the present business center of the town. The title to the property was disputed, and the claimant carried his case to the Supreme Court, and won it. The owner thus finds himself in possession of his mining claim and the buildings thereon, including a large portion of the City of Tombstone. He is now one of the most prominent and best hated men in the camp. The Sheriff has been ordered to evict the trespassers, and with whispering humbleness they are compelled to call upon

Fields, the proclaimed owner, who has been named the "Duke of Tombstone," and come to his terms. A steady stream of crestfallen squatters throng his rooms (where he sits in state, guarded by the City Marshal) all day long, paying tribute to this mighty man. . . . Fields is a character in his way, and has many points in common with the hero of the play after which he has christened his mining claim. Like "Col. Sellers," he is likely to find "millions in it."

I spoke of the complicated and confused manner in which locations have been made in the District; the natural sequence of such a state of things has already arisen, and the conflict of titles begun in earnest. The "Duke of Tombstone" is now engaged in a vigorous warfare with parties whom he claims have jumped a portion of his Gilded Age mine, and the varying fortunes of the fight are affording the Tombstonites much amusement. The Sheriff, under order of the court, dispossessed the jumpers and turned the property over to Fields, who placed a guard of half a dozen men in charge. These warriors, after holding the fort for two days, thinking that five dollars per day was not enough for their arduous services, struck for ten, which Fields refused to give, whereupon the "fighters" laid down their arms and abandoned the works; which were immediately taken possession of by the jumpers, and as I write, a dozen of them are standing guard around the shaft, armed like so many Bashi Bazouls. Between the lawyers—who have gathered around him like so many vultures—and the jumpers, his Highness of Tombstone is having a lively time. . . .

The question of title is one great drawback in the building up of this town. As nearly all the ground is covered by mining claims, and as the suit of Fields is supposed to have been a test case, occupants of other portions of the town are in a state of anxious solicitude and are daily expecting a notice from some owner of mining ground, to step up to the Captain's office and settle. As many of them have already paid for the property they occupy to other parties, it seems unfair and unjust that they should be again compelled to do so. But despite this somewhat unsettled condition of titles, Tombstone is going ahead at a rapid rate, and its people have unbounded confidence in its future. . . .

PAT HAMILTON

*According to the Phoenix Gazette in 1889:*

Edwin Fields, the owner of the "Gilded Age" which brought so much woe to Tombstone property owners, is cooking in a San Francisco restaurant. Thus the "Duke of the Gilded Age" languishes in poverty and obscurity.

*The Tombstone Epitaph received the following dispatch from Chicago in 1896:*

Edwin Fields, who at one time owned a large part of the city of Tombstone, and a mine worth more than half a million, was last night taken to the county hospital in the police ambulance. From the hospital he was taken to the poor house to spend his few remaining years.

## THE EARP-CLANTON FEUD

Tombstone's boom in the early eighties came at a time when Arizona, especially the southeastern section, was overrun by the so-called cowboys, a class including almost all the wild bunch—cattle thieves, horse thieves, stage robbers, and all others of the lawless element. And the lively town of Tombstone came in for more than its share of the deviltry.

Undoubtedly the most tragic and notorious of all the affrays of early Tombstone was the Earp-Clanton feud, the first and bloodiest episode of which was a battle between the law-enforcement officers and the cowboys which took place in 1881 at the O.K. Corral in the heart of the town and resulted in the killing of three men—Billy Clanton and Tom and Frank McLowry, of the cowboys—and the wounding of several of both factions.

Following closely on the heels of this dastardly affair was the attempted assassination of Virgil Earp (City Marshal), and although the assailants were not identified, it was thought to be an act of retaliation by the cowboys against the authorities. Earp did not die, but an arm was left helpless from the effect of shotgun slugs.

Three months later, while Morgan Earp (Deputy City Marshal) and Wyatt Earp (U.S. Deputy Marshal) were inside a billiard saloon, a gunshot blast through a rear door snuffed out the life of Morgan Earp. A few days later, while attending a grand-jury session at Tucson, Frank Stilwell, a friend of the Clantons, was slain at the Tucson railroad station, supposedly by some of the Earp crowd, who were also in that city at the time.

In order to present a clearer picture of the succession of events, it is necessary to go back to what was perhaps the spark that touched off this parade of tragedies. Because some of the newspapers had differing views as to which faction was at fault in these forays, and because the Tombstone Epitaph's accounts, which upheld the actions of the law officers, have been used most often in published stories of the struggle, the following accounts are from the Tombstone Nugget and the Tucson papers, the Star and the Citizen, all of which generally favored the cowboys. An excellent coverage of the Epitaph stories of the succession of events is to be found in Douglas Martin's Tombstone Epitaph, a volume of accounts from the files of that newspaper.

The terrible state of affairs which has done so much to destroy human life in and about Tombstone will be part of the history of Arizona that will be read with interest. The killing of Clanton, the McLowrys, Morgan S. Earp, Stilwell and others, and the wounding of Virgil Earp is such a series of tragedies, that the accounts should be preserved. A San Francisco Tombstone correspondent gives the story of the Feud from almost the beginning, as follows:

The killing of Morgan Earp on March 18th, and the shooting of Stilwell on the 22nd, form the latest chapter in the feud which began on October 26th, 1881, when Billy Clanton and Frank and Tom McLowry lost their lives. This feud had its origin in the unlawful relations existing between the persons interested, and is the natural result of a quarrel between desperate men in a country where murder is rife and justice comparatively unknown. The Earp brothers at the outbreak of this feud numbered five—James, Virgil, Wyatt, Morgan and Warren. James is the smallest of the five and the oldest, as they are named above in the order of their birth. He is professionally a saloon man. He served in the war in an Illinois regiment and is the most agreeable one of the family. He has a smile for everyone but an enemy, and is generally popular with his acquaintances. Thus far he has not taken an active part in the trouble and probably stands in less danger from assassination than the others. He is about forty years old.

Virgil, who comes next, is a raw-boned six-footer, with a sinister expression, and no one who studies faces could fail to see that he is a bold, daring man, not to be trifled with. He had been a Deputy United States Marshal for years. He earned the position by leading the Sheriff and his posse out of Prescott, to arrest two rowdies who had been firing their pistols within the city limits and killing both of the desperadoes himself while the posse were dodging around in the brush.

On the day of the triple homicide he was City Marshal of the town, a place he had been seeking for months, and got it, not by election, for he had tried it, but by appointment from the City Council, as it had been made vacant by the departure of the regularly elected officer.

Wyatt is another six-footer, but has a more refined appearance than any of the rest. He is a professional gambler, cold and calculating, and is the brains of the outfit. He is consulted on all occasions and his judgment is generally law with the rest. He does not know the taste of liquor and only occasionally smokes a cigar.

Morgan, who was killed on Saturday last, was the handsomest of the brothers and perhaps the most reckless, for at times it required the combined efforts of all the others to keep him in check when he got mad. He was just six feet in height and weighed 160 pounds. He gambled for a living, although, at one time before the robberies commenced on the Benson road, he was employed as messenger by Wells, Fargo & Co., but only for a short time.

Warren, the youngest, comparatively a boy, being only 20 years old, but partakes of the Earp character. He was in Colton, California, and left immediately on receiving the news of the trouble and has been on hand ever since. He is quite dark, while the others are decidedly blondes, with blue eyes, and are closely shaven, with the exception of long, sandy mustaches.

The Earps are all married, with the exception of Warren. Old man Earp is said to keep an eating house and saloon at Colton, and it was at this place that the body of Morgan Earp was being carried when Frank Stilwell was shot at Tucson.

Doc Holliday, who has identified himself with the Earps, is a consumptive-looking man, with gray hair, and about 30 years old, and is generally known as a desperado of the first water. It is related that Wyatt Earp owes him his life, which he saved by interfering in a fight while Earp was Marshal at Dodge City, Kansas. He has killed a number of men; how many no one knows. He is also a professional gambler.

The Clanton brothers numbered three—Ike, Finn and Billy. They lived on a cattle ranch on the San Pedro River, about twelve miles from Tombstone, with their father. Old man Clanton was murdered in August by Mexicans, with five others. The Clantons then fell heir to all the old man's cattle, and were pretty well fixed. They are fine specimens of the frontier cattle man. Billy, although only 19 years old, was over six feet in height, and built in proportion, while Ike and Finn are wiry, determined-looking men, without a pound of surplus flesh. They lived on horseback, and led a life of hardship.

The trouble between the Earps and the Clanton and McLowry boys grew out of the robbery of the Benson stage on March 15th, 1881. The stage, with Wells-Fargo & Co.'s express, left Tombstone for Benson with a large treasure, "Bud" Philpot driving and Bob Paul as Wells-Fargo's messenger.

The coach left at 6 p.m., and at 7:30, and while only 200 yards out from the first station, the order to halt was given. Simultaneously with it, two shots were fired, one of which killed the driver and the other perforated the cushion upon which Paul was sitting. The driver fell off, carrying the lines with him, and the horses ran away, Paul emptying his gun, returning shot for shot, but without effect. The horses kept running, and the robbers kept shooting, and in all fired some twenty shots at the retreating stage, with its load of ten passengers, and succeeded in killing one man who was on top. Paul managed to stop the team, gathered up the lines and drove rapidly to Benson, when he telegraphed the news to Tombstone.

Immediately all was excitement. Agent Williams of Wells-Fargo and the Earp brothers were riding around, preparing to hunt the robbers. At 8:30 that same evening Doc Holliday rode up to a saloon in Charleston, ten miles from below the scene of the attempted robbery and inquired for Billy Clanton. On being told that he was not there he started in the direction of Tombstone, which was nine miles distant, and at about 10 o'clock rode up to a saloon on a back street in Tombstone and called for a big drink of whiskey, which he drank at a gulp, without dismounting. His horse at the time was covered with foam. At midnight the agent and the Earp brothers, with Holliday, left town to meet Paul. It was too dark to follow a trail when they arrived on the ground, so they camped until morning. They found three masks made of hay rope and about twenty large-size rifle cartridges. They then took the trail and followed it for three weeks without catching anyone but a supposed accomplice, and he was assisted by some unknown person to escape from the custody of the Sheriff while consulting with his lawyer.

The news of Holliday's ride becoming known, coupled with the facts that he was seen mounted and armed in the early part of the afternoon, ostensibly to go to Mexico, caused many surmises, and not a few made the remark that "the robbers were hunting themselves." Before the return of the agent's posse it became known that Billy Leonard, Jim Crane and Harry Head were interested in the murder, and it was their trail that Paul was following. Wells-Fargo offered a large reward for them, but it was of no use. So matters rested for some time until, as Ike Clanton swears, Wyatt Earp called him aside and told him that he would guarantee him all of Wells-Fargo's reward and one thousand dollars more on top of it, if he would induce Leonard and Head to come to some ranch in the neighborhood of Tombstone so that he (Wyatt) could surprise and kill them. He gave as his reasons that they had failed to realize anything out of the attempted robbery and that Leonard and Head might "squeal" some time. Crane had been killed by the Mexicans with old man Clanton, so there was nothing to fear from him. To satisfy Clanton that he meant business, Earp had Wells-Fargo's agent telegraph to San Francisco asking whether the reward would be paid dead. The answer came back: yes. But while negotiations were pending Leonard and Head were both killed in New Mexico for cattle stealing.

Clanton told of the proposition which Earp had made with him, and this coming to ·Earp's ears, made bad blood between them. During all this time Holliday was under bonds for attempting to kill a saloon-keeper who objected to his presence in the house, and was awaiting the action of the Grand Jury. In the meantime, also, Holliday had a quarrel with the woman he had been living with, and she denounced him before the authorities and swore that "Doc" had a rope mask in his trunk for a month before the killing of Philpot [driver of the hold-up stage] and that she knew that he was implicated in the murder. He was arrested and discharged for want of evidence and the matter was hushed. Finally Ike Clanton came into Tombstone with Tom McLowry from the Clanton ranch, expecting to meet Billy Clanton and Frank Mc-Lowry, who were to come from the McLowry brothers' ranch, and proceed together to New Mexico, where they were to buy a band of sheep. The McLowry brothers were young men who had a cattle ranch about twenty miles from Tombstone and were intimate with the Clantons. Having just sold a herd of cattle they were about to invest the proceeds in sheep. They were both well educated, and Tom, especially, was sober and industrious. Not finding their respective brothers, they concluded to spend the night in town, so they both got into a poker game in one of the numerous saloons, in which Vigil Earp, the City Marshal, was playing.

During the game Holliday walked into the room, and addressing Clanton, said: "You —— cow-thieving —— — — ——, you have been talking about myself and my friends, and you must fight me." Clanton replied that he was just at that time unarmed but would accommodate him at any time. To which Holliday replied: "Heel [arm] yourself and stay that way." Ike and Tom then left the house. In the morning Ike appeared on the street with a pistol in his belt and a rifle in his hand, for which offense Vigil Earp struck him over the head with a six-shooter, and disarmed him. He arrested him and brought him before the Judge and had him fined.

While this was going on Wyatt Earp met Tom McLowry and struck him over the head with a six-shooter, knocking him down saying at the same time: "You are another of those cow-thieving

—— — ——, that wants to fight the Earp brothers." In the Police Court Clanton stood with his head tied up, and in response to a remark made by one of the Earps, replied, "Fight is my racket, and I only want four feet of ground to fight on."

Just at this time Frank McLowry and Billy Clanton rode into town, both armed, and met their brothers near the stable. They dismounted to hold a consultation, and to be out of the way of passers-by stepped into a vacant space between two buildings [O.K. Corral]. Frank and Billy were holding their horses, when the Sheriff came up and said: "Boys, I will have to disarm you." Ike and Tom had no arms, but Billy and Frank had, so Frank said he would not submit to be disarmed unless the Earp brothers were also disarmed. At this moment Wyatt, Morgan and Virgil Earp, and Doc Holliday came down the street. Holliday was armed with a shotgun and pistol and the rest with pistols. As they approached the Clanton party the Sheriff threw up his hands and said: "For God's sake, Earp, don't go down there; these men are unarmed." They paid no attention, but passed on.

Virgil Earp had deputized his brothers and Holliday as special policemen, to assist in disarming the Clanton party. As the Marshal approached he said: "You —— — ——; you wanted a fight; now you can have it. Throw up your hands." Almost immediately the shooting began, which resulted in the death of Tom and Frank McLowry and Billy Clanton. At the first fire Ike Clanton ran, being unarmed, and in the direction of his flight stands a frame building with nine bullet holes in it. He escaped unhurt. Among the Earp party Virgil was hit in the leg and Morgan was hit in the shoulder.

Ike Clanton then had the Earps arrested for murder, and the examination in the Justice Court lasted three weeks, and cost several thousand dollars on each side. Three witnesses swore positively that Billy Clanton and Tom McLowry were shot with their hands in the air, and that Holliday fired the first shot from a shotgun into Tom McLowry. Nevertheless, the Justice discharged the prisoners upon the grounds that they were officers of the law, and were doing their duty. Then the friends of Clanton and McLowry swore vengeance, and since then have, no doubt, been scheming to accomplish it.

A short time later Virgil Earp, having just recovered from his wound in the leg, was leaving the Oriental saloon and going home at 11:30 p.m. when he was fired at with two shotguns. Two of the buckshot took effect, one shattering the left arm and the other lodging in the small of the back and just grazing the spine. He lost the bone in the arm, and just got well enough to be around when his brother Morgan was killed and Wyatt shot at.

—Tucson Star, 1882

While the above story by the San Francisco Tombstone correspondent, as reported in the Tucson Star, states that the cause of the hostility between the Earps and the cowboys was the Benson stage holdup in March, 1881, the Tucson Citizen had an account from the Tombstone Nugget that stated that the bitter feeling between the two factions was an outgrowth of the Bisbee stage holdup in September, 1881. The Tombstone-Bisbee stage was "taken in" near Bisbee and the Wells-Fargo treasure box was robbed of $2,500 and the passengers of several hundred dollars more. As soon as the report of the holdup reached Tombstone, a posse, including Wyatt and Morgan Earp, set out to trail the robbers. Identification of their boot tracks and the tracks of their horses near the scene of the crime led to the arrest of Frank Stilwell and Pete Spence of Tombstone. The Nugget account of the hold-up, and a more detailed account of the O.K. Corral fight follows:

The 26th of October, 1881, will always be marked as one of the crimson days in the annals of Tombstone, a day when blood flowed as water, and human life was held as a shuttlecock, a day always to be remembered as witnessing the bloodiest and deadliest street fight that has ever occurred in this place, or probably in the Territory.

The origin of the trouble dates back to the first arrest of Stilwell and Spence, for the robbery of the Bisbee stage. The co-operation of the Earps and the Sheriff and his deputies in the arrest caused a number of the cowboys to, it is said, threaten the lives of all interested in the capture. Still, nothing occurred to indicate that any such threats would be carried into execution. But Tuesday night Ike Clanton and Doc Holliday had some difficulty in the Alhambra saloon. Hard words passed between them, and when they parted it was generally understood that the feeling between the two men was that of intense hatred. Yesterday morning Clanton came on the street armed with a rifle and revolver, but was almost immediately arrested by Marshal Earp, disarmed and fined by Justice Wallace for carrying concealed weapons. While in the Courtroom Wyatt Earp told him that as he had made threats against his life he wanted him to make his fight, to say how, when and where he would fight, and to get his crowd, and he (Wyatt) would be on hand.

In reply, Clanton said: "Four feet of ground is enough for me to fight on, and I'll be there." A short time after this Billy Clanton and Frank McLowry came in town, and as Tom McLowry was already here the feeling soon became general that a fight would ensue before the day was over, and crowds of expectant men stood on the corner of Allen and Fourth streets awaiting the coming conflict.

It was now about two o'clock, and at this time Sheriff Behan appeared upon the scene and told Marshal Earp that if he disarmed his posse, composed of Morgan and Wyatt Earp, and Doc Holliday, he would go down to the O.K. Corral, where Ike and Billy Clanton and Frank and Tom McLowry were and disarm them. The Marshal did not desire to do this until assured that there was no danger of an attack from the other party. The Sheriff went to the corral and told the cowboys that they must put their arms away and not have any trouble. Ike Clanton and Tom McLowry said they were not armed, and Frank McLowry said he would not lay his aside. In the meantime the Marshal had concluded to go and, if possible, end the matter by disarming them, and as he and his posse came down Fremont Street towards the corral, the Sheriff stepped out and said: "Hold up boys, don't go down there or there will be trouble; I have been down there to disarm them." But they passed on, and when within a few feet of them the Marshal said to the Clantons and McLowrys: "Throw up your hands boys, I intend to disarm you."

As he spoke Frank McLowry made a motion to draw his revolver, when Wyatt Earp pulled his and shot him, the ball striking on the right side of his abdomen. About the same time Doc Holliday shot Tom McLowry in the right side, using a short shotgun,

ıch as is carried by Wells-Fargo & Co.'s messengers. In the mean-
ıme Billy Clanton had shot at Morgan Earp, the ball passing
ıhrough the point of the left shoulder blade across his back, just
ırazing the backbone and coming out at the shoulder, the ball re-
ıaining inside of his shirt. He fell to the ground but in an instant
ıathered himself, and raising in a sitting position fired at Frank
ıcLowry as he crossed Fremont Street, and at the same instant
ıoc Holliday shot at him, both balls taking effect, either of which
ıould have proved fatal, as one struck him in the right temple and
ıhe other in the left breast. As he started across the street, however,
ıe pulled his gun down on Holliday saying, "I've got you now."
ıBlaze away! You're a daisy if you have," replied Doc. This shot of
ıcLowry's passed through Holliday's pistol pocket, just grazing
ıhe skin.

While this was going on Billy Clanton had shot Virgil Earp in
ıhe right leg, the ball passing through the calf, inflicting a severe
ıesh wound. In turn he had been shot by Morgan Earp in the
ıight side of the abdomen, and twice by Virgil Earp, once in the
ıight wrist and once in the left breast. Soon after the shooting
ıommenced Ike Clanton ran through the O.K. Corral, across Allen

Street into Kellogg's saloon, and thence into Toughnut Street where he was arrested and taken to the county jail. The firing altogether didn't occupy more than twenty-five seconds, during which time fully thirty shots were fired. After the fight was over Billy Clanton, who, with wonderful vitality, survived his wound for fully an hour, was carried by the editor and foreman of the Nugget into a house near where he lay, and everything possible done to make his last moments easy. He was "game" to the last, never uttering a word of complaint, and just before breathing his last he said, "Goodbye, boys; go away and let me die."

The wounded were taken to their houses, and at three o'clock next morning were resting comfortably. The dead bodies were taken in charge by the Coroner, and an inquest held. Upon the person of Tom McLowry was found between $300 and $400, and checks and certificates of deposit to the amount of nearly $3,000.

During the shooting Sheriff Behan was standing near by commanding the contestants to cease firing but was powerless to prevent it. Several parties who were in the vicinity of the shooting had narrow escapes from being shot. One man who had lately arrived from the East had a ball pass through his pants. He left for home this morning. A person called "The Kid," who shot Hicks at Charleston recently, was also grazed by a ball. When the mine whistle gave the signal that there was a conflict between the officers and the cowboys, the mines on the hill shut down and the miners were brought to the surface. From the Contention mine a number of men, fully armed, were sent to town in a four-horse carriage. At the request of the Sheriff the "Vigilantes," or Committee of Safety, were called from the streets by a few sharp toots from the whistle. During the early part of the evening there was a rumor that a mob would attempt to take Ike Clanton from the jail and lynch him, and to prevent any such unlawful proceedings a strong guard of deputies was placed around the building.

That evening Finn Clanton, brother of Billy and Ike, came to town, and placing himself under the guard of the Sheriff, visited the morgue to see the remains of his brother, and then passed the night in jail in company with the other brother.

Shortly after the shooting ceased the whistle sounded a few short toots, and almost simultaneously a large number of citizens appeared on the streets, armed with rifles and a belt of cartridges around their waists. These men formed in line and offered their services to the peace officers to preserve order in case any attempt at disturbance was made, or any interference offered to the authorities of the law. However, no hostile move was made by anyone, and quiet and order was fully restored, and in a short time the excitement died away.

At the morgue the bodies of the three slain cowboys lay side by side, covered with a sheet. Very little blood appeared on their clothing, and only on the face of young Billy Clanton was there any distortion of the features or evidence of pain in dying. The features of the two McLowry boys looked as calm and placid in death as if they had died peaceably. No unkind remarks were made by anyone, but a feeling of unusual sorrow seemed to prevail. Of the McLowry brothers we could learn nothing of their previous history before coming to Arizona. The two brothers owned quite an extensive ranch on the lower San Pedro, some seventy or eighty miles from this city, to which they had removed their cattle since the recent Mexican and Indian troubles. They did not bear the reputation of being of a quarrelsome disposition, but were known as fighting men, and have generally conducted themselves in a quiet and orderly manner when in Tombstone.

—Tucson Citizen, 1881

*The Tucson Star of November 3, 1881, printed an editorial and a letter:*

It now appears, after the smoke of the Tombstone bloody street affray has passed away, that but one side of the tale has been told. It is claimed by many that the killing of the McLowrys and Clanton was cold-blooded and premeditated murder, with little or no justification.

It appears that the parties who did the killing were hostile in feeling to those who fell before the bullet, and that threats had been made, and when the shooting occurred the boys who were killed were preparing to leave Tombstone; two of them were unarmed and that they showed no disposition whatever to quarrel or create any public disturbance. If this be so, then those who committed the tragedy, under color of law, should be classed as public offenders. . . .

The communication of "Observer," from Tombstone, which we publish in another column, certainly sets forth a bad state of affairs, and places the killing in a much worse light than has yet come before the public. We have interviewed several prominent gentlemen from Tombstone and they confirm the statements made by our correspondent.

Tombstone, A. T. Nov. 1, 1881

Editor Daily Star:

The Tombstone daily papers have published to the world an account of the affray on our streets, which terminated in the death of Tom and Frank McLowry and young Billy Clanton, at the hands of the Earp brothers and one Doc Holliday. The account is given in a way to make patriots of the murderers, and the voiceless tongues of the murdered boys cannot deny the libel which brands them as thieves, ruffians and row-makers. But this article is not intended as a criticism or stricture of the papers for publishing the account alluded to, so much as an humble effort of one who knows something of the facts, to do justice to those who are dead, and speak one word in defense of those who are now unable to speak for themselves. The victims of this unfortunate affair were boys against whom no public offense has ever been charged. True they dealt in and handled cattle instead of handling cards. They may have bought stolen cattle, and under their reputations were able to dispose of the same publicly in our markets.

Even admit that these boys were thieves, that it was their occupation to steal cattle, yet this fact does not justify, and cannot justify, in the light of a decent public sentiment, the foul murder which our papers seem to commend. Admit the worst that can be said of these boys as proven facts, and they stand in angel robes of innocence as compared with the cut-throat who shot Tom Mc-Lowry with buckshot while he was protesting that he was unarmed.

If want of moral character in the slain is to justify or extenuate the crime of premeditated, vile, foul, cold-blooded murder, what shall we say to the plea when we find it advanced by the bloody hands of a deeper criminal than the man lying dead before him. Let those who rejoice at these humble graves remember the men by whom they were slain, and on their lips the breath of condemnation will change into a sigh of sympathy and regret—sympathy for the dead, and regret that the living did not receive the same death that they gave.

Only one side of the case has been published. That was gotten from the very parties involved in the case. We have heard, from reliable sources, and eye-witnesses, a very different state of facts. From the most reliable we learn the following:

Ike Clanton the day before the shooting was sitting unarmed at a table taking his dinner, when Doc Holliday, knowing that Clanton was unarmed, entered the room and cursed and abused him shamefully. Clanton told him he was unarmed, but if he wanted a fight he could give it to him afterwards. Next day Clanton was on the street armed. Virgil Earp, who is City Marshal, and a friend of Holliday's, went to Clanton, in company with Morgan Earp, his brother, and struck Clanton over the head with a pistol and disarmed him. When Clanton was in the City Court, standing, or preparatory to standing his trial, he was abused and cursed and outrageously treated by Wyatt Earp. Clanton again signified his readiness to fight any of the crowd on equal terms. Some time in the afternoon Ike Clanton, who was still armed, and his brother, a mere boy, and the two McLowry boys, one of whom had left his pistol at the barroom of Moses & Mehan, were all down at the O. K. Corral apparently preparing to leave town. One of the boys had actually got his horse out on the street, when the Earp brothers and this same Doc Holliday came down on them and ordered them to throw up their hands and give up their pistols.

It is said that Tom McLowry, who was unarmed, did throw up his hands and was then shot by Holliday at so close a range that the hand would cover the wound made by the sixteen buckshot. Ike Clanton being helpless ran up and caught one of the Earps, but immediately let go and ran from under the pistols which were directed at him and made his escape. But before Ike ran, or attempted to run, several shots had been fired. There was left after Ike's escape only the two boys, and they stood up against the four assailants like men and died with unflinching courage. They were both literally shot to pieces, and without any cause whatever. They had had no trouble with the Earps or Holliday, except what was forced upon them. They had violated no ordinance of the city, and were not subject to arrest at the hands of the Marshal. The whole matter was a scheme concocted to murder these men, perhaps under cover of official authority, and right well was it carried out.—OBSERVER

—Tucson Star, 1881

*Another Star editorial:*

Our evening contemporary rather takes us to task for saying that Billy Clanton and the McLowry brothers were assassinated. It says that the killing was done in open day, and in a face-to-face conflict, in which two of the Earps were wounded; and after a judicial investigation was made, all the evidence published and the parties discharged by the examining magistrate; the grand jury then in session declined to indict them. The facts, so far as stated, may be true, but the important points are omitted. All the evidence was published, which we studied with great care, and we sincerely believe that no disinterested man can read the same and not come to the conclusion that Clanton and the McLowrys were shot with their hands up, and their wounding of Earp and Holliday was after they were shot down; that the magistrate in releasing the slayers was guilty of culpable ignorance of his duty or was afraid to perform the same, or acted corruptly in discharging them; that the majority of the grand jury was either intimidated from taking action on the case, or were in full harmony with the murderers. No other conclusion can be arrived at from the reading of the evidence as published in the Tombstone daily papers. There is no question of doubt, on the evidence, that the boys who were slain were commanded to throw up their hands, and that they did so, and in this position they were fired upon by the Earp party, and not until then did they attempt to defend themselves. The whole series of killing cannot be classed other than cold-blooded assassination.

—Tucson, Star, 1882

# THE AFTERMATH

### THE DEATH OF MORGAN EARP

*The killing of Morgan Earp in March, 1882, was reported as follows in the Tucson Citizen:*

Shortly after eleven o'clock on Saturday night, after leaving the theater, Morgan Earp, while playing a game of billiards in Campbell & Hatch's saloon in Tombstone, was shot by some unknown person from the rear of the building, who fired two shots through the glass door, one of which entered the right side of Earp's abdomen, below the ribs, passing completely through and shattering the spinal column. The spent bullet then entered the thigh of George Berry, (a bystander) and lodged near the bone, causing a bad flesh wound.

Morgan Earp was immediately removed to a lounge by his brothers and friends and surgeons were summoned. The wound was pronounced fatal, and death ensued in a little less than an hour after the shot was fired. Of the death scene and the theory of the shooting, the Tombstone *Nugget* says:

Although he suffered great agony until he died, no word of complaint escaped his lips, which in a short time were closed and silent in death. The only words heard, excepting those whispered to his brother, before he died, was when his friends attempted to raise him to his feet. He then said, "don't, I can't stand it; this is the last game of pool I'll ever play."

A few minutes after the fatal shot was fired, the brothers, Virgil, James and Warren, with the wives of the first two, were by his side. The scene at his death couch was affecting. Each breath came with a gasp and a struggle as his heart yielded drop after drop of his life blood. Around him were those whose lives were wrapped in his very existence. . . . At the front door of the saloon stood a hound, raised by the brothers, who, with that instinct peculiar to animals, seemed to know that his master had been struck down, and despite of threats or entreaties remained whining and moaning, and when the body was taken to the hotel, no sadder heart followed than that of the faithful dog.

At this hour, while the horror of the assassination is yet fresh, the air is full of rumors, speculations and theories as to who committed the deed, and how it was done. Certain it is that the shots came from pistols; the bullet holes in the door prove this, and their direction led to the belief that one of the parties must have stood upon a barrel, either with the intention of shooting Wyatt Earp or intimidating those inside and thus preventing anyone from going out and obtaining sight of the assassins.

After the shots, those engaged in the affair immediately escaped through a small alley leading out to Fremont Street, but owing to the lateness of the hour and the darkness of the night no clue could possibly be obtained. . . . A short time before the shooting two men were seen standing near the door through which the shots were fired, and immediately after three men were seen running rapidly from the scene of the tragedy toward Frémont Street.

### THE KILLING OF FRANK STILWELL

Frank Stilwell, it will be remembered, was one of the suspects in the Bisbee stage holdup, one of the incidents leading up to this series of reprisal killings. He was a close friend of the Clantons. It was thought that, after the killing of Morgan Earp in Tombstone, the Earp crowd followed him to Tucson. Frank Stilwell was in Tucson to appear as a witness in a trial before the District Court. It was the intention of the Earps, it is assumed, to kill Clanton, whom they suspected of killing Morgan Earp. Seeing the Earp crowd, Clanton was warned by Stilwell to leave the depot and go downtown, which he did before they spotted him. Not seeing Clanton at the depot, the Earps apparently decided to kill his friend Stilwell while they had the chance.

The following account of the killing of Stilwell was published in the Tucson Star in 1882:

The westbound train of Monday evening brought to Tucson Doc Holliday, Virgil Earp, Warren Earp, Wyatt Earp, a man named McMasters and another, supposed to be named Johnson. They were armed with breech-loading shotguns, and got off the cars, taking their guns with them, and stood around the platform and then walked over to Porter's [railroad] Hotel.

Ike Clanton, who had been in Tucson for over two weeks was expecting a man named McDowell, of Charleston, to arrive, he being a witness in the trial of Jerry Barton before the District Court, and he was at the depot when the train arrived, expecting to meet him. Frank Stilwell, who had been subpoenaed before the District Court, to appear at 10 a.m. on Monday, and who arrived by the emigrant train on Sunday morning, was also there. Clanton was seated under the veranda of the hotel when Stilwell approached him and requested him to go downtown, as the Tombstone crowd evidently intended to kill him. Clanton at first refused to go, but was finally pursuaded to leave, as he was not prepared for a hostile meeting. He and Stilwell therefore walked away a few paces near the railing of the hotel park, where they stood conversing for some minutes. Clanton then walked down towards town, and Stilwell walked back around the office corner of the hotel. At that moment all the Tombstone parties went into one of the cars, and several of them returned at once, following along after Stilwell, he continuing to move in the direction of the office corner of the hotel, as that was the only way he could go without facing the armed crowd.

Soon several shots were fired in rapid succession; a loud scream following the first shot, given, it is supposed, by Stilwell. The engineer was with his engine, not over two hundred feet from the shooting, just moving out his train, but the light from his locomotive prevented him from witnessing the assassination. Several railroad hands, just after the shooting, chanced to approach going to their duties, and were warned back by the crowd of shooters, and they thought it best to go, which they did. Just after the shooting the train moved out westward, and it is supposed took along one of the Earps not thought to have been one of the shooting party. [It should be related here that the body of Morgan Earp was on this train, being taken to Colton for burial.] The shooters then proceeded by some means, probably on foot, to Papago Station, nine miles eastward, and at midnight, flagged the east-bound freight train, boarding it and so arrived back in Tombstone next day.

When Clanton heard the shooting he armed himself and returned towards the depot, and meeting some parties inquired the cause of the shooting, and was told they did not know, or that they were celebrating the illumination of the city by gas [a *celebration had been going on*]. He then returned and not until the next morning did he or the public know that Stilwell had been shot. His body was found riddled with buckshot, showing the work of more than one gun. His left leg was broken above the knee by several shots and his body was shot through by several more, all the wounds seeming to have been made by the largest sizes of buckshot.

As to Stilwell being in any manner connected with the killing of Morgan Earp (in Tombstone) on Saturday night, it is extremely improbable, as we have been informed by credible parties that at the time of that shooting he was seated with several others in another quarter of that city engaged in a game of cards, and this fact, it is alleged, can be fully substantiated by the parties who were with him, all reputable men.

The remains of Stilwell were yesterday buried, being followed to the cemetery by one person who was a friend of his in life. Stilwell was a young man of twenty-six years, of fine physical appearance, and although he had been apprehended several times at the instigation of his supposed murderers, he is not known to have been convicted of any crime. He was a native of Texas, brother of the famous Government scout, Jack Stilwell of Texas. He came to Arizona three years ago, and for a time drove team in Mohave County for Ham Light, who speaks favorably of him as a man. He was latterly engaged in keeping a livery stable at Bisbee and Charleston. One of the supposed causes of the enmity of the Earps against him is that he was a known friend of the Clantons.

Yesterday afternoon a warrant was sworn out for the arrest of the entire Earp party, and Sheriff Behan was instructed by telegraph to make the arrest. He accordingly attempted it, but was resisted by the Earps with a force of eight or ten men. They then left Tombstone, and Sheriff Behan, after telegraphing for Bob Paul, Sheriff of Pima County, proceeded to equip a posse to follow them.

### THE TOMBSTONE BANDITTI

The sad condition of affairs which has existed in Tombstone during the past six months, in which several human beings have been hurled into eternity, is assuming a magnitude which calls upon all good citizens to stand abreast and put it down at any cost.

The assassination of Morgan Earp last Saturday night at Tombstone was a foul crime without palliation, but was the natural outgrowth of the cowardly assassinations of Billy Clanton and the McLowry brothers by the Earps and Holliday, under the guise of official authority. Both crimes were equally heinous and the perpetrators should have been made to pay the severest penalty of the law.

But worse than all this was the deep-dyed assassination of Frank Stilwell at the depot last Monday night, when without any provocation a band of four or five slayers pursued a lonely man in the dark and without a word of warning murdered him in cold blood. . . .

As to who the villains were who committed the crime there is no certainty as yet, although the evidence points strongly to the same band that has kept Tombstone in a turmoil for the past year. It is openly boasted by some that they will not deny the crime, and that their mission to our city was for no other purpose than to kill Ike Clanton, and failing in their purpose, sought his best friend and wreaked their disappointed vengeance on him. . . .

It has been stated that Stilwell, the unfortunate man who fell victim, was a bad and dangerous man. This may all be true. He has been twice or thrice arrested, once charged with murder and once on suspicion of stage robbery, but in both cases the Court, or examining magistrate pronounced him innocent. Let us give the man who is silenced in death by the assassin's bullet the benefit of the Court's judgment. He cannot answer his accusors now. . . .

But admitting that he was all that his sworn enemies alleged, that was no excuse for the crime. He was not an outlaw. He was within the jurisdiction of the Courts and the officers of the law, and could have been taken at any time without the slightest resistance. The presumption seems to be all in his favor.

In regard to the Earp party, no doubt but what they have some warm friends who are good citizens. And undoubtedly it is this fact which has given them so long suffrage in Tombstone. If one-twentieth part of what is said of their record is true, they are certainly no desirable acquisition to any community. They are a roving band; their path is strewn with blood. Strange as it may seem, wherever they halt in a settlement stage robberies follow and human life ceases to be sacred. Their late escapades at Tombstone are only their records repeated in other frontier towns; and if we judge the honest sense of justice and peace-abiding disposition of our citizens, they will never dare another such foul murder as was committed last Monday night. If they must take human life they must seek other localities than our city. It will not be tolerated; neither need it for a moment be supposed that crime committed here will end in a sham examination or suborned jury trials. These may seem plain statements, but the situation demands it, and they will be maintained by the law and the people.

—Tucson Star, 1882

In a telegraphic report from San Francisco, dated May 27, and printed in the Phoenix Herald in 1882, is the following:
Virgil W. Earp, of Arizona fame, is now in San Francisco. He came here for surgical treatment. In his last fight he received a severe wound in the left arm by a bullet, which caused the loss of about six inches of bone, which will probably cripple him for life. He will have an operation performed on the limb. In a conversation, Earp admitted that his party killed Stilwell.

What happened to the Earps, Holliday, and the rest of the Clantons? After a few more skirmishes, the Earp crowd disappeared into the desert and wound up in Colorado. They were never brought back to Arizona to stand trial for the lawlessness of which they were accused. But most of them had trouble elsewhere.
All that has been learned of the later whereabouts of James Earp is that he settled in California, where he was living at a ripe old age. James seemed to have avoided the strife and lawlessness of his brothers. Warren Earp was killed in Willcox, Arizona, in 1900.

Virgil died in Goldfield, Nevada, in 1905, and Wyatt, the strong man of the family, died in 1929 in Los Angeles. Doc Holliday died of consumption in a Glenwood Springs, Colorado, sanitarium in 1887. Of the remaining Clantons, Finn died near Safford, Arizona, in 1882, and Ike was killed in Bonita, Arizona, by a deputy marshal in 1887.

# 6

# COURT ON THE FRONTIER

## A BLOODY AFFAIR

One of the bloodiest and most disgraceful scenes that ever occurred in Arizona took place in open court of the Third Judicial District at Prescott on the morning of December 3, 1883. During all the exciting cowboys troubles in Tombstone nothing approaching this ever happened, although it more nearly resembled the street fight between the Clanton and Earp clans than anything it can be compared to. That men trained in the law should so far forget the gentlemanly position they had been admitted to that, from bandying blackguard epithets at each other, they should resort to personal violence which was calculated to draw into the melee their personal friends, is almost beyond comprehension.

Chief Justice French was presiding in the case of Kelsey vs. McAteer, an equitable proceeding, in which certain water rights were involved and to which McAteer laid claim. Mrs. Kelsey, the plaintiff, a widow and most estimable lady, was the owner of a ranch in Kirkland Valley, just adjoining that of Patrick McAteer, the defendant. This case involved the right to the use of one-half of certain waters of Kirkland Creek, flowing by both ranches, and without which hers would have been worthless. This suit had been pending for five years and although Mrs. Kelsey appeared as plaintiff, other settlers were equally interested, among them "Uncle Jimmy" More, who also owned land along the creek. Charles W. Beach, until a short time hence proprietor of the Prescott Miner, was taking an active interest in the suit, Mrs. Kelsey being his mother-in-law. In fact, Beach was managing Mrs. Kelsey's interests, outside the counsel.

Between the Beach and Kelsey families and McAteer, bad blood seems to have existed for some time, and it was claimed that Beach had been warned to look out for McAteer, as he intended to do him harm. Although McAteer had a reputation in Prescott as a man with an ungovernable temper when aroused, Beach apparently paid no attention to the warning and seemed quite unafraid, and willing to rely upon the court for protection of his interests, if not his safety.

It was the third day of the trial and at nine o'clock court was opened and the case proceeded with. Moses Langley, of Kirkland Valley, was on the stand to testify in behalf of the plaintiff, and his direct examination was closed. On cross-examination, Charles B. Rush, District Attorney, who was counsel for McAteer, asked him if he had not, on a certain previous occasion, sworn to a certain matter, at the same time reading a portion of an affidavit to which the witness had sworn and subscribed his name some years previous. To this Mr. Clark Churchill, Attorney General, and counsel for the plaintiff, objected and insisted that the entire affidavit should be submitted in evidence, and referred to taking a portion of it only, and submitting it as a garbled statement. To this charge, of its being a garbled report, Mr. Rush made a very sharp and curt reply, denying it, and Mr. Churchill, insisting on his statement that selecting a portion of the affidavit was only making a garbled statement of the same, and if any at all was admitted, he was willing to admit the entire affidavit. Rush then interfered. Churchill, in a sneering way said he was addressing his remarks to the Court, not to Rush. Rush said: "Mr. Churchill, you must not charge me with garbling an instrument, even to the Court!" Churchill then said, speaking to Rush: "I don't need the Court to protect me, and if you say you did not garble the affidavit, YOU LIE!"

Bitter words passed between them, when Mr. Rush picked up an inkstand and threw it at Mr. Churchill's head, and at the same time grabbed him by the throat. This was the commencement of the row, and from this time out it was a scene of confusion, and it was all done so quickly that it was impossible to get any connected particulars in regard to it. At the same time Rush struck Churchill, his partner, J. C. Herndon, rose in his seat and struck Churchill from behind, some say; others say he threw another inkstand at Churchill. Herndon said, however, he struck him in the face. Chairs, inkstands and all other available missiles were used, and pandemonium prevailed.

George Tinker, the Attorney General's private secretary, and W. O. "Buckey" O'Neill, Court reporter, seeing the odds against Churchill, came to his rescue, and at the same time McAteer, who had become almost wild with excitement, sprang from his chair and drew a large double-edged knife and commenced to cut in every direction. Approaching to where the struggling attorneys were, he endeavored to stab the counsel for the plaintiff. Before he could accomplish this however, he was caught by several of the bystanders. Endowed with the irresistible strength that rage alone can give, McAteer threw aside those who endeavored to hold him, and a scene that would rival the horrors of hell, ensued. Drawing aloft the cruel knife he rushed at More, an old man of seventy years. In an effort to escape the terrible blow, More piteously exclaimed: "Mac, for God's sake, don't cut me!" But to no avail. He drove the knife to the hilt through the left arm of his victim. The blade entered the top of the arm, passing clear through it, severing an artery and entering the breast, under the arm. Withdrawing the knife from the gaping wound, he left his victim to stagger around the room, his blood bespattering the furniture and walls as he vainly implored for help.

Then singling out Charley Beach, he made for him and before anybody could interfere, stabbed him in the left side of the neck, barely missing the jugular vein, and with sufficient force to knock him over the railing dividing the auditorium from the bar. Wheeling around he then made for Court reporter O'Neill, who, while attempting to quell the melee, had excited McAteer's enmity by endeavoring to obtain possession of the knife. In doing so, O'Neill received a severe cut on the left hand between the first two fingers. O'Neill backed up against the wall in attempting to escape from the infuriated man, but just as McAteer had nearly arrived within striking length of the reporter, Beach, who had partly recovered from the stunning effects of the wound in his neck, drew his revolver, a 38-calibre Colt's and fired at McAteer, the ball hitting him in the back, immediately under the left shoulder. McAteer, with a half muttered curse, fell at the feet of O'Neill, his intended victim, who lost no time in securing the knife which had done such terrible execution. With the report of the revolver, reason seemed to assume sway among the struggling men, and the fierce fighting that had been raging among the attorneys and their clients, ceased, and all present who could, turned their attention to the wounded men.

The badly wounded More had wandered out of the court room and started for Dr. Kendall's drug store, leaving a trail of blood behind him. On reaching the door of the drug store he fainted and fell from loss of blood. He was taken to St. Joseph's hospital where Dr. Ainsworth and Assistant Army Surgeon McCreery were summoned to attend him. Charley Beach was conveyed to a lower room of the courthouse, and afterwards to his residence, where his wound was also dressed by Dr. Ainsworth.

McAteer lay on the south side of the court room, and was afterwards taken to the residence of John Ehle, where he had been rooming, and was attended by Dr. McCandless, who pronounced his wound as almost certain to prove fatal. The bullet, as stated, entered the back under the shoulder blade, passing across the back and lodging about one and a half inches under the skin, about four inches to the right of the spinal column. His lower extremities became perfectly cold and motionless, and he complained of pains in the bowels, which indicated that the ball had struck the spinal column.

A gardener, who was a spectator in the court room, also received a cut from McAteer's knife across the back of the left hand. Mr. Churchill received some very severe blows on the head with some kind of missiles, as the bruises and bumps on that organ bore wit-

ness. When the melee closed he was lying upon the floor with his
feet upon a chair and an incipient chair factory piled on him.

Lawyers and all present presented a remarkably sad and dilapidated appearance. The floor of the court room and the stairs leading thereto were covered with blood; the tables occupied by the
attorneys together with all the papers on them as well as many of
the participants in the struggle were smeared with ink; the whole
place looked as if an ink cyclone had struck and expended its fury
on the spot.

During the progress of the affair an elderly but wonderfully excited individual rushed down into the Plaza bareheaded, swinging his arms and urging for God's sake for everybody to go up into
the court room as they were "killing people like sheep there." He
said that they were all piled on top of each other and all killed but
three or four. Of course the affair created the wildest excitement,
and the Plaza was soon crowded with people, and the wildest
rumors set afloat in regard to it. Knots of men could be seen on
every corner discussing it. The reporter of the *Journal* was compli-
mented for the full yet impartial account given of the affair, while
an extra issued by a contemporary the evening of the tragedy was
criticized for its version.

That afternoon Attorney General Churchill and District Attorney Rush were called into court by Judge French and each were
fined in the sum of $500 for contempt of court. A venire for a
special grand jury to inquire into the causes leading up to and
the circumstances attending the affair was ordered to be summoned by the sheriff. Hon. Edmund W. Wells was appointed a
special district attorney to attend the session of the grand jury during its investigation of the court room tragedy. Chief Justice French
made the following remarks:

> In this matter for which I have called a special grand jury
> to appear it was my intention on the close of the Kelsey and
> McAteer case to have adjourned court until the 7th instant,
> in order to give the bar and the officers of the court a rest, as
> the labors of the court have been more severe than ever be-
> fore. I have invited the members of the press with a view to
> expressing my opinions on the lamentable occurrence of last

Saturday. It is my judgement that the least said about this matter until the grand jury considers it the better. I shall instruct the grand jury that they must pay no attention nor base their actions on what has appeared in the press, or the reports that have been circulated on the streets, but consider only the facts and merits of the case from the witnesses themselves. I would request the citizens also not to discuss the matter, and have advised those who were present not to talk about the matter. Since its occurrence I have ascertained that there was no peace officer in court, but it was so instantaneous and quick that it seemed to me and those with whom I have talked that if there had been fifty officers present the affair could not have been prevented. It was one of those occurrences that burst out like a flash of powder and was beyond any control. When the grand jury shall have convened I will try to charge them in a manner I think is best calculated to promote peace, justice and quietness. . . .

—Prescott *Journal*, 1883

The case of Kelsey vs. McAteer, which was in progress when the machinery was thrown out of gear, was continued for the term. Apparently the newspapers followed the Court's admonition, as the only mention of the affair that could be found in newspapers thereafter was the report of the postponement from time to time of the grand jury's inquiry, which was delayed until it could become known whether either or both of the two wounded men, McAteer and More, would succumb. No mention of the eventual findings can be found in the newspapers.

Two weeks after the tragedy it was found necessary to amputate More's arm to save his life, after which he recovered. McAteer lived for a month and a day.

Charles W. Beach, his slayer, apparently was exonerated, or at any rate no information to the contrary is to be found. Shortly after the affray he again became editor and proprietor of the Prescott *Miner* and later went into the cattle business. In 1889 some person fired a double-barreled shotgun at his head while he was seated before a window writing a letter, killing him instantly.

*"Buckey" O'Neill, a member of Roosevelt's Rough Riders, was killed in battle on San Juan Hill in Cuba during the Spanish-American War in 1898. The other participants in the affair died of natural causes, the last being "Uncle Jimmy" More, who passed away in 1903.*

## JUDGE SHELDON'S WRATH

*The following account is taken from two articles on "A Bit of History, Early Days in Graham County," signed by F. L. B. Goodwin and published in the Graham County Bulletin in 1891:*

It was ten years ago [actually November, 1883], said Judge F. L. B. Goodwin, that I came to Solomonville for the first time. I had met Judge A. W. Sheldon, then Judge of the First Judicial District which then embraced the counties of Pinal, Pima, Cochise and Graham. The Judge, one morning at breakfast, told me that he was going to Graham County to hold the first term of the District Court in what was then the youngest county in Arizona, and mentioned the fact that the calendar was large and the term would probably be prolonged and he induced me to come over. I never shall forget the night I landed in Solomonville on "Pony" Duncan's hack. It was uncommonly cold. When we reached the county seat of the new-made county where a District Court had never been held, I thought I was a stranger among a strange people and about that time I was anxiously desirous to find a fire. The lights from the Solomonville saloon, a new-made institution, in the embryo town, attracted my attention and in company with several of my fellow-travelers from Bowie Station, we lost no time in getting close to the stove, which filled with mesquite wood, made the atmosphere of that large building most congenial. I had scarcely looked around before I was made aware that I was not entirely among strangers, for there were many distinguished gentlemen, and a number of "tin horn" gamblers whom I had known at Prescott, all of whom gave me a most cordial greeting.

It seemed to me that the élite of southern Arizona had congregated in that saloon to meet me and I was flattered by their attention and the frequency with which they called for the drinks. Nathan Solomon was behind the bar as pleased as an undisturbed setting hen. Being somewhat weary from my journey from Florence—by stage and rail—about the hour of midnight I inquired of the barkeeper where lodgings could be found. Imagine my surprise when he informed me that there was no unoccupied space in Solomonville, except out of doors, where a man could find a sleeping place. I was about looking around for a vacant chair in which I might locate for the night when "Pony" Duncan came in and kindly inquired if I had succeeded in finding a place to sleep. I told him that I had not and he said blankets were scarce in this place but if you will come with me I will try and make you comfortable. With much alacrity I embraced the invitation. I did not know where it would lead to but any old port in a storm. We came to a corral and the boss of that outfit, and on a pile of grain sacks with a saddle blanket for covering, I passed the night with much comfort.

Solomonville at that time was crowded with lawyers, litigants, jurors, witnesses and friends of parties who had business in court. There was a stage line running to the town of Sheldon on the Arizona and New Mexico railroad and its coaches were full every trip carrying passengers from and to Clifton. The railroad at that time had only reached Guthrie Station, ten miles from Clifton.

The first criminal case was tried on the 10th. Pablo Garcia was indicted for murder. The jury found the defendant guilty of murder in the second degree, and recommended him to the mercy of the court. The judge, no doubt, considered the recommendation for judicial clemency by sentencing Garcia to the territorial prison for the term of his natural life. He was pardoned in 1885, less than two years of his term having been served.

Herman Chavez was indicted for the killing of Juez Fresca and for killing his wife, Maria Chavez. The trial of Chavez for the dual murder excited peculiar interest, as the facts of the case were of a startling and sensational character. The wife of Chavez was supposed to have been the paramour of the deceased Fresca and the friends of the defendant claimed that he took their lives in defending the honor of his home and the sanctity of the marriage relation. Evidently the judge did not take such a sentimental view of the case as his severe excoriations of the jury on the rendition of the verdict proves. On both indictments the defendant was tried and in each case a verdict of manslaughter was returned. Judge Sheldon was incensed to such a degree that he gave expression to his feelings in "thoughts that breathe and words that burn." . . . The verdicts in both cases generally met with the approval of the community and those who heard the trials, especially the members of the bar. Court was held in a small room belonging to Mr. Solomon, adjoining his warehouse, and across the street from his residence. It was at night and the room crowded, when the jury came in on the second trial. After answering to their names the foreman handed the verdict to the court; he read it and ordered the clerk to record the verdict.

It was apparent to every observer that the judge was deeply moved by mental excitement. His features betrayed emotion, and many present were prepared for some manifestation of his disapproval, but none anticipated the crystallization of anger, disgust and seeming contempt which was to follow. . . . The judge with a frown, dark as a starless night, turned in his chair and facing the jury said:

> Gentlemen of the jury stand up. Your labors in this case, with the rendition of your verdict, are closed, but the court has a further duty to perform which it cannot avoid. It is a duty the court owes to itself not only, but to the people of the county. While the merits of this case were under consideration, the court could express no opinion upon the evidence, but now it is at liberty to speak, and while it is an unpleasant task, it nevertheless becomes the plain and sacred duty of the court to express in clear and explicit terms its profound astonishment at the rendition of such a verdict; a verdict so utterly at variance with all the facts in the case, and the law which governs them. Such verdicts, gentlemen, are

mockery of law, and a travesty upon justice, and will render trial by jury a farce.

The respectable, law-abiding citizens of this county look upon the trial by jury as the bulwark which is to stand between them and the bands of outlaws which have made life and property unsafe in this portion of the territory, deluging the ground with blood. To them you must answer for thus nullifying the labors of the grand jury, rendering impotent the efforts of the prosecuting officer and making it impossible for the court to mete out exact justice and rid the country of crime and criminals. If a man can shoot down another in his own house without justification or excuse, and at the same time murder in cold blood his own wife for some trivial remark, and for such a cowardly, unprovoked, brutal and dual murder be adjudged guilty of manslaughter only, then should courts of justice be abolished and the safety of human life and the protection of property be left to Winchester rifles and double-action revolvers. By such verdicts, gentlemen, you assume the responsibility for the terrible condition of affairs which exist today in Graham County, making it, as it is, a foul blot upon the map of Arizona and a disgrace to the civilization of the age.

You will justly be held amenable to public opinion for this status of affairs. For this miscarriage of justice there is or can be no intelligent or legitimate excuse. It could not be arrived at through any process of reasonable induction or honest action. It is an insult to every respectable, law-abiding citizen who is interested in the peace, prosperity and progress of the Territory, or who possesses any regard for the rights of his fellow men, or the rules which ordinarily govern decent society.

Gentlemen, it seems to me that the time has arrived when Graham County should be blotted from the map of Arizona, and its citizens relegated for trial to a locality where juries have some regard for their sacred obligations, and some respect for law and justice; where they are not hampered by ignorance, controlled by prejudice, influenced by fear, or governed by sympathy.

In this county, where murder and bloodshed have run riot, and where the only protection to life and property consists in a strict enforcement of the law, you, by this verdict, have deprived every man of that constitutional right, of protection. You have sanctioned disorder, and have welcomed anarchy, and were it not for the press of business before the Court, and the great expense that would be incurred by the empaneling of a new jury, I would immediately dismiss you from the consideration of any matters before the Court. Gentlemen of the jury, you are discharged, and I only regret that I cannot discharge you for the term.

On each verdict judgement was rendered and Chavez sentenced to the penitentiary for ten years. He was pardoned in 1886, after serving three years. . . .

Three Chinese were convicted of murder and sentenced to be hung. They were executed in the county jail.

The grand jury did an immense amount of business at that term of the court, returning a large number of indictments and ignoring more than one hundred charges.

The result of the criminal business was that nine persons were sent to the territorial prison, three sent to the county jail for one year, three executed, and a number against whom indictments

were found, left the county for the good of society. Of those convicted, nine received executive pardon, some of whom became
exemplary citizens. . . .

In many respects Judge Sheldon was a remarkable man. With
the bar and litigants he was unpopular, but in social circles he was
genial, companionable, elegant, and the incarnation of good breeding and civility. He seemed to think his mission was to enforce
the law and rid Arizona of criminals, hence the severity of his
judgements which were rarely tempered with mercy. He was by no
means exempt from the infirmities of human nature. He looked
with jaundiced vision upon the social and moral condition of the
Territory and regarded Arizona's future from the standpoint of a

pessimist. He was an honest man and fearlessly discharged his duties during the brief period he was on the bench in Arizona. Within a short time after leaving here he died in California from the effects of a wound he had received in the Civil War. If, as the poet declares, "to live in hearts we leave behind is not to die," Judge Sheldon still lives in the memory of many who incurred his judicial displeasure.

## PRICE MUST HANG?

"And it is the judgement and sentence of this Court that you be taken hence and kept by the Sheriff of this county in secure confinement until Friday, the first day of February, 1895, and that upon that day, between the hours of nine o'clock a.m. and four o'clock p.m. you be taken into the yard of the jail of this county and there hung by the neck until you are dead, and may God have mercy upon your soul."

Such were the words which closed Judge Baker's address to William Price, found guilty by a jury of the murder of William Shurbett, on Washington Street in Phoenix on the 8th day of October, 1894.

The court room was crowded with spectators, who stood upon the bench in the rear of the court room to see and hear everything that went on, when William Price was led into the room by Sheriff Murphy. The prisoner was neatly attired and appeared very much unconcerned, falling into conversation with an attorney who sat with him while awaiting the entrance of the Judge.

As soon as Court opened Judge Baker called the case of William Price and Attorney Campbell for the prisoner arose and submitted a motion for a new trial, setting forth five errors in the Judge's rulings and instructions to the jury.

The prisoner was asked to stand up and as coolly as though he was facing a companion instead of a Court which was to sentence him to an ignoble death, he stood upon his feet, his arms clasped behind his back and an unconcerned far-away look in his eyes which were fixed upon the wall over the Judge's head.

The Judge reviewed the progress of the case, the trial by a jury, the verdict of guilty, and the recommendation by the jury for mercy. He stated that the law was lame which gave into the hands of a jury the power to fix a verdict and then made the Court responsible in fixing the punishment. The Judge spoke for about ten minutes during which time the prisoner remained perfectly calm and unmoved. At the conclusion of the Judge's talk he asked the prisoner if he had anything to say why the sentence of the Court should not be passed upon him. The prisoner replied that Judge Fitch would speak, and that gentleman arose while the prisoner under instruction of the Court sat down.

Mr. Fitch made a strong plea for mercy for his client, spoke of his youth, previous good character and the recommendation of the jury for mercy. . . .

Judge Baker replied to Mr. Fitch: "I have been very impressed by what you have to say, Colonel. As to that portion of your remarks as to the hardship of the law which fixes the standard of a reasonable man to guide him on a case of this kind, is an argument that goes to the law makers and not to the Court, whose duty it is to declare the law simply and coldly as it finds it upon the statute books."

The Judge then addressed the prisoner as follows:

> As I partly said just now in reference to the application of the jury for mercy, your whole case is greatly oppressing me. It has stood constantly in my vision both by night and by day since I read the recital of the facts in the case and the result of the deliberations of the jury. It has been like a cloud, like an ever-constant feeling that there was a shadow over me— on the street, in my room and at my house. I have no inclination to say one single word that would add any pang, any pain or any additional horror to the terrible situation in which you now stand; convicted of murder—the very highest crime written upon the statute books of your country, saving and

excepting it be the crime of High Treason to the State itself. For a moment, let us look at the facts as shown by the evidence on the trial of this case, briefly, not to harrass your feelings:

It appears from the evidence that the night before this fatal shot was fired, in a saloon, in gambling, you had some difficulty with the dead man who, peradventure struck you some slight blow, and in this affair some money was temporarily restrained from your possession contrary to and against the customary rules of gambling. You left the house that night no doubt in a towering passion and I must conclude from the evidence in the case, with the fixed determination to get even with your adversary, to square the thing with him. On the next morning you were at the same place armed with a deadly weapon and I want to say, just here, will men never learn to cease to pack arms in this community and in violation of the Statutes of this Territory? Anyhow you appeared at the same place armed with a deadly weapon; you got the money that no doubt was yours of right and came in contact with your adversary on the sidewalk. I am satisfied from the evidence that you were the aggressor, Mr. Price. The jury was so satisfied. I stand with them. You used vulgar language to your adversary—you said that you were armed—you were heeled and that you could not be robbed any more. Those words were indicative of the spirit of revenge that was consuming your soul and which filled the very recesses of your heart.

Under the testimony of the prosecution you pursued him while he was walking away, using vulgar language, until he turned and spoke to you words of defiance, when you pulled your pistol and fired at him point blank. You missed him. Your adversary fled for his life across the street and you pursued him, firing at him, wounding him once. Not enough, you wounded him with a second shot, when he fell prone upon the ground. It looks as if revenge had its cup full, it seems as if the bitterness, the gall of your heart ought to have been sweetened, but to the contrary, you deliberately walked up to your adversary while prone upon the ground, helpless upon the ground with face and hand turned up as if calling for mercy; you then with both hands upon the pistol intending that life should be taken; that the bullet should not fail to hit your victim. You went to him and bent over him and fired the deadly shot. Could there be a case of greater deliberation, premeditation and cool unyielding revenge? Such are the facts of the case for which the jury has returned a verdict of murder against you.

There are other views of the matter that it is perhaps not improper for me to speak of at this time. The law is a rule of action for the guidance of the members of society. It is indispensable; it is absolutely necessary. The object of the law, the central idea in inflicting punishment of this kind is, that others may be deterred from similar acts. The law cannot take any pleasure in seeing the extreme penalty administered. No officer takes pleasure in a thing of that kind—how can the heart find pleasure in it? It is done to deter—to restrain the vicious.

Let me say here: That if there are any pleasures in occupying the exalted position that I occupy among you; if there has been any delight in the discharge of the duties of this office, it has turned it all to wormwood and to gall. All to wormwood and gall.

I say that the idea is that others may be deterred from doing likewise. Man's life is valuable, that is the idea; and no man can take another's life unless it is under the rules sanctioned by our law. You have no right to deprive him of that which God alone has given him or has the power to give to him. If men are not restrained in their passions by the law, then we shall walk in this community armed one for the other, and no man can say when he leaves his house in the morning that he will be able to go back to it, to his family at night; for his adversary may kill him on the street as he walks. That cannot be tolerated. It must be understood in this community that the life of every citizen is absolutely safe and secure; and he who arms himself with a deadly weapon and slays his fellow man and is convicted thereof must expect to suffer the extreme penalty of the law. I am constrained to do this which my conscience tells me I ought to do, in this case. I must obey the law myself; must uphold the law of my country. I must conscientiously do it, whatever the result may be, and that is, Mr. Price, that I must sentence you to death, the extreme penalty of the law.

And it is the judgement and sentence of this Court, that you be taken hence and kept by the Sheriff of this county in secure confinement until Friday the first day of February, 1895, and that upon that day, between the hours of nine o'clock a.m. and four o'clock p.m. you be taken into the yard of the jail of this county and there be hung by the neck until you are dead, and may God have mercy upon your soul.

Judge Baker then called on the prisoner to rise and asked him if he had anything to say for himself and the prisoner replied that he had not. At the conclusion of the sentence the prisoner who had remained standing without a trace of emotion upon his face, while the spectators shuddered at the awful words, was led away. As his back was turned to the Judge and he passed through the great crowd in the court room, a smile spread over his face and he walked as though he was going to liberty instead of death.

It is said that after regaining his cell his attorneys called on him to offer consolation in the appeal which they would take in the case, when he told them he wanted no appeal; that at the best he would be sentenced to imprisonment for life and he would rather hang.

Two weeks after the sentencing, Price escaped from the county jail. The news spread through the city and created a great deal of excitement. Upon investigation the following is the account of the escape as learned from the officers:

Adjoining the rear of the old courthouse the new jail is being erected, and which is almost completed. Between the two buildings is a scaffold reaching from the ground to the top of the new jail. From that scaffold friends of another prisoner, Jim Young, the counterfeiter, must have passed to him a couple of files through the narrow grated windows near the roof of the jail.

The day before, at 4:15 o'clock in the afternoon, Price was released from his cell and he joined the other prisoners at dinner in the corridor and the jailer locking the door went into the front of the building leaving the prisoners alone.

The jail door from the jailer's room is of heavy strips of iron crossing each other at a distance of a couple of inches and which is fastened by three heavy chains and padlocks. One chain extended from the bottom of the floor. One of the other chains was fastened about a foot from the floor to the door and casing on the left side, and the other about a foot from the top of the door, on the same side. This door opens into the jailer's room from which a door opens into the jail yard which is surrounded by a close board fence twelve feet high with braces on the outside, the inside being perfectly smooth.

About 4:45 o'clock as Under-Sheriff Widmer was standing on the front porch of the courthouse, having just returned from an examination of the outer walls of the jail, Hackett, the stage man, came rushing up and told him that he had just met a couple of prisoners running down First Avenue towards the river. Widmer told him he must be mistaken as a few minutes before he had found everything secure. But he proceeded to make an examination, assisted by Deputy Prethero, when it was found that the information was correct and that murderer Price and counterfeiter Young were the men who had made their escape.

The examination showed that as soon as the jailer had locked the door and retired from the room, the two desperate prisoners had gone to work on the two lower chains, which they sawed apart, and then springing back the door crawled through between the bottom of the door and the floor. Once in the jailer's room the rest was easy. Taking a chair and a shovel they went into the yard and placing the chair against the wall they mounted it, caught the blade of the shovel over the top of the wall and pulled themselves up to where they could get a hold on the wall and dropped to the ground on the other side, free men.

The officers immediately started in pursuit but not a trace could be secured and as darkness fell in a short time the chase was abandoned till morning when Sheriff Murphy, Deputy Prethero and others started out again.

As Price was under a death sentence, the officers were keeping him as closely confined as they deemed necessary, but had failed to place a death watch over him. They kept him confined and only allowed him the use of the corridor at meal-time for about an hour.

Young, who was a desperate character, was allowed the corridor at all times, but was encumbered with a ball and chain. He had sawed the ball off and part of the chain, but was still encumbered with a part which was the only fact that led Hackett to know that they were escaping prisoners when he met them. . . .

A week later a telegram was received stating that Price, the condemned murderer, and Young, the counterfeiter, who had escaped from the county jail on Christmas afternoon, had been captured, and that Price was badly wounded and would die, Young had a broken leg, and Deputy Prethero had a broken arm. No further particulars were received but that was sufficient to cause everybody in the city who heard the news to express their gratification.

From a special correspondent at Gila Bend these particulars were

received of the capture and terrible fight which ensued before the desperadoes were compelled to show the white feather:

Deputy Prethero, with Billy Moore of Mesa City and Kellog of Agua Caliente, left Gila Bend in a buckboard leading three saddle-horses, going south towards the Mexican line. Reaching Ajo [ah-hoe] they secured the services of Tom Childs, Jr., as a guide and after a short search found the trail of the fugitives. The trail showed that Harris and Richards, who had gone out ahead, were following close and the party started off at a rapid gait expecting to overhaul Harris and Richards and join or relieve them in the chase.

Following the trail they found that Harris and Richards had left it and started due south for the Mexican line with the evident intention of heading off the fugitives who were without doubt making Mexico their objective point. Prethero and party decided to follow the trail to the end, let it lead where it would. They stayed with it until it led into a box canyon, when young Childs led them around to a pass on the other side of the mountain which they entered, and dismounting, crawled from rock to rock until they saw Price and Young, who were camped in the canyon. They had arranged their camp behind the boulders so that they had a good view of the canyon and could see almost its entire length without being seen themselves and could easily have defied a large number of pursuers and killed them without danger to themselves.

Not expecting danger from the rear they took no precautions for protection in that direction and the pursuers succeeded in getting within twenty-five yards of them before they were discovered. As soon as Price and Young found they were discovered they seized their rifles and began firing. The posse returned the fire and for a few minutes bullets flew thick as hail. A shout from the fugitives caused the posse to stop firing and when the smoke cleared away the pursuers saw both of their men lying upon the ground writhing in agony. Deputy Prethero had also been wounded, a bullet striking him in the arm, breaking that member. Of the prisoners, Price was mortally wounded. Three bullets had passed through his body and he was suffering terribly. One ball had struck Young in the leg, breaking it.

Moore, Kellog and Childs bound up the wounds of the injured

men as well as they could and, after a short rest, the horses were brought in, the prisoners mounted, supported as much as possible by their captors and the start was made for Gila Bend. Prethero and Moore started off ahead leaving the prisoners with the rest of the party, and upon reaching Gila Bend, called for the doctor there. After the doctor had cared for Prethero's injuries, Moore and the doctor started out to meet the injured prisoners, Prethero remaining at Gila Bend awaiting the arrival of the party.

When the posse arrived with Price and Young, Price was dead and Young was suffering terrible pain from his wounded leg. A coroner's jury was empaneled and an inquest held on the body of Price. Young was taken in charge by the doctor and everything possible was done for him.

In Phoenix, Judge Baker issued an order that Price, dead or alive, must be brought to this city if captured and the entire posse with the body of Price and the injured Young proceeded to Phoenix by train. Young had been placed on a cot in the baggage car and was carried from the train into the waiting room at the depot, where he lay smoking and talking. To the reporter he gave the following account of their movements since leaving the county jail by way of the back fence on Christmas afternoon:

> On scaling the wall we ran south on First Avenue a short distance, when we turned due west until we reached the edge of town. Here we secured two horses, a gray and a bay, saddles, one Winchester rifle, two 44-calibre and one 38-calibre revolvers, five boxes of Winchester cartridges, one round of cartridges for the 44 and two cartridges for the 38. [Whether this cache was awaiting them, or how they procured the arms, is not indicated.]
>
> That night we traveled sixty miles west, by Buckeye and across the Hassayampa. Next day meeting Chauncy Gunn and wife we followed them to a ranch where we got hay for our horses and continued on to Sentinel. Here provisions and a sack of grain was secured and after resting all night we left next morning, going almost due south. We followed no trail or road and in fact knew none. Our sufferings for water were

considerable and at the time of our capture our horses had had no water for two days and had been ridden hard.

Shortly before the capture we had given up all hope of finding water and had retraced our steps about fifteen miles intending to make the Gila River. On one of our back marches we found that Harris and Richards had crossed our trail only a few rods behind and we knew we were being pursued.

We made camp about ten miles from Tom Child's ranch and about sixty miles from Gila Bend. It was our intention if our pursuers should come up with us, not to shoot if there was any chance of escaping by running. Price had said that he did not want to kill anybody if he could help it, but if it came to a show-down he would be driven to it.

Prethero, Moore, Kellog and Childs came up to within seventy-five yards of where we were camped, safely fortified behind a bank in the sand wash. We were not exactly surprised as we were looking for them all the time and if Price had not run when the posse approached we would have killed every one of our pursuers without a particle of danger to ourselves, so strong was our position, but Price was after liberty and not blood and as soon as he saw the posse he made an attempt to escape, running up the bank in full view. Seeing him run I followed.

The officer fired a volley, a ball striking me in the leg and I fell. A ball struck Price in the shoulder and he returned the fire with his Winchester getting in three shots. He then turned around receiving a ball in the stomach. When the last shot struck him he threw down his gun and surrendered, saying as he gave himself up that he wished he had kept on shooting. The only shooting done by us was the three shots fired by Price. I did not fire a shot. The shot which struck Price in the shoulder was, I believe, fired by young Childs as he had a small calibre gun and the bullet in the shoulder was smaller than the other. Who fired the fatal shot I do not know. . . .

Price died when about a half mile from Gila Bend and

made no statement other than that he wished to die. He had said previously that he would fight till he died rather than be hung. . . .

When told that Burson and Hamilton had been arrested at Phoenix on a charge of assisting in his escape he said: "Who is Burson? I don't know him, neither do I know Hamilton."

Regarding the escape he said Price had half a dozen saws concealed for some time and had probably got them from some friend. He said: "I took one with me to saw the chain from my legs."

When asked about their horses and guns, he said the horses belonged to Price and that when they reached the southwest corner of town he waited while Price went off and got the guns. He did not know where they came from. Price had $160 in money with him.

Young said he knew of no outside assistance. The escape was planned by Price some time ago, the intention being to follow the deputy out of the corridor, try to disarm him and fight for freedom. Young talked him out of it. Price had begged him to help him and out of pity he had consented, as he did not wish to get out himself till he did so legally. . . .

The body of Price lay in the courthouse yard, and later, was buried in the potter's field. At least five hundred people visited the jail yard and viewed the remains, to satisfy themselves that it was indeed the condemned murderer who through his thirst for satisfaction had killed one man and had himself been killed.

—Phoenix *Herald*, 1894-95

## FRONTIER COURT INCIDENTS

In the early days, judges, governors, marshals and various other appointive officials of the Territory of Arizona were not appointed because of their great knowledge and ability, but in most instances because they were possibly treading on the heels of some politician in power in the particular State he hailed from. He might be a profligate son who had to be cared for and could fill the bill, and yet many of these fellows made good, having the brains to care for the job.

In 1872, the counties of Yuma and Mohave comprised the Second Judicial District, and two terms of court were scheduled each year in both counties. The judge lived in Yuma and when the river steamer was scheduled to make a trip up the Colorado River north as far as El Dorado Canyon, he would book passage for Hardyville, where court was held, that being the county seat of Mohave County.

There was no rooming house at that place and the witnesses and jurymen had to pack their blankets to that place and the mesas and washes thereon were dotted with little fires, where some of the miners cooked their own meals, while others patronized the dining room of Wooster Hardy, who also ran a forwarding station at that river point, where the teamsters to Prescott, Fort Whipple, Camp Verde and other places along the line, delivered goods.

A murder trial was on in court and the judge had two days of witnesses, and during that time miners who had been free of booze had tanked up quite readily. Of course, the judge had to get in while the booze was flowing freely and the second night of the court he had been having a great time sleeping on Hardy's bar. He awakened and sat up astride the bar, calling out: "Mr. Sheriff, please bring in the prisoner." The sheriff was seated in a barroom chair tilted back against the wall, as drunk as it was possible to get. Seeing the uselessness of getting a rousing reception from the sheriff, an assault was made on the chief deputy, who was lying on his blankets on the flags, in front of the building and under the porch. He was told of the situation and then replied that he would not get out of there for all the judges with injunctive power in the country. Then the kind-hearted fellows, seeing the uselessness of trying to open the first night court in the country, used their good offices to mollify the court and with a few more drinks he settled down to a restful night on the bar.

The case was given to the jury the following day, and when the men sallied into the jury room, which was the dining room, they immediately elected a foreman, who told them of the character of the crime which was the killing of a non-commissioned officer in the army, these fellows being at a low ebb in the estimation of the miners and others, that any man who believed the defendant innocent of the crime to throw their hats on the table. And on the table went all the hats, virtually holding open season on all soldiers and officers of the regular army. This ended the term of court, and the river steamer returning the following day took the judge back to his abode at Yuma.

—From a series of early-day stories by Anson H. Smith,
pioneer editor of the Mohave County Miner, 1882-86,
published by the Miner in 1933

Not many years ago there officiated in a precinct in the Tonto district of Gila County, a justice of the peace. Within the same judicial borders there also dwelt a very impoverished man with his wife and ten small children, dependent upon him for support. At this time the cattle business was supreme; the herd owner and cowboy held sway, and but little mercy was accorded to the man caught stealing cattle.

A calf was missed from the ranch of a prominent stockman of the district and the loss was charged to the family man. He was promptly arrested and brought before the justice for trial. At the trial the proof of guilt was very strong, showing among other circumstances that the hoofs and hide of the animal had been found beneath the floor of his cabin; while the prisoner offered no defense.

On the evidence the justice found the prisoner "guilty of murder in the first degree"; and passed sentence of immediate hanging. The cowboys were there and ready to execute the sentence. The rope had been passed over a limb of a giant mesquite, when it occurred to them that it was rather extreme punishment for just a calf, and that probably the prisoner's family would suffer if deprived of its only bread-winner. They therefore sent a committee to the justice to state these facts and endeavor to secure a modification of the sentence. The justice listened and ordered the case continued for one week. At the appointed time court was again called,

and announcement was made that the case had been fully considered; that he must still find the prisoner guilty of murder in the
first degree, but, as he was a poor man with a large family dependent upon him for support and the calf was undoubtedly
needed for food, he would order an acquittal on the ground of
self-defense.

—Yuma *Sentinel*, 1903

One of the most disgraceful scenes that ever occurred in any
court room took place at the Post larceny trial. A disagreement
occurred between the lawyers in regard to the sheriff delivering
Hudson to the deputy sheriff of Cochise County. The matter was
discussed on its merits by both sides. Lawyer Baker in the heat of
argument made some strong statements which caused the district
attorney to inform him that he had lied. Baker in turn vented his
spleen with a string of vile and abusive epithets and proceeded to
pull a mountain howitzer out of his pocket. He was immediately
held by spectators and the aforesaid mountain howitzer taken
from him by the sheriff. Quiet was soon restored. After the close of
Baker's argument Judge Alsap, another lawyer in the case, took
the floor and in the course of his remarks made some allusion to
the acts of the sheriff; which he had not time to finish when Mr.
Orme, the sheriff, applied strong language to the judge and backed
his assertion with a chair. Three or four men stepped in and
stopped the racket and the trial went on. The sheriff was fined ten
dollars by the court when he said he would pay when the balance
were fined for their actions. Thus ended the first chapter in the
Post trial.

In regard to pugilistic lawyers, too much indigation cannot be
expressed by both press and people against the shameful proceeding
in the Justice's Court. . . .

The presiding Justice of the Peace was deeply wrong in not fining
the whole quartette fifty dollars each for contempt of court. It is
to be hoped that no such disgraceful a scene will ever occur again
in our courts. Let the fair name of Maricopa County be preserved
at all hazards even if a half to a dozen or more lawyers be severely
censured for it.

—Phoenix *Herald*, 1882

In the early part of the Territory's existence Judge Fitzgerald, an imported jurist, occupied the bench of the First Judicial District, at Tucson. The judge had a most exalted idea of his own importance and dignity, and proposed to check the laxity of decorum that he thought he found in his court room. The attorneys were informed that smoking would not be tolerated, and that coats must be worn under pain of displeasure of the court. The grand jury was called for the first time. Among the jurors summoned was a brawny miner, who appeared in his usual costume of dark shirt and overalls.

"What do you mean sir," thundered the magistrate, "by appearing in this court room in your shirt sleeves? Where is your coat?"

"At home, Judge," mildly responded the juror.

"Then go and get it. Not a word sir, or I'll commit you for contempt!"

The miner went silently out. He didn't return for that day nor on the next, and the judge, after issuing a bench warrant for him, had to swear in another juror.

About two weeks after, the original miner, dressed as the court had demanded, again stepped within Judge Fitzgerald's range of vision. To the irate court he tendered the explanation that his home and coat were both in the Harshaw Mountains, near the Mexican border, over a hundred miles away. . . .

—Phoenix *Gazette*, 1893

In '81 and '82 old Jim Burnett was justice of the peace in Charleston, on the San Pedro, below Tombstone. Charleston at that time was a howling camp, full of freighters, miners and the wooliest of cowboys. The whiskey sold wasn't of the mildest brand, and consequently tribulation sate within the community, and the Justice Court was always open. Jim did a rushing business, and at the end of three months duly reported to the board of supervisors, sending in his bill for the amount due him from the county. The county fathers cut down the bill by about half. Three months later the county treasurer wrote Burnett to forward him his quarterly statement. The reply came promptly back: "Go to hell; this court after this will be self-sustaining." And so it was, in great shape.

Every time a cowboy would get exhilarated and shoot up the town, the judge would fine him several hundred dollars, and "sink" what remained after paying four or five constables.

One day old man Schwartz got excited and killed a man. After the justice had finished the inquest, he had Schwartz hauled before the bar, heard a few witnesses, found the defendant guilty and fined him a thousand dollars. Schwartz wanted to appeal the case, but couldn't get his papers from Jim Burnett. When he went up to Tombstone (the country seat) about it, some of the ablest lawyers in the territory called him a cussed fool, and told him that if he had any respect for his neck he had better pay the money. He took their advice and planked down the cash for the papers wherein Justice Burnett gave him release from the law's oppressions. But the county never saw any of that money. Those who figured on the proposition said that Burnett came out $22,000 ahead on his office in two years.

Mark Smith was defending a cowboy on one occasion before the Charleston judge, and his client was found guilty and fined $1,000.

"But," yelled Mark, in dismay, "Your honor, you have no jurisdiction to impose a fine of that magnitude, and I give notice of appeal. Now, if your honor will fix the bond we will furnish it."

"Mr. Smith," gravely answered the judge, "you don't understand this court. You have been practicing law before one-horse judges in Tombstone, sent from the East, who take the law from d——d books; but I want you to understand that that horse thief of yours there will pay that $1,000 fine or I will have him taken out behind my corral and shot, and now take your choice, and get a move on you."

Mark looked at his client, who was getting well scared, as he understood that Jim Burnett never made idle threats, and allowed his eyes to wander over the office, with not a book of record or otherwise in sight, but four large revolvers conspicuously close to his honor, and after a hasty consultation the money was handed over to the man of law, and Mark and his client lit out for higher land, glad to get away at any price.

—Phoenix Gazette, 1893

The following letter was written to a leading attorney in Tucson by a well-known character in southern Arizona, and is fraught with originality and sarcasm. The names of the parties are withheld by request:

Solomonville, February 8, 1891

As has been well said, human resolutions are weak and entirely broken. You will remember that in my letter to you at Florence a little more than a year ago, I told you that I thought I would adhere strictly to my family precepts, keep sober and keep out of trouble. I did so for more than a year and succeeded admirably, but alas it seems as though my life must be a series of misfortunes, and the fates and the courts have again decreed that I must be deprived of my liberty for a period of six months.

My object in writing to you is to furnish you a statement of facts in my case, and ask your opinion and assistance in the matter. I was in a Mexican saloon drinking with a crowd of "bad greasers"; hot words arose between one of them and myself, and he threatened to hurt me and abused me. I pulled a six-shooter to defend myself and in the melee the weapon was discharged accidentally, the bullet striking a chair, and glancing off struck or rather grazed a Mexican's arm. Now the prosecution soon discovered that it would be useless to prosecute me for assault or for carrying deadly weapons because I was assaulted as I was leaving town, and had just put on my pistol, as the law allows. However it would not do to let "Cyclone Bill" off without prosecuting him in some way and I was arrested for carelessly discharging fire arms in a public place.

I demanded a jury trial and proved to the satisfaction of a portion of the jury that the shot was unintentional and purely accidental. After remaining out all night the jury failed to agree and was discharged. I then secured a change of venue to an adjoining precinct, the trial by jury resulted in my receiving the following sentence: To serve a sentence of sixty days in the county jail, after which I am to pay a fine of one hundred and twenty days or dollars, making in all six months imprisonment because I had no means with which to pay the fine. Immediately after sentence was passed, I gave notice of appeal in answer to which the "learned magistrate" informed me that if I would furnish bond to the amount of $300 within three days, and, said he, it will "have to be a mighty good bond (and if you give bond in this case I will order your arrest upon a charge of assault with a deadly weapon), I will grant you an appeal. If not, your right to appeal will be denied."

Now as you well know I am ignorant of law, but this much I do know that in Texas the poorest man, if he be not satisfied with the judgement of an inferior court, is entitled to appeal to a higher court, and even though he be unable to give an appeal bond and remains in custody. Upon the arrival of the district court at its regular term, he has the right to appeal before such court. Now I wish you would write me your opinion upon that point. I persisted and compelled this arrogant magistrate to enter upon his docket my notice of appeal. His remarks in open court about having me re-arrested, which he intended as a menace of threat, had the effect of preventing me from giving the appeal bond.

During the trial the magistrate allowed, over my objection, the district attorney to examine all of my witnesses but one before I put them on the stand, and when I put the one remaining witness on the stand, after he had given his testimony the court would not permit witnesses' testimony to go to the jury, leaving me entirely without a defense. During the course of the examination of the various witnesses, while one of them who was summoned by the state was giving his testimony, which was decidedly in my behalf, the court, in a threatening and angry manner, and with violent gestures, told the interpreter to tell the witness that if he testified falsely or kept back any fact that he knew to be detrimental to my case, that he could order the witness placed under arrest. This had the effect of frightening the witness so that he deliberately testified falsely and to my detriment.

The most remarkable part of this wonderful trial, however, was this: after all the evidence was in and the district attorney and myself had addressed the jury, the court said: Gentlemen of the jury the court charges you as follows:

> The defendant is charged with carelessly discharging a deadly weapon in a public place. If you find from the evidence that he is guilty of said offense you will say in your verdict, we the jury find the defendant guilty as charged. If

however you should decide to find him not guilty as charged, and you see it proper to find him guilty of any other or a different crime from that charged in the complaint, you shall find him guilty of that crime even though the complaint does not charge him with the crime of which you find him guilty and the court will accept your verdict and punish him accordingly.—WILLIAM ELLISON (CYCLONE BILL)

—Tucson *Star*, 1891

The last act of the drama, beginning with the killing of Billy Kinsman, took place in the district court when May Woodman, his slayer, convicted of the crime of manslaughter, was brought in for sentence. Prior to pronouncing the fatal words that should consign her to the walls of a penitentiary the judge reviewed the affidavits introduced by the defense on motion for a new trial, and stated that he did not consider them sufficient, and overruled the motion. The counsel on both sides agreed to a period of ten days in which to file a bill of exceptions. During the remarks of the judge in this connection the prisoner, who was accompanied by her mother, sat near her counsel, apparently unmoved by the denial of the motion. Upon the request to stand up, and asked if she had any reason to offer why sentence should not be pronounced, the prisoner broke into a paroxysm of tears, and exclaiming: "For God's sake let me die," and sank into her chair. The judge then proceeded to state that, having been found guilty it became his duty to pass sentence; that while his sympathy, as well as that of the community went out to her, being a woman, his duty as a magistrate prevented him from allowing it to warp his judgement, or stand in the way of justice. That the custom so prevalent in this country of using weapons upon slight pretext for the purpose of redressing wrongs must be stopped, and the practice of carrying concealed weapons, especially at night, was commented on and condemned in the severest terms.

The judge in conclusion, informed the prisoner that her term in the penitentiary could be utilized by her in preparation for a higher and better life. That the full limit of the law was a comparatively light sentence taken in connection with the crime, and he felt that his duty compelled him to sentence the prisoner for the term of five years, the utmost limit prescribed for this offense. At the conclusion of the sentence, the prisoner, who had been sobbing bitterly, wheeled in her chair and looking at the judge with flashing eyes, cried out: "May God curse you forever!"

—Tombstone *Republican*, 1883

Neil Munro had a case before his honor Justice Wright which attracted considerable attention. About eight months previously, Neil bought a baby burro, and kept it in his yard for his children to play with. Recently it was turned out, and failed to return. After it had been absent several days Mr. Munro offered a reward for its return. It was brought in by a Mexican, and the reward paid. It had been branded during its absence. A few days later a Mexican came along and claimed it, but Munro would not give it up. The Mexican brought suit before Justice Wright for the burro. Munro and several of his neighbors swore to the identity of the burro. The Mexican who claimed it swore positively that it was his, and that it had not left his possession since it was born, and this he substantiated by several witnesses. The testimony was so contradictory that the justice continued the case until the following day. The Mexicans, in order to make their case still stronger, brought the alleged mother of the burro to the justice's office and hitched her in front of the door. While the judge was arranging his papers, a burro colt, about the same age as the one in question, rushed across the street and up to its mother and commenced taking nourishment. This, of course, settled the case in Munro's favor.

—Clifton *Copper Era*, 1901

"I understand," said Judge Street to a Yuma juror, "that you are opposed to capital punishment, and that you have publicly expressed yourself as such. Is that so?" The lanky Arkansan from down the valley looked at the judge and convulsed the bystanders by this reply:

"Generally speaking I'm agin capital punishment. But not in this case. I think this scoundrel deserves all that we can give him, and I will vote to hang him."

—Phoenix *Gazette*, 1901

# 7

# THE GALLOWS

THE GALLOWS

In order to set the stage for this chapter by putting the reader in the proper frame of mind, so to speak, it may be said that the reporting of the hanging of a human being is not a very pleasant task, to say the least. And it is not a morbid streak in the Editor's mentality that prompts the inclusion of these gruesome last scenes in the lives of condemned men during Arizona's turbulent days. The thought in mind is to present what seems to be the most interesting aspect of each of these chronicles, the victim's final earthly thoughts and his very last words before paying the awful price— the hours during the last meal, the last interview, the walk to the gallows, and the final minutes and seconds. Some of the condemned men appeared gay and carefree; others sombre and unconcerned; some repentant and remorseful. Most of them were brave men to the end.

Many of the gunfights of early-day Arizona were saloon brawls— a combination of whiskey and weapons. Other cases were cold-blooded, calculated murder by apparently sober men. Although it was customary to carry a gun on the frontier for self-protection, a law-unto-himself attitude on the part of some desperate men caused them to use their weapons for other purposes than self-defense, and few of them were forced to pay the extreme penalty for their crimes.

In the stories that follow we have ended the actual hanging scene with the springing of the trap, although some of the accounts went so far as to chronicle the heart count, minute by minute following the drop, until zero.

## THE HALDERMAN BROTHERS

All that human agency and legal skill could do to save those whom the mandate of the law had marked as its own was done in behalf of Thomas and William Halderman, but justice wept and would not be comforted; the blood of two peace officers of Cochise County cried aloud and hushed the voice of mercy, and at 12:40 o'clock on November 19th, 1900, these two men forfeited their lives to satisfy the ends of the law.

The importance of this case caused the bringing to bear upon those in power the strongest influence, both from those in high public station and private life. But the pardoning power was satisfied after a most thorough examination, and the men had a fair and impartial trial; were defended by able attorneys, and their conviction and sentence was legal, although twice the gallows, with its ghostly shadows flung across the prison windows, was in readiness and twice was the hand of mercy reached forth to give them a small respite from their impending fate. The first respite was given when the appeal to the Supreme Court was taken; the next was granted by President McKinley, and lastly by Governor Murphy, who fixed today as the time which was the last.

If a feeling of sympathy was inclined to steal over the hearts of those who knew the boys on account of their youth and their conduct in prison during the long months they had been waiting their doom, it was overshadowed by the cold-blooded and cruel manner in which they dealt out death to their unsuspecting victims for which they must pay the penalty.

A *Prospector* reporter called at the jail and saw the condemned men.

They had not changed in mood and showed a determined spirit to face their fate unflinchingly. When asked if they cared to make a statement both answered they were ready to die and were prepared to meet their doom. Thomas Halderman stated: "The officers have been kind and we feel thankful for our treatment which has been very fair." "Yes," added William Halderman, "thank everybody for us who have shown us any favors. We are ready to die and die in the Christian faith; I forgive everybody and I hope they will forgive us. I die always believing I acted in self-defense and it is all over now."

"I am going to hang because I held a gun," said Thomas Halderman, "for I never fired a shot, but I am ready to die. We regret what will happen on account of our people but it looks as if we will hang and we will make the best of it. We have prayed and we are ready." When asked if they expected to make a statement on the gallows both condemned men replied in chorus, "Yes, we may say a few words."

At this moment Sheriff White appeared and asked the orders of the prisoners for their meal, which was to be the last. Any delicacy was theirs for the asking but the prisoners merely replied, "anything will do," and finally ordered commonplace fare though a good substantial meal was later served. The prisoners were calm and collected and showed remarkable composure.

The time set for the execution was between the hours of noon and one p.m. A large crowd was present and anxiously awaited the time when admittance would be had to the prison yard where the execution was to take place. All the windows in the courthouse on the second floor facing and overlooking the prison yard were lined with people to witness the execution. About one hundred persons were in the prison yard at the time of the execution. When the iron door leading to the jail was swung open a solemn hush prevailed and all eyes turned in that direction. Shortly after, the condemned men appeared. Thomas Halderman was in the lead in charge of Deputy Sheriff Johnson, and William Halderman followed in charge of Deputy Sheriff Bravin, while Sheriff White and Reverend Elliott followed closely in the line down the narrow steps to the scaffold.

Thomas Halderman, the younger prisoner, had just emerged from the jail door and facing the crowd said, "Hello hombres." Then placing his hand to his eyes to shade them from the sun's rays said, "the sun's hot, ain't it?" The prisoners walked to the scaffold and mounted the steps with a firm tread and exhibition of nerviness that was most surprising. They showed no signs of the least faltering and with rare courage and remarkable boldness and fearlessness advanced to the platform and even assisted the attendants in the final arrangements.

William Halderman stepped to the front under the dangling noose and surveying the crowd below said with a wave of the hand, "Nice looking crowd." He even smiled and remarked, "Some of you fellows are shaking already!"

Thomas Halderman who was equally nervy held the rope and also looked over the crowd below and turning to his brother, observed, "Those people look all right." He looked at the noose and mechanically placed it loosely over his own head. He then listened attentively to the reading of the death warrant.

Sheriff White read the death warrant which was quite lengthy. During the time of the reading, Thomas Halderman paid marked attention throughout but the elder brother on the other hand paid no attention whatever and was the while engaged in conversation with Deputy Sheriff Bravin. At the conclusion of the reading Sheriff White asked if they wished to make a statement. Thomas Halderman spoke up promptly and in a clear voice said: "I have nothing to say and guess it would not do any good anyway. I forgive you all and hope you will forgive me." William Halderman said: "This will be an experience that ought to benefit all of you. I hope I will meet you all. I pray for you and hope you will pray for me." The straps were tied about the body and ankles to hold the arms and legs of the condemned men firmly together.

During this the prisoners noted some acquaintances below and made a few personal remarks or nodded to each.

While standing on the trap door and firmly strapped, William Halderman addressing Sheriff White said: "Kindly give us time for a little prayer." Reverend Elliott who had constantly been with them and afforded them much religious consolation, stepped forward and after having the two condemned men clasp each other's hand, read a solemn prayer which was most impressive. The pastor invoked the mercy of Him on their souls and in turn shook hands with both of the men bidding them goodbye.

The black caps were then drawn over the heads of the prisoners and as it shut them out from sight of the faces below, both men said in chorus: "Goodbye boys. Pray for us." Each again said: "Goodbye," and the crowd answered: "Goodbye," and the trap was sprung.

The crime for which William and Thomas Halderman died was the murdering of Teddy Moore, a boy of about eighteen years, the son of Mart Moore, an old-timer of the Territory. The evidence adduced on the trial of the case showed that a warrant was placed in the hands of Constable Ainsworth of Pearce for the arrest of the Haldermans, upon a charge of violating the Livestock law; that Ainsworth, appreciating that he was to arrest the Haldermans at the Wilson ranch, or at a remote place in the Chiricahua Mountains, took the precaution of stopping at the Smith ranch, on his way, and asked one of the Smiths to accompany him and assist in making the arrest. For some reason or other, Smith refused to accompany Ainsworth, presumably for the reason that his brother was the complaining witness against the Haldermans on the cattle charge. But Smith then advised Ainsworth to go to the Moore ranch, not over three quarters of a mile away, and get Teddy Moore to accompany him in effecting the arrest.

Ainsworth went to the Moore ranch; got Teddy and together they went up the canyon to the Wilson place where the Halderman brothers were. Arriving at the Wilson house, and while sitting on their horses, they called out and the Haldermans came out, whereupon Ainsworth told them that he had a warrant for their arrest for cow stealing, and would have to take them to Pearce for examination. They pleasantly answered: "all right; we will go"; whereupon, and it being early in the morning, Ainsworth asked them whether they had breakfasted. They said they had not. Then he said: "go and do so and we will wait."

Moore and Ainsworth waited some time. The Haldermans breakfasted and then came out of the house, and said to the officer, we must get some clothes. Ainsworth said all right go and get your clothes boys, and then we will start for Pearce. The Haldermans went back into the house, for the last time, but when they returned, one in each door, it was with their rifles in their hands. The Haldermans owned one of these rifles, but the old man Wilson, at whose house they were stopping, owned the other, and when they reached the doors one of them shouted to the officer: "hands up," and they both immediately opened fire upon the constable and his assistant, killing the constable outright, he falling from his horse within forty feet of the house, while Teddy Moore wheeled his horse and started toward his home, his mother's ranch, as fast as he could, the Haldermans the while shooting at him—the last shot, at a time when Teddy was 150 yards away, taking effect in his back and which afterwards proved to be the fatal one. He reached home; was helped from his horse by his mother and sister, and he narrated to all those present all of the circumstances. He lived but a few hours.

Well knowing what they had accomplished the Haldermans fled, taking with them old man Wilson's rifle and their own; crossed the Chiricahua Mountains afoot and finally reached a place on the Upper Gila River in New Mexico, where Sheriff White's deputy, Sid Mullen, and his posse run them down, bringing them back to Tombstone where they were tried and convicted of murder in the first degree, and both sentenced by the jury's verdict to be hung for the murder of Teddy Moore, and today, November 16th, 1900, paid the penalty.

—Tombstone *Prospector*, 1900

# EPILOGUE

It is not a pleasant task of newspaper work to witness a hanging. Perhaps no class of work brings one in closer touch with humanity, its demands for sympathy and its hardening of the sensibilities for the graver tasks which befall the newspaper worker. To give up to the morbid sense is repulsive and to cultivate it means a wasting of the best and sweetest sensibilities of life. After the Halderman boys were hung at Tombstone one of the men who witnessed it said he was ready to see another hanging anytime. It was not half so bad as he expected. The effect upon this man was brutal; it hardened his sympathies and left him worse off for having witnessed the tragic end of two human beings. It is a question whether men should be allowed to witness hangings, and if the effect upon all was the same as this man expressed, there would be no excuse for it, save the public representation which the sheriff in a measure is entitled to. But the effect was not the same upon all. There was that depressing influence which one has a right to expect in the crowd that stood before the gallows as these two boys were about to be dropped to eternity. Men stood with bared heads, faces paled by the emotions of the strange experience, and eyes fixed upon the men who stood upon the scaffold as the sheriff read his warrants of death.

The Citizen correspondent spent the last hour of their lives with the condemned men. A half hour before the death hour he received a telegram from Phoenix which said that the governor would not interfere. Seated upon a stool the younger brother conversed with the reporter freely while the elder one ate heartily the last meal of his life. Outside in the sheriff's office a crowd had gathered and the loud talk and laughter made its way to the cell. It was ominous merriment for the condemned men, and the younger brother looked at me as though he felt that if anyone should feel sympathy for him in that trying last hour it should come from a young man—for he, too, was young [Thomas was nineteen; William, twenty-three] and a dangling noose a hundred feet away was ready to receive him and end his life. Never was there a better exhibition of nerve, of genuine bravery, than this young man displayed. A few minutes before the time for the hanging came he said that he was innocent, but that he proposed to walk out of the jail and die like a man. "I think," said he, "that when a fellow finds that he can't get away from a thing he should take it like a man." Those were the sentiments of a brave man. A man in battle finds himself spurred on by the inspiration of those who surround him, one who fights an antagonist is aided by his own anger, but the man who is in possession of his full reason and calmly awaits for the officers to lead him out to his death represents the highest standard of bravery when he meets it with fear of none but his Maker.

Standing on the scaffold with the noose placed about his neck by his own hand this young man listened attentively to the words of the sheriff as the death warrant was read. As the straps were tightened about him he raised his eyes from the crowd in the jail yard and looked far off upon the peaceful scene of mountain and canyon, scanning the hills with a lingering, dreamy look which was pitiful to witness. It seemed as though that picture of nature must have been photographed upon his mind, so earnestly was its comfort and solace in that trying moment grasped by the condemned man. He seemed to bring the mountains close to him, drawing in the folds of the great panorama and wrapping himself in its embrace. It is this picture that remains with me, and I wonder if nature did not yield to this young man the comfort that he sought in its solemnity and purity.

—Tucson *Citizen*, 1900

## "TURN HER LOOSE—GOODBYE"

On the evening of July 15th, 1882, Joseph Casey was in Calabasas. There he possessed the reputation of being a desperate character, willing, even anxious to undertake any evil deed that might suit his devilish purposes. On the night in question he was especially wild, and in his malicious meanderings about the town, at a late hour, he with revolver in hand deliberately robbed a man and woman, whom he found in a house of prostitution. He then proceeded to an adjacent saloon and endeavored to "stand up" the proprietor, but in this he was frustrated.

The same night Sheriff Paul (of Pima County) arrived in Calabasas from La Noria, having in charge Morton, the murderer, and a party named Graham, charged with horse-stealing. The next morning he arrested Casey on the charge of robbery, and the three men he put in charge of William Cunningham, as guard, while he returned to the line after the man whom Casey had robbed, as it was necessary to have such party as witness against the culprit. The prisoners were placed in a partitioned part of the brick basement of the Santa Rita [Hotel]. During the night Casey gained his liberty by slipping unseen through one of the windows of the apartment, and immediately sought a brick yard, an eighth of a mile distant, as a place of refuge. Justice of the Peace, G. W. Atkinson, went after him with a double-barreled shotgun. Upon reaching him, the latter turned with the ferocity of a brute and exclaimed:

"You damned —— of a ——, I will take that gun away from you, and shoot you with it!"

There would probably have been a terrible hand-to-hand struggle, had not William Edwards arrived upon the scene at that moment and lent his aid in capturing the fugitive. Casey was granted a preliminary hearing before Judge Atkinson, and was committed to jail to await the action of the grand jury. Sheriff Paul then brought his prisoner to Tucson.

Casey remained in jail until October 23rd, of that year, when the notorious delivery took place, and he, with Murphy, Gibson, Moyer, Hurley, and others gained their liberty. Nothing was heard of him until the December following, when officers captured him at El Paso, and telegraphed to Sheriff Paul. The Pima County officer promptly hastened to El Paso, and while there he learned that Tim Hurley, another of the escaped prisoners was in Chihuahua. Leaving Casey under what he had reason to believe a strong guard, he went to Mexico, but when he returned he found that Casey had again escaped. Notwithstanding the most diligent search, the slippery rascal evaded the officers until early in March, 1883, when he was captured in Colorado City and successfully escorted back to jail in Tucson. He was registered at the Pima County prison on March 17th.

The fellow kept quiet for a couple of months, and then followed the outbreak and its fatal ending—the murder of Holbrook. It was on a Sunday morning, April 29th, that Jailer Holbrook received his death wound. He was looking after his routine duties at his room and about the jail. Some fault had been found by the prisoners with the manner in which the dishes had been washed, they claiming that none of them were properly cleaned. Holbrook had just stepped out of the door into the jail yard to direct the dishwashers to be more careful in their work, when, after but a moment or two had elapsed, he was surprised to hear the door, which was tied open, sharply close behind him. He at once returned to the jailer's corridor and turned to the right into his room, where he was confronted by Casey, who held a pistol at his breast and told him to throw up his hands. The jailer immediately grasped Casey's pistol hand, and turned the muzzle away from him just in time to avoid receiving the bullet, which struck the door casing. As he was about to engage with Casey, being himself unarmed, he saw Henry St. Clair with another pistol leveled at him. Knowing that if he succeeded in overpowering Casey, St. Clair would come to the rescue by taking his life, the jailer started to retreat outside the door to call for help. He found the door closed behind him, and just as he was in the act of opening it, Casey fired again, the ball passing through Holbrook's body from his back. He heroically succeeded in opening the door and passed out, and knowing that the jail breakers would try to escape through that door into the jail yard and then scale the fifteen-foot wall to gain their freedom, he held the knob of the door with a determined strength, at the same time calling loudly for help.

It was some minutes before his alarm was heard, and when it was, men appeared at an open window of the sheriff's office, which commands the jail yard, and with loaded guns prepared to shoot down anyone who attempted to pass out; called to the jailer to let go of the door and come to the window, where a step-ladder was lowered and he ascended to the window, passed in and was assisted to a cot. The guards then entered the jail yard. They found that Casey and St. Clair had left two of the three pistols they had secured from beneath the mattress of the jailer's bed, on a shelf near the door of the jailer's room, but the third pistol was gone.

Casey had passed through the aperture he made in the grating above the cells by springing an iron bar from its socket, and was quietly sitting on the top of the farther end of the cells. Knowing that another pistol was missing, they called to him to come forward and throw up his hands, at the same time leveling their pistols at him. He came down the ladder from the top of the cells and dodged into the vault at its foot. He refused to come out until four shots had been fired through the light wooden screen partition of the vault, which passed over his head, he having crouched down on its floor. On coming out he told the guards that the pistol was in the closet of the sink, and it was found where he said it was.

Notwithstanding every possible attention, the wounded jailer died at the hospital on the evening of the day he received his fatal wound. There was universal indignation over such a brutal murder, and a strong effort was made by citizens to lynch Casey. At the following term of court both St. Clair, previously charged with highway robbery, and Casey were indicted for murder in the first degree. St. Clair pleaded guilty of murder in the second degree, and was sentenced to prison for life. Casey stood trial, and, being convicted, was sentenced to be hanged. His counsel appealed the case, but the action of the lower court was affirmed.

A good many prominent men agreed that if Casey had stood trial in the original charge of robbery at Calabasas, he would have been acquitted. There were, in the first place, two men connected in the onslaught upon the house of prostitution. One escaped. Casey was the only culprit captured, and when the trial was called in the district court here, the important witnesses against him had become scattered, and it was impossible to subpoena them. The only testimony that could have been brought against Casey would have been made by the person robbed, and that was conflicting. It is well known that he made his escape from the county jail the night before the trial. If he had remained incarcerated, the next day might have brought him his liberty. He would also have escaped the gallows, it is presumed. It is, however, believed that he did not break jail to escape the penalty of his latest crime, but for fear that other charges, for past criminal practices, might be brought against him, and lead to more serious results to him. . . .

The doomed man did not go to bed until one o'clock this morning [the day of his doom]. During the early part of last evening he devoted to card playing with his guards, Skinner and Kirby. Afterwards he entered into conversation with Mr. Otis, Chairman of the Board of Supervisors, and Sheriff Paul. The talk was genial and Casey was particular not to divulge any secrets of his past life. At this juncture it may be well to state that a few days ago Casey sent for Mr. Otis, and after their first interview, took quite a liking to that gentleman. The Supervisor had been with the criminal a great deal since, and, in sympathy for the unfortunate man, he went to the personal expense of purchasing a funeral suit of black. When Casey retired for his last sleep before execution, he was apparently in good spirits. He slept soundly and did not awake until six o'clock this morning. He then exhibited no signs of nervousness over his approaching dissolution. A hearty breakfast was spread before him, and he gave vent to a very liberal appetite. The menu consisted of scrambled eggs, porterhouse steak, mutton chops, a plate of cakes, a little bacon, and a pot of coffee.

During the morning Casey devoted the most of the time with his spiritual adviser, Father Antonio Jouvenceau. He also underwent the ordeal of a close shave. Afterwards he dressed himself in his new suit, and for an hour thereafter devoted his time to receiving a few welcome visitors, among them a couple of Sisters of Charity. When a couple of newspapermen attempted to call upon him (not Citizen representatives) and obtain an interview, he called out to the guard: "Will you do me the favor of sending these reporters away? I don't wish to be bothered with them."

Shortly after twelve o'clock, Casey seemingly enjoyed a cold lunch of chicken, roast beef, pie and hot tea. At a quarter to one o'clock the great crowd that had assembled outside were allowed to enter the jail yard. As they were tramping through the hallway of the jail, the multitudinous footsteps of the throng must have been especially annoying to the man about to meet his doom. A

*Citizen* reporter was near him at the time, and it was noticeable that Casey was unusually restless. Instead of quietly sitting on his bunk, with an unconcerned air he paced up and down his cell, unremittently. The cigar between his lips was puffed vigorously, and he was really ill at ease. At one o'clock precisely, Sheriff Paul entered the corridor, and asking Casey whether he wished the death warrant read in jail or on the scaffold, the prisoned preferred to hear the document delivered privately. The sheriff therefore proceeded to fulfill his unpleasant duty at the bars of the cell. Hardly a dozen specators were present. Casey listened attentively but uttered not a word. Then, as the key clanked in the lock of his cell, the murderer arose, straightened himself out, and walked steadily into the corridor. Thence he proceeded through the jail to the scaffold.

Outside fully two hundred spectators, many there from morbid curiosity, were awaiting his arrival. But he did not show the least signs of flinching. It was evident that he would die game. Ascending with a firm step the stairs of the scaffold, and just behind Father Jouvenceau, he quietly seated himself in the arm chair there provided for him. The butt of a cigar, which he had compressed between his lips as he made his last earthly trip, was carelessly thrown away when he sat down. The officers on the scaffold, including Sheriff Paul, Detective Len Harris, Sheriff Ward, of Cochise County, Deputy Sheriff Vosburg and Deputy Appel, lost no time in preparing the criminal for execution. Casey was on the scaffold at four minutes past one o'clock. The leather straps were at once wound around his legs, and while this operation was in progress he, still seated, spoke as follows to an eager crowd. His voice never faltered:

"I want to make a few remarks. I did kill Holbrook, but I did it under the impulse of the moment; I had no intention of killing him. I believe in all my life I never did anybody any bodily injury before, and did not mean to do it to him. I forgive everybody and hope all forgive me. I want to make a statement in regard to Harry St. Clair. He had nothing to do with the shooting. He is a young man, and I hope he will get out. He's got no friends to help him. I hope you will do something for him. I die a Catholic and resign my body in care of the church."

Not a sound was heard in the yard when the speaker arose after his remarks, and permitted the leather bands to be placed around his arms. Just before the rope was drawn around his neck he exclaimed:

"We all got to get there sometime, boys; all have to get to the jumping off place."

When the rope began to squeeze his neck, again he called out:

"Very uncomfortable necktie."

At the last moment, just as the black cap was drawn over his face, the desperate man called out:

"Turn her loose, goodbye!"

Then Sheriff Paul cut the pulley rope.

This occurred at seven minutes past one. A soul was ushered into eternity in almost a second. Casey was in fact a dead man when the rope that held his body became taut.

—Tucson Citizen, 1884

## THE RIVERSIDE HOLDUP

The famous Riverside stage holdup occurred on August 10, 1883, when the eastbound stage from Florence to Globe was attacked a few miles above Riverside by the Red Jack gang of road agents. They shot and killed Johnny Collins, the Wells-Fargo messenger, took $2,800 in silver and gold dust from the box he had in charge, and took from a Riverside merchant named Le Blanc, a passenger on the stage, money which the latter carried on his person.

The Red Jack gang was an organized band of criminals which had been operating in the area, usually making their headquarters at the ranch of Len Redfield on the San Pedro, a rendezvous of robbers where food and fresh mounts were available to members of the gang fleeing from the scene of their robberies. Prominent in this ruthless gang, aside from Jack Almer, alias Red Jack, were

Len and Hank Redfield, Joe Tuttle, Frank Carpenter and Charley Hensley.

The Florence Enterprise of 1883, in its account of the affair, goes on to say:

The robbers had laid their plans carefully. They sent one of their confederates, known under the aliases of Jack Averill, Jack Almer, and Red Jack, to Florence to watch the stage and see when the treasure box had the appearance of being well filled. This man of many names remained in Florence nearly a week, and was looked upon as a hard character. He had been seen in the Sulphur Springs Valley under very suspicious circumstances a month or two previous. But there was no evidence at hand to warrant the officers in arresting him. He had sold his horse and claimed that he was going to Riverside to obtain work in the mines. He was observed at the stage office every day when the agent was loading the Globe stage, and on Friday, when he saw that it required two men to lift the treasure box into the boot, he suddenly concluded that he must go to Riverside on that stage. He paid his passage and informed the agent that he would get aboard the stage farther down the street, as he would have to go down that way to get a saddle he had to take with him.

In the meantime the two men who were to murder the messenger and capture the treasure, had established a camp in the mountains near Riverside, where they could watch the road and see who was aboard the stage. They were under a large mesquite tree, and against the tree leaned their rifle and shotgun, and their horses were hitched nearby. When the stage passed by this point Red Jack commenced to sing, for the purpose, we presume, of assisting his partners to recognize him. His presence on the stage was the signal that the treasure box was full. As soon as the stage passed, the assassins mounted and followed at a distance till twilight came, then they pressed on and were only a few yards behind the stage when the driver pulled up at Evans & Le Blanc's Riverside station to change horses and afford his passengers an opportunity to take supper.

As the robbers came up they made a careful survey of the stage to make sure that Red Jack was aboard. They rode by the station a short distance then turned out of the road towards the river and rode along the river bank to avoid being seen at Riverside. Having reached the ford, a hundred yards above Riverside station, they crossed the river and rode on a mile and a half to the point they had selected for the robbery and murder. They had evidently inspected and prepared the place for the robbery some time during the previous week, for the branches on the bush behind which one of them stood, were carefully parted and tied back so as to give the robber full command of the road toward Riverside without exposing himself to view.

After accomplishing their dastardly work the robbers took a trail circling to the right from the place of the robbery and leading over the hills to the San Pedro road, at a point about two miles above Riverside. When they came to the San Pedro road they stopped, and the tracks would indicate that they did so for the purpose of dividing the treasure into two packs and strapping it on to the stage horse which they had taken with them for that purpose. At this point they dropped a nickel-plated shotgun shell, number 12 Winchester fire. From here they followed the San Pedro road and passed Dudleyville at a full gallop, one leading the pack horse and the other riding behind and whipping up the almost exhausted animal. Each man held a revolver in his right hand and both men were as silent as a tomb. The boys in front of the Dudleyville store hallooed to them and demanded the reason for their hurry, but they made no reply. About five miles above Dudleyville the robbers turned out of the road into the timber, and their tracks could not be followed, owing to the fact that the ground was covered with a thick growth of summer grass. They probably killed the stage horse in this timber and buried the money. This view of the case is sustained by the fact that when the robbers passed Mesaville, five miles farther on, they did not have any pack animal with them. At five o'clock on Saturday morning the robbers passed Perdue's place, and were noticed by both Mrs. Perdue and Mrs. Pearson, who was a guest at the house. They were still riding at a high rate of speed. They could not be traced above Redfield's.

The news of the robbery did not reach Florence till about ten o'clock Saturday morning, thus giving the robbers a good start. As soon as possible after receiving the news, Sheriff Doran, of

Pinal County, who was at Pinal, telegraphed that he would meet
the posse at Riverside. Under-Sheriff Scanland and Fred Adams
then left for the scene of the tragedy. Upon arriving on the
ground, Scanland and Adams took the track of the fugitives with
orders to follow it as long as a trace remained. In the meantime
Ex-Sheriff Gabriel, who was at Riverside on mining business, commenced an investigation and learned that Red Jack had got off
the stage at Evans & Le Blanc's station and inquired if two men
left a horse for him there, and that upon being answered in the
negative, had raved about their treachery and asserted that he
would make it warm for them if they should fail to keep their
agreement. He learned further that Red Jack had brought with
him on the stage a saddle and bridle, and that he had started up
the river on foot, leaving the saddle at the station, and taking the
bridle with him. These facts convinced Pete Gabriel that Red
Jack was a party to the robbery and he determined to follow up
and capture him. The editor of the Florence *Enterprise* had arrived at Riverside, on his return from a visit to Globe, an hour
previous to the discovery of this information by Gabriel, and
accidently meeting him he informed us of his purpose and extended us an invitation to join him in the expedition. No proposition could have suited us better, as the dead messenger had been
our friend. Going to Putnam's to secure a horse and arms we
found Sheriff Doran, who had just returned from inspecting the
robber's camp in the mountains; we informed him of the purpose
of Gabriel and ourself. The sheriff saddled up his animal while
Putnam was having a jack saddled for us, the only available saddle
animal he had that night, and joined us.

At ten o'clock we were off in the direction of the San Pedro.
Some time after midnight we reached Dudleyville, where we ascertained that Red Jack had given one of Mr. Finch's sons $15 to
take him as far up the river as Captain Cage's and that he had
said to the boy during the journey that he must reach Redfield's
that night if he had to steal a horse to accomplish the journey.
This information confirmed us in the belief that Red Jack was
a party to the robbery, and borrowing two Winchester rifles and
a six-shooter from the Dudleyville store, we pushed on with all
possible speed. Just before daylight we arrived at Mesaville, where

ve found officers Scanland, Adams and Harrington, who had
pent the night there. They came out from under their blankets
promptly, saddled their horses and joined our party.

Noon found us at Frank Shield's residence. Frank furnished us
with fresh horses. While we were waiting for dinner, young Hunt-
ey came up and said that he was the man who had started to
ake Red Jack to Redfield's. When questioned he said that Frank
Carpenter had met Red Jack and himself about one half mile
above Shield's place, and that Frank and Red Jack had got off
their horses and gone out to one side where they had a very con-
idential talk. After finishing their talk they returned to Huntley,
and Frank gave Red Jack $10 with which to pay Huntley. Then
Frank gave Red Jack his horse; the latter went on to Redfield's
and the former came on down to Mesaville. We learned subsequently that Frank had agreed to meet Red Jack with a horse.

Dinner over, we mounted our fresh horses, divided our party—
three taking one side and three the other side of the river—and
pushed on to Redfield's. We reached the ranch about seven
o'clock and swooped down upon the occupants unexpectedly.
Two of our men were in sight and three suspicious-looking strangers were camped in front of the house. But Red Jack had passed
on at one o'clock that afternoon. We had anticipated a lively
fight at this ranch, but were agreeably disappointed. The two in
sight, Joe Tuttle and Len Redfield, were as meek as doves and
shook from head to foot. We unsaddled our horses and went
into camp, keeping our guards through the night to see that our
birds did not take wing or attempt to take our scalps.

Next morning Sheriff Doran placed both Tuttle and Redfield
under arrest and then made a careful search of the premises. The
three suspicious-looking strangers who were camped in front of the
house had disappeared. We found a number of suspicious articles,
among other things a United States mail sack. After the arrests
it was decided that Pete Gabriel should continue the pursuit of
Red Jack, while the rest of the party should return to Florence
with the two prisoners, and take in on the way Frank Carpenter,
who had in the meantime been apprehended at Mesaville and
arrested as a member of the gang. On the way down we found at
the mouth of the Arivaipa a portion of the stage harness reins

lost by the robbers. At Dudleyville, Carpenter, who is a nephew of Redfield, gave the latter completely away, as the saying goes. Under-Sheriff Scanland had on his saddle the saddle-bags found at the scene of the robbery, and as soon as Carpenter saw them he turned to Len Redfield and said:

"Len, these fellows have got your saddle-bags!"

"Shut up!" replied Len.

Carpenter evidently did not know that the saddle-bags had been lost.

Sheriff Doran arrived in Florence with the prisoners, and they were brought before Judge Thomas for examination. There was sufficient evidence to convict all three of the prisoners as soon as it could be collected. Joe Tuttle is one of the principals in the crime, and Redfield and Carpenter are accessories. There are two other parties known to be connected with it, Red Jack and Charley Hensley, still at large. It is probable that others are connected with the crime, as the men mentioned belong to a regularly or ganized band of criminals, making their headquarters at Hensley's and Redfield's. Sheriff Doran, accompanied by Packer and Brent detectives, left last night with the intention of capturing Hensley. Pete Gabriel, accompanied by Bob Hatch and others, has also turned back this way in pursuit of Hensley and Red Jack.

The Tucson *Star's* Florence correspondent gives the following description of the captured stage robbers now in confinement there:

"Len Redfield was not locked up when first brought down here, but on information furnished the detectives since, he has been incarcerated with the others. Although somewhat self-possessed and showing more nerve than the others he can not conceal the deep anxiety under which he is suffering.

Carpenter is a tall, very slim young man, with a high prominent forehead, restless hazel eyes, thin lips, rather thin features, the lower part of the face being covered with a thin straggling, dun-colored growth of beard. His hair has a stand up, Andrew Jackson-like tendency, and he has the general 'Look-out-for-me, I'm-a-comin'!' air of a would-be desperado.

Old Joe Tuttle is the worst broken-up criminal that I ever laid my eyes on. The appearance of conscious guilt, and hor rible forboding of impending doom in his case, is marked and unmistakable. His limbs tremble, his pale blue, restless eyes wander from his nerveless hands to the floor, and he never looks anyone in the face. Two or three times he has lately given way to fits of crying and sobbing like a child. He is an old, gray-haired man of 55 years, with long aquiline nose, heavy, overhanging brow, narrow retreating forehead, and generally forbidding features."

The remains of Johnny Collins, [the Wells-Fargo messenger ·ho had been killed in the holdup] were brought down to Florence nd the Coroner held an inquest at which the following testi- ιoney was taken and verdict rendered:

Watson Humphrey, the driver, testified:

On the evening of the 10th of this month I left Riverside station to go to Globe. After leaving Riverside I crossed the river, and about a mile above Putnam's postoffice was fired into—the first I knew anything was wrong. The messenger, Johnny Collins, was killed at the first shot. He received other shots after that. I think the first shot was fatal. He fell against me, slid down along my left leg, and lay prostrate across the boot, face downward. I should have said we were fired into from both sides. Then I spoke to the man on the left who had ceased firing. The man on the right was still firing at me:

"For God's sake don't shoot any more! You've killed a man already. What more do you want"

He ceased firing at me, and then shot my off-wheel horse and off-leader, stripped the harness off my near-lead horse, and then led him back and tied him to the side of the wagon. The man on the left, who shot the messenger, then discovered a passenger, Felix Le Blanc, inside the coach, ordered him out, and told him to drop his money; and then told him to throw the treasure-box out, saying:

"You son-of-a-b——h, if you don't throw it out I'll shoot you!"

They called me the same name and ordered me to help them. We tried, but found it hard work, and wanted to move

Collins' body on to the ground, out of the way. The robber called us "sons-of-b——s," and said if we didn't get the bo out they would shoot us. We finally got it out, after hard work. They then made Le Blanc drag the box partly back o the wagon in the shade. It was moonlight. They then made Le Blanc take a hatchet they provided and break open th box. Then they drove us toward Globe, and said if w attempted to return to the station they would shoot us. W went up the road some two and a half miles and waited unti the buckboard came down, and held them there till morning and then came back to the place of assassination and rob bery. We found one horse dead, one mortally wounded, and one gone. One horse was all right. We took the harness of the dead horse and hauled him off the road; took the leader from the buckboard and unharnessed the wounded horse backed the stage around, placed the messenger's dead bod and the treasure-box in the buckboard, put the leaders on the wagon and returned to the station. We prepared the body the best we could and sent it in to Florence. It seemed to me five or six shots were fired on the messenger's side. I can count five on my side, three at me and two at the horses One shot cut my whip-stock in two, one raked my leg a little above the knee. I saw only two robbers. I did not know either of them. I can describe them only in height. I should judge the one on the messenger's side was five feet three and the other taller, rather slim, over six feet high. Don' think I could recognize the voices. They spoke plain English Can't tell whether they wore masks or not. The man on my side had a rifle. The body was still on the boot when I ar rived there in the morning. I have heard that Collins wa born in Virginia. He gave his age to me as twenty-three.

[*The testimony of the passenger, Felix Le Blanc, supported tha of Humphrey, the driver, in all essential points.*]

The remains of Collins were brought in on the buckboard and buried in the Florence cemetery. . . . In his mother's last lette to him she wrote that she had a presentiment that something ter rible was going to happen to him if he did not quit running as messenger, and urged him to resign the position.

Public sentiment was running high, unanimously in favor of hanging the robbers, and it was decided that as soon as it was positively known who the guilty ones were, they should be taken out; given a fair trial before a citizens' committee, and then promptly executed. . . .

*A later issue of the* Florence *Enterprise continues:*

On Monday morning about five o'clock, Deputy U.S. Marshal Evans arrived in Florence from Tucson with a posse of seven men, and accompanied by Len Redfield's brother Hank. Evans was armed with a writ issued by Judge Pinney, commanding him to remove Len Redfield to Phoenix for safekeeping, word having reached Tucson of the unrest and talk of a lynching bee at Florence. It was the plan to secure the prisoner and depart with him before daylight. The district attorney at Florence telegraphed Judge Pinney asking him to suspend the order as the people of the town were arming and would hang the prisoners should Marshal Evans attempt to take Len Redfield from the jail. The judge made no reply.

As soon as the presence of the marshal from Tucson, and the knowledge of his purpose became known to a few of the citizens, the alarm was given which spread rapidly and aroused the people to the highest pitch of indignation. It was finally determined that Len Redfield should not be permitted to leave the town alive. Later in the morning the business men closed their stores and every able-bodied man in the town quietly shouldered his gun and repaired to the courthouse and jail. Several guards were stationed at strategic places in order to repel any attempt that might be made by the Tucson posse to interfere, although the Tucson men, realizing the futility of their mission, were not to be found in the vicinity.

The main body of the citizens' force, numbering nearly a hundred, filed into the jail yard. They took Deputy Scanland and his assistant prisoner, and placed them under guard. They were then searched for the jail keys, and the key to the outside door was found. The jail was opened and Joe Tuttle and Len Redfield were quietly taken out into the corridor and hung.

The ropes were thrown over the braces between the joists. Although strangled they both died without a struggle. Redfield was game. When the men went into the cell to bring him out, he coolly looked around and said, "Who is the leader of this gang?" And as the rope was placed around his neck he remarked, "Well, boys, I guess my time has come." Tuttle broke down completely when the men entered his cell. He placed his hands over his face and sobbed, "Let me talk; give me time to talk!"

"You didn't give poor Collins time to talk and we will serve you the same way," replied one of the men. This ended it. After the two men were hanged young Carpenter was brought out of his cell and told to look at his uncle and Tuttle and take warning of their fate, that he was young yet and could turn from his course and make a man of himself. He was pale as a ghost when brought from his cell but recovered when assured that he would not be hanged. He desired to make a statement about his connection with Red Jack and was ordered to proceed, but he talked about everything else except his connection with Red Jack and was ordered back into his cell.

The crowd guarded the hanging men till a physician pronounced them dead; then the committee disbanded and went about their business as though nothing had happened.

Out of the hundred men engaged in the lynching not one was under the influence of liquor and the work was done in the most orderly and quiet way possible. Not a loud or harsh word was spoken, and the people outside the jail yard hadn't the slightest idea that any hanging was taking place, although they knew the jail yard was full of armed men. Even the officers in the jail building did not know the men had been hung for twenty minutes after the work had been done. One man, who came down to take a hand in the hanging and arrived on the ground after the citizen party had gone into the jail yard and closed the doors behind them stood with the guards outside for half an hour after the men had been hanged, totally unconscious of what had taken place, and finally becoming disgusted with the supposed failure of the citizens to come to time, he shouldered his gun and marched off, saying, "D——d if I am going to wait here any longer; they ain't going to do anything; they ain't got sand enough to hang anybody."

As soon as it became generally known among the Spanish population that the robbers had been hanged, hundreds of Mexican men and women flocked to the jail to see the dead bandits, and to convince themselves that they had really been hanged. It had been the common complaint among the Spanish population that none but Mexicans and Indians could be hanged here and they could hardly believe that they were mistaken, till they gazed upon the evidence of the fact.

An inquest was held over the bodies. The verdict of the jury was that the men came to their death by being hanged by persons to the jury unknown. After the inquest the coroner had the bodies taken down and laid out, and Marshal Evans telegraphed to Hank Redfield, at Tucson, informing him of the fate of his brother and asking him what disposition should be made of the body. The answer was: "Send it to Tucson." The remains of Tuttle were buried after sundown in the cemetery at Florence.

Following up the points made in a confession by Tuttle, Detective Thacker, Sheriff Doran and Dan Stevens recovered the $1980 in silver coin, but the gold was lost.

On October 3, according to the Florence Enterprise, Sheriff Paul, of Pima County, obtained a clue as to the whereabouts of Red Jack and Charley Hensley, who were supposed to be near Willcox. He thereupon organized a posse and proceeded to Willcox by an engine furnished by the railroad company. After obtaining horses and provisions they left Willcox that evening and came upon the robbers near Percy's ranch, twelve miles distant. Firing was opened by both parties at once; in the exchange Red Jack was killed, being riddled with balls. Hensley was badly wounded but escaped toward Point of Mountain with six well-mounted and armed men in pursuit. Not one of the posse was seriously injured, although one received a slight flesh wound in the ankle.

Next morning Hensley met the same fate that had befallen Red Jack the night before. He was found by the Sheriff's posse near Point of Mountain, ten miles from Willcox, lying in a gulch. He had been wounded in the breast and abdomen the night before. He fired three shots at Sheriff Paul, shooting the Sheriff's horse from under him. Hensley was game to the last, shooting as long as he was able to pull a trigger. Both Hensley and Red Jack had declared their determination only three nights previously never to be taken alive but to fight to the death.

Frank Carpenter, the remaining member of the gang, had been released on bail, but before he was brought to trial his death was reported, in November, 1883. It is said that he died from nervous prostration occasioned by the fright he received while in the jail at Florence.

Thus ended another bloody episode in Arizona's turbulent frontier history.

The stations of Dudleyville and Mesaville, often mentioned in the account above, were neighboring stage stops on the road which branched south from a junction a few miles east of Riverside, off the Florence-Globe stage road. This road led toward Tombstone and the Mexican border. Mesaville, which is no longer in existence, is not to be confused with the present lively city of Mesa, sixteen miles east of Phoenix.

## THE BISBEE MASSACRE

Along in November, 1883, six men, John (Johnny) Heith, Omer W. (Red) Sample, William E. (Billy) Delaney, Dan (Big Dan) Dowd, Daniel (Yorky) Kelly and James (Tex) Howard, were in and about Clifton. They were men without regular occupation, and were generally considered bad in example if not in deed.

On the morning of the 27th of November, Heith, an old saloon keeper at Clifton, went to a saloon opposite a residence which he said he had purchased, and handing the proprietor a key, asserted:

"That is my home across the street, and I expect my wife here in a few days. I am going out with the boys, to be gone a short time. When I come back I will have plenty of money, and don't you forget it."

Heith and Tex Howard left Clifton the same day together. According to Heith's own evidence, he ran across Sample, Dowd and Kelly, out of Clifton some ten or fifteen miles. They journeyed to Bucklin's ranch. There they met Delaney, who at that time was going under the name of Johnson. They knew him to be escaping from Clifton for having killed three men in a saloon brawl a few months previous. Having become desperate, he was only too glad to join the gang. While at Bucklin's they conspired to take in Bisbee. It was understood, after the preliminary arrangements were made, that Tex and Heith should proceed to that town first and gather points. The other four men were to remain at Bucklin's camp, or somewhere in the near vicinity. Heith guaranteed to pay all the expenses of the crowd.

Heith and Tex then went to Bisbee, and put up at the same hotel, and fed their horses at the same corral. Heith, upon entering there, pretended to be looking for a business opening. After some apparent investigation he entered into partnership with a man by the name of Wade. They were to start a dance hall. Heith made strenuous efforts to open it by the 8th of December. On that day the Copper Queen Mining Company paid the monthly wages of the men they had employed. It was customary at that time and for a long time previous, for the general merchandise and banking firm of Castaneda & Co., of Bisbee, to cash the checks of the miners. These papers were drawn on San Francisco, and of course, the above firm demanded a discount for profit.

Just before payday, Castaneda & Co. placed a sufficient sum in hard money in their safe to meet these profitable demands. This Tex and Heith learned, and upon this information they acted. Tex was immediately dispatched to Bucklin's ranch, thirty-five miles distant, to tell the other to be on hand on December 8th, and that they were expected to take in the store of Castaneda & Co.

Heith only opened the dance hall to draw the crowds of hard-working miners from the streets, so that his colleagues in crime, summoned by him from the ranch, could accomplish their purpose without much molestation.

When Tex Howard was dispatched upon his errand to Bucklin's

ranch, it was his intention, pursuant to orders from Heith, to continue his journey to Clifton. There he was to remain until the theft, and murders if necessary, had been accomplished, and then from that point to give succor, in the way of provisions and assistance to the other participants, when they escaped from Bisbee. It was agreed that Heith should remain in his temporary dance house and saloon, and, the day after, to enter into presumably active search for the criminals. He believed that he had the cunning to lead the authorities from the right track of the fugitives, and thereby allow the latter to get to a place of safety.

However, Tex, before leaving Bisbee, heard that Deputy Sheriff Daniels had said that he suspected Tex of being one of the Gage train robbers, the prevalent theory being that the same gang recently robbed the Southern Pacific train at Gage station, near Deming, New Mexico. This made Tex mad, and he swore he would return to the town with the gang and make Daniels suffer by taking a hand in the Bisbee onslaught.

The gang left the camp in a body, and stopped on the fatal morning of December 7th, three miles from Bisbee. People passing at the time very definitely identified Kelly and Dowd, during their trial, as being in the camp.

Tex Howard, as agent for Heith, arranged the plans that were carried out that night. At seven o'clock of the evening of the 8th, five of as bad characters as were ever known to border civilization, rode along up the main street of Bisbee.

According to plans, Kelly, Howard and Sample entered Castaneda's store, leaving Dowd and Delaney outside. It is understood that the latter two were to order every person passing in close proximity to the store to enter it. When they had taken their agreed positions, a scene occurred which has few parallels in the history of frontier fatalities.

Inside the store stood Tex Howard with a revolver in each hand, and compelling the few customers he found there to keep their hands above their heads and utter not a word. Every man or woman passing was forced into the store by Dowd and Delaney, and were obliged to acquiesce to Howard's demands or suffer death. In the meantime Kelly had ordered the clerk of the store to open the safe. He took all the cash therein found. Sample in the same few moments was robbing Castaneda who, lying sick in a back room, was unable to defend himself.

While the last-mentioned three men were holding at bay a dozen persons in the building and robbing the premises, the work of death was proceeding without. Delaney seemed bent upon killing somebody, and kept up a continual fire. The first fatal ball struck Deputy Sheriff D. T. Smith, who approaching the two men announced his office and ordered them to keep the peace. This ball, it was later proven, was fired by Dowd. Johnny Tappenier and a man named Nolly were also shot dead for not wishing to enter the store as directed. Mrs. Roberts, who was watching the terrible scene from a doorway across the street, was struck dead by a stray bullet. She was eight months with a child.

The two men in the store accomplished their part of the business in a few minutes, and passing out, mounted horses, and with the rest of the gang rapidly left town, firing indiscriminately as they went.

Heith, the man who planned the murder and robbery, during the exciting time stood smiling behind the bar of his dance hall, endeavoring by his generous hospitality to keep all in who were there, and draw all he could from the streets.

Leaving Bisbee with only about $3,000 and some jewelry, the gang proceeded eastward till they reached Soldier's Hole. Here they divided their booty, Dowd and Delaney going into Sonora, and Howard, Kelly and Sample turning to the north, bound for Clifton.

A sheriff's posse under Deputy Daniels followed their trail thus far, guided by Heith and one Frost. The two latter here left the posse and came to Tombstone, where they were arrested on suspicion, although Frost was discharged on examination.

Passing through the Chiricahua Mountains they [Howard, Kelly, and Sample] were discovered in camp near Galeyville, about three days after the raid, and given chase by U.S. Deputy Marshal Saunders, of Deming. In his posse were J. M. Wilkins and A. Guzman, of Tucson, who happened to be in Galeyville on business at the time. The three robbers escaped in a snow storm. Saunders mistook them for the Gage train robbers for whom they were looking.

Continuing their way north they left Kelly at the railroad, who stole a ride to Deming on a freight train. Immediately on his arrival he was arrested on the supposition of being a train robber, but was subsequently turned over to Sheriff Ward on December 11th.

Sample and Howard, on their arrival at Clifton, told their mistresses the whole story of the Bisbee raid, and showed their spoils. They then left Clifton and camped in a box canyon about forty miles above the town, where they were captured by a sheriff's posse, on December 17th, under Deputies Hovey and Hill. The posse had proceeded in the canyon about three miles, when suddenly they came upon and surprised the robbers' camp in which Sample was sitting, cleaning two rifles and two revolvers, with not a cartridge in any of them. On him was found a hunting case gold watch, with William Clancey's name on the inside and the initials W. C. on the outside; and about $200 in money. On Howard was found $160; $50 of which was in Mexican dollars and halves. Sample had a bullet wound in the back, received from the posse who fired at him in the Chiricahua Mountains. At the time of the Bisbee raid the parties took two gold watches from Castaneda's store. They had been left there and the party leaving them had taken a minute description of them, which he subsequently gave to Deputy Sheriff Bob Hatch.

When Dowd and Delaney left their three companions at Soldier's Hole, they turned into Sonora, and traveled together as far as Bavispe. Here Delaney left Dowd, and went to Magdalena where he was recognized. He pretended to be seeking work, and was directed to Minas Prietas, where many miners were at work. The superintendent was instructed to give him work, and thus detain him till his arrest could be made, which was effected about January 15th.

Meanwhile Deputy Sheriff Daniels got on their track and arrived at Bavispe just one hour after Dowd had left to cross the Sierra Madre for Janos. Daniels followed on alone through a perilous Indian country. Arriving at Janos he found Dowd had just gone to Corralitos. He went there and by the help of the superintendent of the mines there arrested Dowd on New Year's day. He was driven to a station on the Mexican Central Railroad called San José, a distance of 110 miles from Corralitos. Here

Dowd was locked in an express car and brought on to American soil without the formalities of red tape.

The prisoners were incarcerated in the Tombstone jail. On February 8th, they were indicted. All excepting Heith were placed on trial, he having demanded and was granted a separate hearing. On the 11th of the same month the five were convicted of murder in the first degree. Their counsel applied for a new trial. This was denied, and on February 20th they were sentenced to death.

Judge Pinney, in sentencing them, said they were to be pitied rather than abused that they should so far forget their duty to their country and their God, so far forget the teachings of Christian mothers as to permit themselves to be lost to humanity and society, to become so lost to everything human and decent as to commit the heinous crime of which they were convicted. He concluded:

> It is indeed a pitiable sight—pitiable to see men in the very prime of life and physical vigor, so utterly destitute of moral courage, such very cowards in life as to be willing to resort to robbery to gain money, thereby acknowledging their inability to stand the test of manhood, which requires long, faithful and honest endeavor. It is this quiet, persistent test that shows manhood and moral courage. As men grow weaker and weaker, in these, they resort to illegitimate means of obtaining money, till finally they so far forget their manhood as to murder their fellow men, in the most cowardly manner, for the purpose of gaining a few dollars. The act has not the least spark of bravery or of nerve; on the other hand, it is but the act of braggadocio—the arrant coward. Their act will cost in the end nine lives, four by their cowardly rifles and five by the vengeance of the noose. [*Little did the judge realize that within a few days another life by violence would be added to the frightful toll, with the lynching of Heith.*]
>
> It is not a pleasant duty for any man placed in my position to pronounce the sentence which the law imposes. Nothing that I could say would aid you here. It only involves upon me to perform the last act that can be performed here. The sentence of the court is that you be taken hence to the county

jail and there confined until the 28th day of March, 1884, and on that day between the hours of ten o'clock in the forenoon and five o'clock in the afternoon, each of you be hanged by the neck until you are dead.

Heith's trial followed. Strangely, the verdict in his case was in the second degree. He was sentenced to prison for life. This occurred on February 21st. At an early hour next morning about one hundred men, principally miners from the Contention and Grand Central mines, which had been shut down, went to the courthouse. Selecting seven of their number from Bisbee, they went to the door leading to the jail, and rapped for admittance, the remainder of the crowd staying outside. It was about the hour when breakfast is brought to the prisoners and the jailer, Billy Ward, thinking it was a man with food, opened the door without looking to see who his visitors were. Instantly he was covered with weapons, and a demand was made of him for the keys of the jail. Seeing resistance was useless he quietly gave them up and a party proceeded to enter Heith's cell and unshackling him, brought him into the corridor of the jail. It was the first intention to hang him to the bannister of the stairs leading to the second story, but this plan was abandoned and the crowd started for the telegraph line at the lower edge of town.

At the door of the courthouse they were met by Sheriff Ward who, throwing up his hands, exclaimed with a show of authority, "Stop this! You have got to stop this right here!" Before he could realize what had happened, he was picked up and thrown down the steps and the crowd proceeded with the prisoner down Toughnut Street until reaching a certain place selected for the execution. The trip from the jail to the point mentioned was made on a run, Heith keeping in the lead. Arriving at the place Heith pulled a handkerchief from his pocket and said, "Boys, you are hanging an innocent man, and you will find it out before those other men are hung. Tie this handkerchief over my eyes. I am not afraid to die. I have one favor to ask; that you will not mutilate my body by shooting into it after I am hung."

His eyes were bandaged as desired, and in a moment his body was dangling at the end of a rope from the cross bar on the telegraph pole. Heith throughout showed great nerve, and had it not been for the absolute certainty of his guilt, his life would probably have been spared. No attempt was made to molest the other prisoners under sentence of death, the community waiting to see them legally hanged.

—Tucson *Citizen*, 1884

*In the Phoenix* Herald *in* 1884 *was this item:*
The coroner's jury found a verdict that Heith came to his death in Tombstone on the 22nd of February, 1884, from the effects of emphysema of the lungs, which might have been—and probably was—caused by strangulation, self-inflicted or otherwise, as in accordance with the medical evidence.

A placard was posted on the telegraph pole where Heith was found suspended and dead, bearing the following inscription:

JOHN HEITH
was hanged to this pole by the
Citizens of Cochise County
for participation in the Bisbee massacre
as a proved accessory
At 8:20 A.M. February 22, 1884
(Washington's Birthday)
ADVANCE, ARIZONA!

*The Tucson* Citizen *representative commissioned to report in full on the hanging of the Bisbee murderers, wrote:*
The chief topic of conversation on the streets [of *Tombstone*] is the legal tragedy of next Friday. This is a matter of no wonder when it is known that a particular occurrence is to take place on the 28th, never before superceded in the history of this country, namely the hanging of five men at the same scaffold, simultaneously. This alone would subject a people to unusual excitement, but in taking into consideration the brutal and fatal foray upon a small frontier town, the murder of four respectable citizens, and the robbery of a mercantile house, it is astonishing that such excitement does not turn into a panic, far beyond the powers of officials to control.

There have been, and are still at this writing, grave rumors of trouble. There is a desire, among a certain class of people here, to have the hanging public, in open view of everybody whose morbid curiosity, or other interests, might tempt them to attend. This, certainly, under the circumstances, would have been wrong, as the sheriff stated, the criminals had friends in the vicinity, and if it became known to such parties that there was to be a public hanging, they would be liable to create bloodshed, in attempting in a body, and by a sudden attack to rescue the murderers. Such men must be kept away from the scene by high, strong walls.

Another rumor was rife—the disposition for a public hanging was so great, especially among the miners, that a threat had been made that just before the hour of putting the doomed men upon the scaffold, the walls of the jail yard would be shattered by explosives. As the hanging was to occur that Friday according to law, there would be no time to rebuild the barrier, and consequently the exhibition would be public.

There was still another fear in the minds of the reflective citizens. Although Sheriff Ward proposed to see that no one entering the jail yard to witness the execution could carry firearms, a speculative citizen was erecting, on private grounds within a few feet of the walls, an elaborate structure, upon which he proposed to seat 600 people. Of course he intended to charge them a big fee for a seat. The walls surrounding the jail yard being thirteen feet high, in order to support his 600 at that elevation, and higher too, he would have to use some very strong supports. And then there was the possibility of a fatal crash. This, however, was not the primary cause of anxiety. The murderers, having friends, a man would quite naturally prefer being shot than hung. What if such friends, and good shots, should select front seats on this platform, and just before the drop plant well aimed bullets through the bodies of the Bisbee desperadoes? . . . .

The scaffold was completed and tried the day before the hanging was to take place, and pronounced by experts to be one of the strongest ever erected in the Territory. The platform, eight feet from the ground, was twenty-four feet long and fourteen feet wide, with a five-foot drop. It should excite the admiration of the most experienced hangman. . . .

Sheriff Ward stated that after their sentence the prisoners had been furnished with extra rations. Besides receiving the usual food allowed the county prisoners, they were supplied with fruits, cigars and liquors, the latter, of course, not to superfluity. Their allowance in this respect was three drinks of whiskey per day. The only complaint they ever made was that the sheriff had covered them with too many irons. This was merely a security he was bound to adhere to. He purchased for each of the doomed five a broadcloth suit and white shirts—burial garments. He was bothered continually by applicants for passes to the jail yard, though all the cards printed had been disposed of, numbering a thousand.

Calling upon the sheriff for permission to interview the prisoners, the courteous official answered: "Why certainly, but it is of no use. They won't speak to reporters. You will not get a word out of them."

"Well, let me try, please." A knock on the outer, iron-girdled door brought the question, "Who is there?" The reply, "Ward," caused the inner door in the same cell to open an inch. The eye of a keeper peeped through. Recognizing the sheriff, both doors were opened, and the officer and the interviewer passed within. Another grated barrier was unlocked before a look could be had into the corridor to which the cells of the doomed men opened. The reporter waited while the sheriff gave orders to let two men, confined in one cell, out into the corridor. A lever from without was turned, a cell door flew open and out stepped two strongly built, broad-shouldered and ruddy-faced men. Neither could have been over thirty years old, and neither was less than five feet ten in height. Stepping to the corridor grating they laughingly asked, "Well, what is it?"

The sheriff informed this reporter that the two men standing there were Tex Howard and Billy Delaney. Then facing them he said, "Here is a reporter who wishes to talk with you."

Fearing an immediate retreat of the desperadoes, I quickly said, "Boys, I am from Tucson, not Tombstone. I would like to publish what you have to say in the *Citizen* there, and promise you faithfully not to misrepresent your remarks in any manner; and also that nothing will be printed until after Friday."

This seeming to satisfy them, Delaney was asked his opinion regarding the lynching of Heith. "I don't know anything about

Heith! I tell you I never saw him from November 27th until he came to jail. He oughtn't to be hung anyhow."

"What have you to say about yourself?" Delaney replied, "I can say we hadn't a square trial. If we had we wouldn't be here. I am innocent."

"You remember that Castaneda stated that he lost something like $1,000 from his safe. That money has never been found. Do you wish to tell where it is?"

"I don't know anything about the money," exclaimed Delaney. And then Howard who stood near interrupted by saying: "The man that's got the money knows where 'tis."

Delaney being asked how he felt over his approaching execution, answered: "No man will stand up better than I." At this juncture Dan Kelly, who was locked in a cell called out: "Tell him how the lawyers defended us." Howard replied: "Didn't defend us at all." In reply to a question, Howard said his family did not know where he was and would never know. The subject of the trial again coming up, Delaney said that if everything was as fair in the proceedings as Judge Pinney's charge, they would have been all right. "He might have done better!" exclaimed Howard. "By the way," interrupted Delaney, "The jury had a lot of Mormons on. How many? Six, anyhow, and you bet, when some witness said I had a horse with a Mormon brand on it, that hung me sure. Why, I don't even know how to steal a horse!" "Yes," added Howard, "nary witness told the truth. The whole evidence was false, and the jury was no better."

This ended the conversation with Delaney and Howard. It was evident to the reporter from the first that the men were not ready to make any honest confessions as to the parts they took in the Bisbee affair. If they had been on a spring picnic they would not have been more contented. Laughing and joking continually, it seemed incomprehensible that the two men were on the verge of the grave. They seemed as reckless of death as they were proven to be of the law. Before the reporter had been with them five minutes, they took advantage of what they considered their condescension to be interviewed by calling upon the sheriff for whiskey.

Kelly, Sample and Dowd were then released from their cells, and the corridor contained the five. All excepting Dowd wanted to engage in irrelevant talk at one time. The latter was quiet, and the reporter only ventured to ask him if Dowd was his right name. He answered, "Well, that's what I'm known by here, and no one will know any other while I live."

"Kelly was quite talkative. He said that Heith was wrongfully hung. He left Heith November 26th in the Chiricahua Mountains. "How will I hang? Well, I will walk up. The sheriff will not have to carry me, and if I hang as brave as I walk I'm all right." He said he had no relations, but being more closely questioned he said he had some in the old country. He said: "I only left there two years ago." This made the sheriff laugh.

Continuing the conversation himself, he said he believed Judge Pinney appointed as able counsel as could be procured. Howard snapped: "But the jury?" They all expressed contempt for the jury. Delaney said: "If the jury had not hung us, the jury would have been hung."

Sample was the last man to speak. "No," said he, "I believe Heith was hung wrong. He never put up the job with me to rob Bisbee. The fact is Howard and I were together, and if the court had given us time we would have procured two witnesses to prove that we were many miles from Bisbee from 7 o'clock of December 8th to 9 o'clock the next day."

What was said of the manners and appearance of Delaney and Howard, will also describe the last three interviewed. They were boisterous and apparently little in earnest. Kelly was the only pale-faced man in the party, and his tongue made up for that. The reporter seeing that further questioning would not bring facts, told the prisoners he would call next day, and then perhaps they would have more to say, as their execution would be nearer at hand. "No! no! Come tomorrow morning. We don't want to see you at night!" exclaimed three of the party as the reporter passed out. "Well, young man," said the sheriff, "you are the first reporter they have allowed to interview them since they were sentenced."

—Tucson, *Citizen*, 1884

*At nine o'clock on the morning of the execution, the Tucson* Star *reporter was granted an interview with the doomed men, which he recorded as follows:*

William Delaney in answer to questions put to him, replied in detail:

"I have no particular objection to talking. I might as well occupy the time now, as I will not have much opportunity in the future. I was born on July 11, 1856, in Scranton, Pa. But I was supposed to have left Harrisburg under suspicion of a murder, of which I am innocent. I have lived in this Territory for four years, prospecting and mining. I have been indicted in Graham County for shooting a man through the heart, who interfered with a quarrel between a Mexican woman and myself, but I am entirely innocent of this crime, and we are victims of men who procured our arrest on account of our bad reputations, in order to receive the rewards offered. This is an unfortunate circumstance, and I am no more guilty than you are. I was not a particular friend of John Heith, and only knew him for a few months. He never put up a job with me to raid Bisbee, and as far as I know, had nothing to do with the affair. I believe he was hanged in the wrong. I have been told that the public expect us to weaken on the scaffold. You see how we act now, and at the last we will die brave. Although our knees may buckle a little. I think we will not make any speech on the scaffold. I am glad the miners tore down the platform outside of the jail yard that was to give so many people a free exhibition. Five hundred men sitting up there, in addition to eight hundred in the yard would make us a little shaky."

At this juncture Delaney remarked with considerable animation, "We had a good breakfast this morning, and we got away with it," to which Sample replied, "Yes, you bet we filled ourselves, but we are liable to buck when we get there."

Delaney is a short, well built man about five feet, four inches in height; he has clear, intelligent eyes, black hair, a well developed forehead, and expresses himself in gentlemanly language. Dan Kelly is twenty-five years of age, five feet, six inches in height, and of a very dark complexion. He would not give the name of his native state. Omer W. Sample, a native of Missouri, is twenty-four years old, six feet, one inch in height, and is a splendid specimen of physical manhood, but of brutal countenance. He has been suffering from a gun-shot wound in the side. Tex Howard is twenty-four years old, and was born in Texas. He has an intelligent, manly face, and has been called "Handsome Tex." Howard, he says, is an assumed name.

Daniel Dowd is twenty-seven years old and weighs 180 pounds. He has lived in Arizona, and was born, to use his own words, "not far east of this place." He seemed apathetic, and showed traces of great suffering, although he endeavored to bear himself quietly.

Each of the condemned men endorsed in almost identical language the statement of Delaney, that they knew very little of Heith, and believed that he was lynched for a crime of which he was innocent—as innocent as themselves.

Promptly at one o'clock, p.m. the procession to the scaffold moved from the condemned cell, headed by Rev. Fathers Antonio Jouvenceau and Gallagher, and Sheriff Ward. Each prisoner was attended to the gallows by an officer of the law. The caps and nooses were adjusted by Sheriff Paul, of Pima County, and Deputy Sheriff Crowley, of Willcox. Tex Howard and Bill Delaney were cool and composed, and smilingly greeted their numerous acquaintances in the jail yard. Red Sample and Dan Kelly faltered and showed a little nervousness, the former almost losing his muscular control. He managed, however, to speak as follows: "Well, my friends, I bid you goodbye. I am to be hung for a crime I never committed. Heith had nothing to do with the Bisbee murders, and he never put up a job with any of us. I desire a Christian burial, and hope to meet you all in Heaven." Dan Kelly said, "I also desire a Christian burial, and that Father Gallagher shall take charge of our bodies." The rest said, "I say what he says," referring both to Sample and Kelly. There was a pause of a few seconds, when Kelly cried, "Let her loose," and the sheriff immediately followed with, "ready." The drop fell at exactly eighteen minutes after one o'clock.

—Tucson Star, 1884

*By two o'clock the bodies had been cut down and conveyed to the morgue. As all the mines in the area were shut down for the day, as were many of the Tombstone business houses, hundreds thronged to obtain a view of the dead faces of the executed men.*

*Thus, with their burial, ended the final episode of one of the* most fearful and bloody tragedies ever enacted within the borders of Arizona.

Castaneda & Co., the store that was robbed, was also known as Castaneda & Goldwater, Joe Goldwater being in partnership with A. A. Castaneda. Heith's name was often spelled Heath, and Deputy Daniels' name was sometimes spelled Daniel. The spellings used in the account of the Bisbee Massacre are as they appeared in the various newspaper articles used. At that time Tombstone was the county seat; the county seat was removed to Bisbee in 1931.

Footnotes on the Bisbee Massacre, as reprinted in the Prescott Journal in 1884, are of more than passing interest:

Garcia, the Mexican who accompanied the Sheriff in his chase after big Dan Dowd, was found hanging to a tree and his body riddled with bullets near Tombstone. It is supposed to have been the work of Dowd's friends.

Kelly and "Tex," confined in the county jail, awaiting trial, says the Tombstone *Republican*, were temporarily enjoying the freedom of the corridors, when they became involved in an altercation which resulted in their coming to blows. "Tex" was getting the best of the fistics, when the jail officers separated the combatants and locked them up in their respective cells. As they were being separated "Tex" said to Kelly, "I hope they will hang you first, you black-muzzled son-of-a-b——h; I want to see you kick."

A dispatch from Tombstone says that: When the Bisbee murderers were called for sentencing, their attorney moved for a new trial. This would cause a delay of a year before the death penalty could be carried out. The community won't stand this, as the defendants had a fair trial and the proof of their guilt was overwhelming. If the law don't hang them the mob will.

The gallows on which the five Bisbee murderers are to be executed, says the Tombstone *Republican*, is now in course of construction. The gallows frame will be made of 6x8 square timbers, securely framed and braced. The platform clear of the drop is 8x16 feet, and will accommodate about twenty-five or thirty persons. The platform will be about eight feet from the ground, and the cross-beam of the gallows is eight feet above the platform. The drop will be supported by several triggers or bolts. These triggers are attached to a through brace, and will all be drawn back together by means of a heavy weight that will be let drop from the platform. The five men will drop together, and the drop will be sufficient to insure instantaneous and painless death. The party who is building the gallows proposes to have everything work perfectly.

## "ADIOS TODOS AMIGOS!"

It was just past midnight on the 18th of December, 1895, when Paul Becker of Becker & McCormick's store in the mining camp of Morenci, closed the place and went out for a few minutes' recreation before retiring. He left a light burning in the store, where he slept, and he returned a short time later with the intention of going to bed.

Upon entering the store he heard a noise in the back room, which was used as a barroom, and he went back there to investigate. Upon entering the door of the barroom he was confronted by two Mexicans, one with a six-shooter, the other with a large knife. Although unarmed and seeing the gun pointed at him, Becker grabbed it with one hand, and as the other man advanced, he grabbed the knife with the other hand and a struggle for the weapon began, which of course ended by Becker getting the worst of it. The man having the knife pulled it through Becker's hand, cutting it in a fearful manner.

Becker was then at the mercy of the robbers, who after taking from him about $25 in money, two watches and the safe keys, ordered him to open the safe, which he steadfastly refused to do. The gunman pointed the pistol at him and said he would kill him if he did not open the safe. Again Becker grabbed hold of the gun, when the other man plunged the knife into Becker's side.

Thinking they had killed him the two men quickly made their

escape, the way they got in, through a transom at the rear of the store. Becker, with the knife still sticking in his side, went out of the front door and ran around to Short's saloon and, sitting down in a chair, asked a bystander to pull the knife from his side, which he did. Officers were notified, and Becker told the deputy sheriff what had happened.

Early next morning Deputy Sheriff Davis and others trailed the blood stains leading to the house of one Contreras, and when within seventy-five yards of the house, Augustin Chacon, a well-known outlaw, and four others emerged from the house, each carrying a Winchester rifle and a six-shooter. As the officer and his posse approached, the robbers broke out and started up the side of the hill at the rear of the house, firing as they ran.

Pablo Salcido, one of the posse, being acquainted with some of the men in the party (who were assertedly a gang of horse thieves of which Chacon was said to be the leader) started to go up to them to have them surrender. As he started up the hill, one of the gang, supposedly Chacon, rose from behind a rock and shot him through the head. The fight continued and Chacon was wounded and captured. Two of the bandits were killed, while the others escaped through the hilly terrain in the excitement.

Chacon was tried in Solomonville in June and sentenced to be hanged on July 24, 1896. His lawyers appealed and the case was taken to the Supreme Court and in January, 1897, the decision and judgement of the lower court was affirmed.

In the meantime, after the appeal was granted, Chacon was taken to the Tucson jail for safe keeping as it was rumored that friends would make an attempt to rescue him from the Solomonville jail, this town being the county seat [of Graham County]. He then was brought back to Solomonville for re-sentencing after the case was affirmed. When brought before the judge the prisoner talked freely with the guards and in the course of a conversation he remarked that he had never seen anything yet that he was afraid of, but that he had never tackled the gallows before.

June 18th, 1897 was the new date set for the execution. When Judge Rouse passed the death sentence on Chacon the court-room was well filled and many people were standing, all trying to get a glimpse of Chacon's face, Chacon, the notorious outlaw they had

heard so much about on account of his many escapades on both
sides of the Mexican border. But if they were expecting him to
show any signs of emotion, they were badly disappointed. He
slowly stroked his black mustache and bowed in assent. Chacon was
a powerfully built man, tall, with thick, heavy shoulders, good form
and very erect. He wore gray woolen pants, blue woolen shirt, no
suspenders; gray canvas shoes tipped with tan or russet-colored
leather. His mustache was short and thick; eyebrows heavy, prominent and lowering, covering small black, piercing, restless eyes.
His nose was straight. He had a heavy head of hair, coal black with
few gray hairs. His age was about forty-one.

Chacon, after the re-sentencing, was remanded to the officers and
again placed in the jail at Solomonville. An appeal was made before Governor Franklin for a commutation to imprisonment for
life at Yuma prison and Chacon's lawyers presented a petition
signed by many influential citizens of Graham County, who
thought the sentence too severe. Among those signing the petition
were several members of the jury who found Chacon guilty. The
jurors said that they would not have returned a verdict of guilty
if they had known that Judge Rouse, the trial judge, intended to
sentence the man to be hanged. They said their verdict was accompanied by a recommendation of mercy.

Less than a week before the execution date, District Attorney
Jones received a letter from the Governor in which it was stated
that the Executive had made careful examination of the Chacon
case and had refused to commute his sentence to life imprisonment.

But Chacon was gone. On that very day, early in the morning,
when a jail trusty entered the sheriff's office to sweep, he noticed
a hole through the partition wall next to the jail large enough to
throw a dog through. He at once notified Jailer Burkner and an
examination showed that Chacon had made his escape. The wall
through which the hole was made was ten inches through, thick
adobe lined, on the inside, with a double layer of two-inch pine
boards behind that, spiked together with five inch spikes. Some
kind of a small saw had been used to get through the boards, when
the adobe was easy work. Jailers Reaves and Burkner had charge
of the jail and its contents at the time. Reaves was sleeping in the

empty cell at the west end of the jail, while Burkner was sleeping in a little office opposite the cell occupied by Chacon. In cutting the hole considerable noise must have been made; a board two inches thick and twelve inches wide and eighteen inches long was first sawed from the wall. The board was pried out, pulling the large spikes with it, and necessarily would make considerable noise. The next layer of boards ran up and down the wall and they were similarly removed.

It was thought some of Chacon's friends or confederates must have slipped him a small file and a short iron bar. He had been visited by some lady relatives a few days prior to his escape, with whom he was allowed to converse for a considerable time, although there was no appparent cause for suspicion on this occasion. It was understood that the jail had not been examined for some time prior to the escape, and that in Chacon's bed was found a long, three-cornered file. The escape, like all previous ones from that jail, was possible only because no guard was on active duty at night. The jail was notoriously unsafe and any prisoner not watched could easily break out of it. Chacon was heavily ironed at the time of his escape and it appeared almost miraculous how he managed to accomplish the feat undetected.

—Composite of newspaper accounts, 1895-97

*The Phoenix* Republican, *in commenting in 1897 on Chacon's escape, said:*

The prospect of a hanging in Graham County is not quite so flattering as it was on Wednesday, when Governor Franklin refused to commute the sentence of Augustin Chacon to life imprisonment. The governor received a telegram from District Attorney Jones saying that Chacon had escaped from jail the night before. He cut his way out of the adobe structure by means of a saw which an admiring confederate on the outside had passed in to him. The chances are many to one that Chacon will never be taken. He is a Chihuahua Mexican, as most of the Mexicans about Clifton and Morenci are. There is a continual passage between that part of the country and Chihuahua, Mexico.

Whoever may be to blame for the escape, Chacon certainly was not. There are several things that contributed to his departure. It is said there is a sentiment in Graham County amounting almost to a religious fervor, against hanging. The jail is the most insecure in the Territory. Chacon in deference to the sentiment of the community on the subject of capital punishment and probably holding antagonistic views himself, naturally took his departure, having been informed that the governor meant to do nothing for him. His precipitate going just at that particular time is regarded as an exhibition of bad taste on the part of himself and those who were supposed to be engaged in guarding him. If he had remained in jail, say a week, he would still have had time to get away before the date of his execution. Public opinion would not then have been so sharply drawn to the coincidence of his flight and the governor's refusal to exercise executive clemency. The governor received a letter yesterday from Judge Rouse, who had sentenced him (Chacon) to be hanged. The judge writes that at the time he imposed the sentence, he believed death would fit his crime. Since then he is of the opinion that the sentence was too harsh, but when the case came back, affirmed from the supreme court, he was unable to mitigate the punishment in resentencing him.

Before the governor received Judge Rouse's letter he got the telegram informing him that Chacon was beyond the need of gubernatorial mercy. His escape has also likely estopped the *habeas corpus* proceedings which his attorney was going to begin at Tucson yesterday, for what is the use of a *habeas corpus* when the corpus is roaming about, nobody knows where or whither?

This is not Chacon's first escape from jail. A year ago he walked away one evening, just before dark. The officers went about the vicinity making inquiry for him. The inquiry developed into a hunt in which many public-spirited citizens joined. Among them was W. B. Kelly of the *Bulletin*. It was not quite dark and Chacon was hiding in a ditch concealed by a dense underbrush with which the suburbs of Solomonville are much embellished. He was waiting for night, which was going to attend him on his journey to Mexico.

In the course of Mr. Kelly's investigation in that vicinity he stumbled and fell into the ditch upon Chacon. He advertised his discovery on the first page next to pure reading matter and sat around on Chacon waiting for answers to his advertisement. The other searchers came up and Chacon was taken back to his place of alleged confinement.

After his conviction he was taken to Tucson. The chance of escaping from the Pima County jail was so slight that he was removed back to Solomonville after the Supreme Court announced its decision to let him hang.

*Five days later the Phoenix Republican said:*

Word comes from Solomonville that no trace has been obtained of Chacon, the escaped murderer. What is more discouraging, none is expected to be obtained. The mystery of the escape of Chacon has received solution. The mystery was how he could have sawed out of the jail without making noise to have attracted the attention of at least somebody. It appears that the supervisors of Graham County, fully cognizant of the insecurity of the jail, had employed three guards at a salary of seventy-five dollars a month apiece. The supervisors expected them to watch, but as no specific contract had been drawn up, the guards imagined that they were hired to sleep. They were all conscientious guards, and a conscientious man will earn his money or throw up his job. A man ought to sleep very well on a salary of seventy-five dollars a month. These guards not only gave the county a fair, honest sleep, but introduced novelties in the way of snores, for which no extra charge was made the county, or if any such charge was made, it does not appear from the records that the claim was ever allowed. So the snoring was no doubt thrown in for good measure. The generosity of the guards was well-meant, but ill-advised, so no fault can be found with them. If the board of supervisors could have rent the veil of the future and have forseen the embarrassment and inconvenience which the somnolent zeal of the guards was going to occasion some time, they would have begged and even demanded that the snoring should be eliminated, for it was this very snoring that enveloped the sound of the patriot, Chacon's saw, while he was carving his way to liberty, the inalienable right of every man who can get out of jail and remain out. If anybody in Solomonville had heard the rasping of the saw, he would probably have taken it for a later development in the faithful guards' style of snore.

Five years later, Chacon was again in the hands of the Graham County sheriff, and the gallows frame which was built for him in 1897 was still standing ready to fulfill its purpose. As Chacon was a Mexican citizen, an official of the Mexican government came to Solomonville and investigated the case but declined to make any effort in his behalf; he inferred that he was satisfied that Chacon deserved hanging. In fact, the official stated to some of the citizens of Solomonville that Chacon had confessed to him having killed fifteen Americans and thirty-seven Mexicans in his lifetime.

An article in the Clifton *Copper Era* in 1902 says:

The credit for the re-capture of this noted outlaw, who had been the terror of Graham and Cochise Counties for years, must be awarded to Captain Burton C. Mossman of the Arizona Rangers. All during his reign as Captain his chief obsession was to capture Chacon. So it was that he gave of his time and energy in the enterprise, even though he had then retired from the Rangers. He was, however, a Deputy United States Marshal, and with that authority, could go after Chacon.

The capture of Chacon was the culmination of a deep-laid plan, using two former officers, who had later turned outlaws, Burt Alvord and Billy Stiles, and which was most successfully executed. [Burt Alvord later stated that he effected Chacon's capture in Mexico and delivered him to Captain Mossman through Billy Stiles.]

Word had been received by Mossman by special messenger that Chacon would make a raid on a horse pasture located about seven miles this side of the Mexican line. Mossman and Billy Stiles awaited his coming, but their vigilance was unrewarded. They retired to a nearby ranch, and on the following night were again in their places, close beside the pasture gate. They did not have long to wait, for about midnight a horseman rode into a small canyon nearby, and instead of making a raid on the pasture at night, this night being very dark and cloudy, evidently Chacon decided to wait until daylight. Stiles and Mossman commanded Chacon, in Spanish, to throw up his hands as he approached the pasture gate. Mossman was close beside him when the command was given and had him covered. Stiles was on the other side of Chacon ready to shoot him if he made a move.

Chacon did not get rattled. He had long since learned to hold his nerve in check in face of danger. He looked up into the face of Mossman, his brows contracted slightly, and fixing those sharp, black eyes on his captor, said in Spanish, "Kill me! Why don't you go ahead and kill me! I know you will kill me!"

Captain Mossman assured Chacon that he would not harm him if he would come along peaceably, and then ordered Stiles to disarm him, which was done and Chacon was relieved of a six-shooter and bowie knife. Saddles were quickly placed on the horses and with Chacon safely handcuffed, Stiles in the lead and Mossman bringing up the rear, the three on horseback started across the country for the nearest railroad station, which was Naco Junction.

Captain Mossman took his charge to Benson and turned him over to Sheriff Parks of Graham County, who was there on his way to Cochise County, having been advised that Chacon would soon be in the hands of the officers. At Benson Chacon was seen by the writer and was allowed to talk to him by Sheriff Parks. The Mexican outlaw, who knew not the meaning of fear, took his capture in a philosophical manner.

"Where are you going, Chacon?" was asked by the reporter.

"I suppose they are taking me to Solomonville," said the outlaw, "and I want them to kill me this time. I prefer death to a term in the penitentiary."

Chacon had broken rapidly in the five years since his escape. His form was bent and his beard tinged with gray. To be hunted like an animal for five years left its mark on the outlaw, and now to be returned to the jail from whence he had escaped from the hangman's noose, five years before.

A later article in the Copper Era says:

In the district court at Solomonville, Augustin Chacon was again sentenced to suffer the death penalty, the new execution date set being November 21st, 1902. His lawyers set up the plea that the law under which he was convicted had been repealed, which rendered his sentence void. Judge Doan held that the supreme court had already passed on that question, which left him no alternative but to pronounce sentence. It was reported that the supreme court would be again appealed to and the prisoner's release asked for on habeas corpus proceedings, but all to no avail.

*Following is Chacon's statement on the scaffold in the jail enclosure at Solomonville as interpreted by Nick Van Alstine, Court Interpreter; it appeared in the Clifton Copper Era in 1902:*

I have much to say [asks for a cup of coffee]. I desire to speak to all classes of people. I only have three enemies in this country. The names of those three enemies that I think I have in this country are, one Chavaria, the other is Dr. Davis and the other is a Mexican, which I have forgotten his name. He lives at Morenci with a Mexican woman by the name of Zenovia. It is these three men who have caused my death. Not because I am guilty of what they accuse me of. My conscience is clean. They have tried to give it to me and have succeeded in doing so. They used the law to bring me up to the scaffold where I am going now to hang. I do not have anything to say against the law. God would help us if there was no law, for that reason I say to all of you to be careful and take warning, and have nothing to be guilty of and not have to suffer. I have nothing to say against the relatives of Mr. Pablo Salcido. I do not even have anything against his wife Louisa. I do not want any of you to believe that I am guilty of the crime. I would not have done it for anything. There are many people here who pretend to know what they are talking about, but they do not know. In regard to my escape from the Solomonville jail five years ago, I want to say that Joe Reaves and George Burkner [the jailers in charge] are entirely innocent. They would not let me say or do anything that was not so. I wish that God will punish me if I am telling a lie. If I am guilty I wish to be expelled from His presence like mother Eve was from Paradise. I carry my conscience clean and bright. I did not do it but I expect to pay for this crime, because a good many people are in the habit of saying a good many things that are not true as Mr. Chavaria did. He is the one who ought to be hanged in my stead and for that which I am going to be hanged for today. That man did not know what he was doing because he did not see the killing of Salcido. Nobody can be more satisfied of this than I am myself. I have a clean conscience. I am sure that this hand [raising his right hand] has never been guilty of committing murder. I may have stolen and done a good many other things, but I am innocent of this crime, from my own knowledge. [Asks for cigarette papers and rolls cigarette and smokes.] It is nothing but right that when one is going to die that he be given a few moments of time to quietly smoke a cigarette.

I have been told by several people that I have been in this country since I got away from here. I was here four years ago myself with another party. That party is now dead. I was here for the purpose of knowing how my business was getting on and to hear what was being said about me. That is when I came here. I did not come here to do any wrong or harm anybody. I have been told that I have been here since, at different places and at different times, with a band of twenty men and that I have been seen here and there with a band of twenty men. This is not so. At the time I heard this report I was a long distance from here. I was brought here by a party who told me a lie. This man went to Nacosari [Sonora] and asked me to come from there. From there we came to near the line—within nine miles. There I was delivered to the chief of the Arizona Rangers. I have been told since that the man who gave me up is in jail at Tombstone. He is said to be in jail and will be dealt with according to law. I could say a good many things against that party, but I will not do so. God will deal with him. I do not wish to see anybody in trouble on my account. I would rather see them out from their troubles than in jail. I wish that God will give him his liberty so that he may not suffer as I have suffered myself. If I am going to suffer death on his account, I wish God to forgive him. I have done lots of favors to get him away from the officers of this country.

I went to the Yaqui River and enlisted as a soldier at the time the soldiers [Mexican] were there. I was there as a soldier, and the soldiers' quarters were most as bad as it was in jail. I asked permission to go out to meet him as I knew that he was near the place at which I was stationed and he sent word that he wished to see me. I asked him what he was doing, and he told me what he had done and that he was trying to hide away from the officers of the United States. I did not believe his statement. He asked me to travel with him in his company, and my answer to him was that I could not because I did not wish to return to the United States and that I did not have horse, saddle or ammunition. He then told me that he would provide all those things for me. Fortunately that day I was discharged from the army—honorably discharged from the army. Then I had to make a night ride for the reason that I wished to get away from him. After that, in September, he was with me again. He told me to come with him that he was going out on an adventure, to look at some mules. I told him that I would not go with him because the mules were not his, but they were stolen, and that I did not wish to be in a bad fix with my own country as I was here in the United States. We left that place and the mules were delivered to him by the owner, or rather the one who claimed to be the owner. When we left that day it was raining. Next day about this time we were overtaken by the legitimate owner of the mules. Then he asked me what shall we do, and my answer was that we were in a bad fix. I told him that we would try to scare them off by firing on them but not trying to hit any of them and that would give us a chance to get away. As those mules were stolen, we left them there.

That is the way I have been guilty here and everywhere. It is said that this man [a local Mexican in the audience], a friend of mine, has assisted me in different ways, in my adventures. It was done in this way that whenever I came to his ranch and asked him for any little favors he complied with my requests as gladly as he would have done with anybody else.

I would like if there is anyone around here who has anything against me to come out and say it. Is there anyone here who has anything to say against this man? I do not think there is anybody in Clifton or Morenci who can say that I have wronged them. My family is entirely different from what I am and never was accused of any crime whatever. If I have ever done anything wrong it was here in this country, and I think that all reports about my friends is nothing but a lie.

I would like to have you all take care of yourselves and take warning from my case, and not do wrong, for if you do you will be dealt with according to law. According to my understanding and knowledge the law is dealt out slowly but surely, with dumb instruments. The law never lets up and never gets out of order. If any of you intend to leave I would like to have you all remain here until the last moment, and now I would like to smoke a cigarette slowly. [Sits down on the scaffold and rolls a cigarette and smokes it slowly.]

Interpreter asks if that was all and Chacon replied that that was all. Chacon spoke for thirty minutes. A number came forward to shake hands with him. These he greeted saying goodbye to them. He requested that he be permitted to live until three p.m., but was told that his time was up. To one who was coming up to shake hands with him he said: "It's too late now. Time to hang." He asked that his face be not covered, but while the cap was being adjusted, shouted "Adios Todos Amigos." He assisted in the tying of the bands about him, and removed his shoes himself. He straightened up for the drop and gave the signal to Sheriff Parks to spring the trap. His neck was broken by the fall.

# 8

# SUPERSTITION LORE

## THE LOST DUTCHMAN MINE

Arizona abounds in tales and legends wild and fanciful, told by old-timers over many a campfire and in barrooms—tales of fabulous wealth and lost mines. There is a saying in the Southwest that the mines men find are never so rich as those they lost, and this mine is no exception. Of all the legends told, that of the Lost Dutchman is perhaps the most familiar, and while the telling is never quite the same twice, it has created more intense interest throughout the years than perhaps any other.

The mystery of the Lost Dutchman mine has been recounted in various forms from one end of Arizona to the other. One tale places the scene in the Mazatzal range, near Four Peaks; another credits it to the Harqua Halas; another asserts that it is the mother lode of the nearby Silver King, while others assert that the lost mine was over in the Superstition Mountains to the east of Phoenix. Some claim that there were three of the mysterious "Dutchmen" connected with the legend, while others tell of a lone miner and his wife. Some say that the wife of the Dutchman, an ancient Negro woman who lived in Phoenix, was given a map of the supposed location of the mine, while others say this colored woman was a friend who cared for the old Dutchman during his last illness and that perhaps he gave her some idea of the directions to the mine. At any rate, no one has ever been able to locate the place, although thousands have tried.

In 1887 a generally mild earthquake rocked some sections of Arizona and was felt in all sections. Some remarks of Dr. W. W. Jones, who was a prominent pioneer of the Salt River Valley area, were reported as follows in the Phoenix Herald:

He was just in from his cattle ranch some thirty miles above Phoenix on the Salt River, and that he was more pleased by the recent earthquake than by anything he had seen in Arizona. From his ranch he had a splendid view of the northern edge of the Superstition Mountains and when the earth commenced rocking he rushed for his field glasses and enjoyed a very interesting view of some of the toppling cliffs of that range, which being of sandstone, were easily shaken from their foundations. Two of the tallest buttes, which guarded the entrance to the canyon, toppled over and met each other in mid-air, and the noise of their fall was plainly heard, though nine miles distant.

Perhaps this is the key to the "closing of the door" to the fabulous Lost Dutchman mine. Quien sabe?

The long series of very interesting legends dealing with this rich gold mine begins with that of a young Mexican lover fleeing the wrath of his sweetheart's father and seeking refuge far north in the forbidding Superstitions. He is supposed to have found the great gold deposit in an area that was still a part of Old Mexico although the Gadsden Purchase, whereby the United States acquired the region including this site, was about to take place. Therefore the young man's entire Mexican community formed a great expedition and made the long march into the Superstitions. There they mined as much of the gold as they could carry and set out jubilantly for home. But the Apaches ambushed them and killed the entire party of four hundred men, except for two young boys who were concealed under a bush. These two found their way back home and grew up with the knowledge that they alone knew the location of the mine. When they were old enough they took a third partner and went to the Superstitions, finding the mine without difficultly. They had hardly begun to dig when the Dutchman came along.

The Dutchman was a prospector with a long white beard, and his name was Jacob Walz (also spelled Waltz). He had been prospecting in the Superstitions, and a band of Apaches had driven him into a part of the mountain he had never seen before. He stumbled into the camp of the Mexican boys and became so friendly with them that they told him about their mine. Walz killed the three boys, and from about 1870 until his death in 1891, the mine was his.

As stories of the Dutchman's gold ore spread around Phoenix and Florence, many prospectors tried to trail him into the mountains, but he outwitted them or killed them. Walz is said to have admitted killing eight men, including his own nephew, because of the mine. He died in Phoenix in 1891 with a shoebox full of the wonderful ore under his bed. Almost with his last breath he gave a friendly neighbor directions to the mine, saying that they must be followed exactly, as the mine entrance was concealed under ironwood logs covered with rocks. Unfortunately, the most important landmark in Walz's directions, a palo verde tree with a peculiar pointing branch, could not be located then or later.

Since then literally thousands of prospectors, both professional and amateur, have searched for the Lost Dutchman mine, and their luck has been uniformly bad. Some have never come back at all; others have returned with pieces of human skeletons and accounts of almost dying of thirst, and still others have been mysteriously shot at in the wild canyons. The tragedy and violence connected with the Lost Dutchman have added to the strong conviction of Arizonans that the Superstition Mountains are cursed. Some people say Jacob Walz never had anything in the Superstitions, but there are those around the town of Florence who say that he used to disappear periodically after running out of funds, to reappear days later with a fresh supply of wealth. He got the ore somewhere, and with seemingly little difficulty, and judging by the number of prospecting expeditions into the Superstitions annually, it would appear that skepticism can never command as large an audience as faith—the faith that still believes the gold is there somewhere.

Several books and pamphlets as well as numerous articles have been written about the Superstition Mountains and the Lost Dutchman mine. These accounts vary as to names and places and differ on other pertinent points. The following stories, taken from various early Arizona newspapers, are presented as they were written and for what they are worth. No attempt has been made to check them against other published accounts that claim to give the "authentic" story of the Lost Dutchman. They are presented without regard to whether they are fact, fiction, or just plain fantasy.

Tucson, Ariz., Aug. 29, 1913

Editor The Observer,
St. Johns, Arizona.
Dear Sir:

As you know, Mr. James usually begins his stories with a "solitary horseman," etc., etc. My story, however, has no solitary horseman; on the contrary, it deals with a solitary Dutchman with a burro.

Many, very many years ago, a German lived in Phoenix with a Mexican woman for his wife. This Dutchman, so called, was none too bright in his top loft, nevertheless, like many of those so mentally endowed, he was quite cunning in his own estimation and conceit.

At divers times this "cunning" Dutchman would leave Phoenix and be gone for an indefinite time, after which he would appear on the streets of Phoenix with more or less gold dust, which he sold to the various merchants of the town. At one time he sold to Mr. Blank $1,800 in dust, but to all questions as to where he got the gold, he always replied, with a cunning leer, "somewhere," but no more. He invariably went alone, and always unbeknown to anyone in the town; even his Mexican wife never knew where he was going or when he expected to return. On one of his trips, and it proved to be his last one, he decided to take his wife along. Together they went to the Rio Verde, where they encamped for the

night. Some time before dark, he pointed out the direction of his
gold placers, and said, "tomorrow or next day we will reach there."
It was not to be so, for that night he was taken seriously ill, and his
wife returned with her sick husband to Phoenix. The sick man was
confined to his bed for several days, but to all importunities by
friends or others to tell them the location of his gold placers, he
turned a deaf ear and absolutely refused to divulge his secret. He
soon died, and his secret has been known from that day to the
present time as the "Lost Dutchman."

Suffice to say, those placers have never been rediscovered to this
day, and it now remains for your humble servant to make this important discovery. To this end, I leave here September 1st to search
for the "Lost Dutchman."

The above is the story in brief of the "Lost Dutchman," which
has been known to me for many years; yet, in all these years, I
never made any attempt to find the place. Should I be fortunate
enough to find it, then—but that's another story.

A. F. BANTA

*Alfred Franklin Banta, a pioneer of 1863, owned and edited various
newspapers in Arizona and was a prolific writer of Arizona history,
although his accounts were often found to be at variance with the
facts, perhaps because of hazy memory. The above account of the
Lost Dutchman, published in 1913, mentions the Dutchman, by
whom he obviously means Jacob Walz (or Waltz). That Walz
war a married man is doubtful. According to the Phoenix papers
of 1891, he was living in an adobe near the Salt River, south of
Phoenix, and during the flood of February, 1891, his place was
washed away, he being rescued by neighbors. Developing pneu-
monia, he died in October of that year. He was cared for during
his last days at the home of a friend, Mrs. Thomas, a colored
woman, in whose home he passed away.*

Here is an earlier account, published in the Phoenix Gazette
in 1895:

Robert McKee, a well-to-do prospector who has been all over
the west, is in the city to gather data that will enable him to find
the mythical mine once known by Dutch Jacob, who in 1891 died

in Phoenix. Mr. McKee is not a broke man looking for a stake but an intelligent prospector who came to Arizona two years ago from Colorado. He once owned the tin mines near Rabbit, South Dakota, that since have been capitalized at $16,000,000. Since, in Arizona, he has hunted and prospected alternately, and in two years eighteen mountain lions have been captured, the result of his trapping, besides numerous bears. His outfit is a curiosity, consisting of seven burros, one an excellent saddle animal, a number of dogs, pure bred Shepherds and collies that are used in bear hunting, several good guns, a very complete camping outfit, a well-filled purse and a fair bank account.

Mr. McKee read in a recent *Saturday Review* of a trip to the Superstition Mountains made by Frank Luke and Frank Kirkland, also about a former trip by P. C. Bicknell. As the story goes, more than thirty years ago two German prospectors were fifty-six miles south-east of Phoenix, where they found six Mexicans working a rich gold mine. They were using the crude Spanish method but getting lots of gold. The Dutchman wanted the claim and took it by the easiest method, by killing the Mexicans. Dead men tell no tales.

As civilization advanced Jacob and his partner became familiar with the people. Finally the partner disappeared, probably by the same hand that dispatched the Mexicans.

Finally the aged Jacob moved to the vicinity of Phoenix, but he made frequent trips to the Superstition Mountains, each time bringing back with him bountiful supplies of gold. Old Jacob became a recluse and later was seen in Phoenix but once a year, just to vote the Republican ticket on election day. During the remainder of the time no one knew he was on earth.

He made his last trip in '84 and brought $500 in two little sacks. He was now growing feeble. During his declining years a woman ministered to the tottering Jacob as did Ruth in days of yore. To her he left his property, consisting of a town lot. He also divulged to her the secret of the hidden gold mine.

In a gulch in the Superstition Mountains, the location of which is described by certain landmarks, there is a two-room house in the mouth of a cave on the side of the slope near the gulch. Just across the gulch, about 200 yards, opposite this house in the cave, is a tunnel, well-covered up and concealed in the bushes. Here is the mine, the richest in the world, according to Dutch Jacob. Some distance above the tunnel on the side of the mountain, is a shaft or incline that is not so steep but one can climb down. This, too, is covered carefully. The shaft goes right down in the midst of the rich gold ledge, where it can be picked off in big flakes of almost pure gold.

After Dutch Jacob had been buried the woman took a miner with her and spent an entire summer looking for the mine, but she was unable to find even the ruins of the house. She tried again the next year, but failed owing perhaps to changes wrought by the heavy rains that annually fall in that section.

Many had hunted for the mine even twenty years ago, and since the death of Dutch Jacob, J. E. Bark, P. C. Bicknell, the journalistic prospector, and many others have made frequent trips in that locality. In the fall of 1894 Bicknell stumbled on the stone house in the mouth of a cave. He felt as though he had obtained the secret but his grub stake was played out and he was compelled to seek civilization. It was covered with slag and looked as though it had been used in reducing ore. An old drill was also picked up.

With these facts Mr. McKee proposes in a few days to go and make an intelligent hunt for the mine. He wishes to see the lady first and if possible get a minute description of what she knows.

The Dutch Jacob mine is a reality, and although it may not be found, it is highly probable it will be. One thing certain, the old man took great precaution to conceal the property which must be very rich as he got gold almost single handed.

*Some of the legends surrounding the Superstitions are fascinating, to say the least, and a few of the early newspaper accounts relative to them should prove interesting. The Phoenix Herald had this story in 1879:*

Some excitement is being created among the Mexican population of Phoenix by the story of a Mexican who arrived last evening from the Reno Mountains. He came into town under cover of darkness, as he was nearly naked. His hands and feet were torn and bloody, and his face was gashed in a fearful manner. His story was told with the air of a man who had been terribly frightened and had not recovered. With a companion he started out prospecting about a month ago, going up Salt River. They left the river when opposite the Superstition Mountain. Their prospecting began at this point.

While climbing up the mountain, in a little gully, through black sand, and down which a large stream of water had evidently passed years ago, they were astonished to find that in this sand were large quantities of fine gold. In some places the sand was only about half an inch deep over the granite. The gold in pieces the size of a bean and smaller, was found in the little fissures in the face of the bedrock. Very little washing was necessary, and they found a little spring of water which furnished them what they needed. They obtained, they think, about $600 worth, or half a day's work. About two o'clock in the afternoon, they were surprised to see an Indian woman come to the top of the gulch above the spring and start to come down. Upon seeing them she ran back over the hill. In less than ten minutes, they were surrounded by fifty or sixty savages. The Indians were very small and seemed to be of a different nation than they had ever seen in Arizona.

The Mexicans were not armed except with knives, and the survivor says they were almost instantly caught with lariats. The Indians took them up the mountain and put them in a cave. They tortured and killed his companion and his fate would have been the same but for his escape. He succeeded in getting away with only a few knife gashes on his face. They lost their gold with all their outfit. The Indians seemed to be cave dwellers, and were evidently excited over the place being found by outsiders. Our reporter's limited knowledge of the Spanish language, makes it impossible for us to obtain all the particulars of the affair. For the benefit of non-residents, we will say that the Superstition Mountain derives its name from the fact that no white man has ever been seen again, who attempted its ascension. It is a tradition among the Mexicans that large deposits of free gold are to be found in its gulches and ravines. It is not known whether there is water there or not. We shall endeavor to obtain further particulars regarding the matter and will publish them as soon as obtained.

*Two items concerning war clubs found in a cave in the Superstitions appeared in early Phoenix newspapers. The Phoenix Herald had this to say in 1884:*

Messrs. Asa and Babcock, of Tempe, have been prospecting for some time in the Superstition Mountains, and report the discovery of a cave of considerable dimensions in which they found some two hundred wooden prehistoric war clubs. These clubs are hard wood, ranging from fifteen to twenty inches in length, with a grip carved on one end somewhat after the style of a policeman's club, and the other end is perhaps three inches in diameter. The wood of which a portion of them is made is exceedingly hard, something like manzanita, while others seem to be of tough mountain oak. Many of them are painted and roughly carved, the latter work apparently having been done with some rude instrument, possibly their stone axes. The preservation of these clubs is somewhat remarkable, considering the ages through which they must have lain and their present perfect condition. Besides, they are one more evidence of the character of that apparently semi-civilized people who have at some time occupied this whole section, with their peculiar and, in many respects, remarkable institutions.

Asa and Babcock brought away with them quite a number of these remarkable instruments for presentation to their friends and as samples of what they had discovered.

*The Phoenix Gazette printed a letter sent to the editor from Willow Springs, in the Superstitions, in 1886. It was signed by "Bick," and reads as follows:*

This picturesque range of mountains which is plainly visible from Phoenix, has for many years borne an unsavory reputation throughout the territory. Strange stories have been circulated concerning mysterious disappearances of luckless prospectors who have dared to penetrate its unknown gorges in search of fabulous deposits of rich ore, and it is even asserted that quite a party of prospectors who entered the range on an organized search for the "mother ledge of the famous Silver King," were never heard of after. The Indians are said to hold these mountains in superstitious awe, and in fact all these myths and fables originated with the Pima Indians many years ago when two hundred of their warriors followed a thieving band of Apaches into the range and were there ambushed by their treacherous foe, and cut off to a man. I have visited the scene of this tragedy and found only a few shattered war clubs and a fragment of a rawhide shield—all that remains to mark the scene of this Pima Waterloo. Not many years ago there were numerous bleached skulls and scores of clubs still on the ground. Some of the latter were taken to Phoenix where they adorned the shelves of cabinets.

*The Phoenix Gazette had this story from the Pimas in 1893 as to the origin of the name of the Superstition Mountains:*

We have often been asked the origin of the name of the mountain; whether because of its rugged grandeur, its castellated domes and aspiring turrets, cut and furrowed and abraded and corrugated by the beating storms of past ages, or whether from the fact, as prospectors tell us, that when heavy winds blow against the south and east sides of the mountain, the terrified listener hears the most piercing and heart-rending and unearthly sounds proceeding from out the caves and caverns and inaccessible crevices of the mountain. We have been at some pains to ascertain as much concerning the origin of the name as possible and in furtherance of this object we interviewed one of the old sub-chiefs of the Pimas, who officiates as medicine man and carried the tradition of his tribe written upon memory's tablets to be transmitted to his descendants.

The tradition of the origin of the name as he gave it to us is about as follows, in the fewest possible words: Montezuma was a great chief and ruler over thousands of souls, the inhabitants of very large cities and populating the extensive plains of this country. Fearing that a great calamity was about to befall him and his people, he caused them to assemble on the plains adjacent to the mountain and then, with his magic wand, he caused an opening to be made in the side of the mountain, into which he and his people went. Then the stone gateway was closed and to this day Montezuma and his people dwell within the center of the rugged mountain. Some day, the tradition says, he and his people will come forth as white people to again occupy the land, build great villages and till the productive soil of the plains.

*Another story regarding the superstitious awe the Indians have for this mountain was told in the Phoenix Republican in 1893:*

The recent discovery of some rich nuggets of pure gold has given a new impetus to the mining excitement in the Superstition Mountains. W. E. Pomeroy of Mesa has a specimen obtained from an Indian that carries at least fifteen dollars of the yellow metal in one chunk. This is only one of many rich specimens that have been brought in by the red men, and there is a determined effort to find the ledge from which these nuggets were obtained. The Indians seem to be familiar with gold ore and know where the rich deposit is located, but a superstition keeps them from revealing the fact.

This fear is based on the tradition that in early days Montezuma enslaved the natives and compelled them to work the mines from which the immense treasures taken by Cortez were obtained. Later, under Spanish rule, the yoke of bondage was still more galling until there was a general uprising of the Indian tribes of Central Arizona that swept their oppressors from the face of the earth, leaving only the ruins of Casa Grande and similar landmarks as monuments of the age of bondage and oppression. After ridding the country of the early Spaniards, every gold mine was covered, and to this day no good Indian has ever revealed the secret of their location, although silver and copper mines have often been located through their guidance.

*In a letter to the editor of the Tempe News, which appeared in that paper in 1893, "S. C. H." writes:*

We gained an early start and a six hours drive from Tempe brought us to the now celebrated Mammoth Mine, in the Superstition Mountain range. A unique sight met us when we reached the camp. Around a big watering trough we saw a crowd of miners, all busily engaged in the washing of gold ore samples, by means of pans and horn spoons. We alighted and wonder and astonishment overtook us as we watched the result of these washings of ore, mostly new finds that had just been made in the surrounding hills. Yellow, glittering gold, and a perfect string of it, became disclosed in pan and spoons after the washings, and those who had so far been incredulous onlookers, became imbued with the excitement, and forthwith packed their burros, mounted their mustangs and struck out after new discoveries.

"Do you know, gentlemen," spoke up an old grizzle-bearded miner, "that you are standing right now on the costliest carpet that you ever put foot on in your lives?" We thought he was off, for surely we were not tramping on any woven texture, but simply on a rather loose lot of what resembled mother earth more than any-thing else.

"Well," he explained, "this lot of earth under you was taken out of the Mammoth a few days ago and eight hundred dollars in gold would not buy it. Watch me," and with this he took a pan-ful of the ground, and commenced washing. A few minutes twist-ing and turning of the pan in the watering trough soon removed the pebbles and earth and a lot of gold—at least a dollar's worth, remained in the pan. It was a revelation. "Why," we exclaimed, "and such rich ground you permit to lie around like this." "Oh well," he said, "nobody will steal it, but come with me and I will show you stuff that will make your eyes sparkle."

He led us a few yards away to a new shaft that is being sunk on the Mammoth and opened one of a number of sacks of ore that had been piled around the shaft. He plunged his hand into one of the sacks and handed us pieces of rock that were virtually bound and held together with wires of gold. "Try and twist them off," he requested of us, but all the twisting could not loosen them. "Each of these sacks," he continued, "contains a thousand dollars worth of gold at least, and as depth increases the ore becomes richer."

He would not allow us to go down into the mine. He claimed having received strict orders not to admit anybody. This in a cer-tain measure made us suspicious, and we thought we would try and obtain additional information, from more disinterested per-sons, and we were not long in discovering one, a discharged em-ploye. He was just our man, for he could have no motives in exaggerating anything pertaining to the mine in which once he had found work and wages. He commenced telling us of the first discovery, some three months hence, of the Mammoth and the subsequent development of this property. . . .

We thanked him for his information. We knew now that we

stood before the greatest gold mine not only in Arizona, but probably in the United States. We predict the greatest rush to these
gold discoveries in the Superstition Mountains of any that have
taken place since the Leadville discoveries, and what is still more,
we predict more wonderful ore finds than any that have ever been
made during such rushes, for the reason that the whole region
seems to be lined with gold-bearing ledges, some with bold out-
cropping and others blind. But I will conclude. Look out, however,
for the Superstition Mountain gold mines, for they are going to
astonish the world.

During the fall of 1913 [*said the Phoenix Gazette in 1916*] José
Perez, a Mexican, although born and raised in Phoenix, was on a
prospecting trip in the Superstition range. One day while riding
down the rocky bottom of a rugged canyon, whose sheer walls
towered far above him, he noticed a slight indentation in the rocky
sides about two hundred feet from the bottom, which appeared
like the entrance to a small cavern. Curiosity overcoming him,
Perez investigated and struggling to the spot discovered a small dark
opening about two feet in diameter which seemed to lead directly
into the mountain. He wriggled into this opening for a distance of
about twenty feet when the cavern suddenly widened into an im-

mense chamber. From this chamber a large passage in which a man could walk upright led into the heart of the mountain. By the aid of a number of matches which he fortunately carried Perez was enabled to follow back for a considerable distance, passing through several chambers like the first one. In one of these chambers reposing on a flat rock the Mexican found several nuggets of high grade gold placed in the form of a dagger or stiletto. Above this on the rocky walls of the cavern were some rudely drawn cabalistic signs.

The now thoroughly excited Mexican hurried from the place and mounting his horse at once rode over the hills to Miami, where he told his tale to a mining engineer, Roy Thomas, in whom he had the most implicit faith. He declared that he believed the "Lost Dutchman," about which he had heard many tales, had been discovered.

Gathering together the necessary equipment for exploration, Perez and Thomas, accompanied by a newspaperman, returned to the scene of his discovery, where a thorough investigation was made. The cavern led back into the mountain for about two hundred yards but no visible indications of mineralization were evident, although some signs of previous occupancy were present. The mouth of the cavern was so small and situated at such an angle that only by the greatest accident could it be discovered from the bottom of the canyon. Thomas and the writer returned to Miami while the disappointed Perez wended his lonesome way.

A couple of years later Perez was in Phoenix a greatly excited and much scared Mexican. Lured by the call of the gold and unable to forget the experience he previously had he had returned to the cavern and there, to his amazement, on the same flat-topped rock in the cavern chamber reposed some nuggets of gold grouped in the shape of a dagger and above it rudely drawn in the rocky walls the sinister sign, "Keep away! Death!" Below was the rude drawing of a dagger. The Mexican, thoroughly frightened, immediately left the cave and hurried to Phoenix and then, to cap the climax, last night as he was walking down the street, a form suddenly emerged from the darkness, thrust a paper into his hand and then as suddenly disappeared. When the frightened man reached the light and opened the missive it contained a rude drawing of a knife with the following words: "Stay away from the Superstitions!"

Whether all this is merely a gigantic hoax on the part of some practical joker or whether, indeed, through the mysterious veil of the past, there looms up the magic and sinister ghost of the "Lost Dutchman" is a matter for further discovery. At any rate Perez will in the future stay away from the Superstition range and its mysterious warnings.

*Here is an interesting letter which appeared in the Miami* Silver Belt, *dated Globe, Oct. 16, 1913:*

H. A. Sidow returned to Globe after an exploration of the entrance to the cave described by Pete Moraga, the French-Mexican prospector, during his recent visit to Globe. It was the description and the samples of gold running from $5,000 to $50,000 per ton which caused so much excitement among the members of the Mexican colony and started the stories to the effect that the Lost Dutchman mine had been found.

Sidow says that while he is not willing to go on record to a statement that Moraga is on track of the Lost Dutchman, he is willing to say that Moraga has discovered a good-sized cave in a remarkable formation, the mineral found somewhat resembling bismuth. This mineral is not the ordinary bismuth, but even if it were bismuth, this in itself would not discourage old-time prospectors since gold is often found in conjunction with bismuth.

Sidow says that Moraga is not willing that he should make public the location of the cave since he is anxious to make further locations in that immediate locality without taking the general public into his immediate confidence. But he is willing to talk about the general features of the cave itself and the chances for the finding of the gold.

"I have often noticed the spot where Moraga showed me the entrance of the cave," said Sidow. "As I have been prospecting for gold in the mountains and as I have been looking for the Lost Dutchman, I have passed the place a good many times; but I never thought about it as the entrance to a cave.

"Moraga claims that it was at the entrance to this cave that he several weeks previous had found pieces of the black rock supposed to be bismuth. And close at hand to this black rock or bismuth, Moraga picked up the four extremely rich specimens of gold. The entrance to the cave is located about twenty-five feet above the level of a creek bed and it might easily be passed by by any person not thinking of the existence of a cave in that immediate vicinity.

"I did not start out with Moraga on this trip. But I did meet him as he was returning from a prospecting tour. He willingly offered to show me the cave, provided I would not tell anybody where he picked up the gold samples. He was very frank about the matter and said that he was not satisfied in his own mind that the gold had come from that immediate district. But he wanted more time to explore the country and he asked me to promise not to reveal the location of the cave.

"The time that Moraga discovered the cave and the gold, he went into the mine only a few feet. The entrance is so small that a fat man could not crawl through it. I started to go in head first, but after I had crawled in a few feet I did not like the looks of the thing and not knowing where I might land I crawled out again. Then Moraga started in feet first and I crawled in after him, also feet first. After we had gone in about twenty-five feet the entrance commenced to widen and at times it widened to a diameter of a hundred feet, I should say. Then again it would grow narrow. Then again it would widen out again.

"It was not the abandoned workings of a mine I am satisfied, but rather the entrance to a cave. I examined it as carefully as I could to determine whether or not we had not stumbled into an old mine. At times the floor was so uneven that we had the greatest difficulty in getting over some of the obstructions. Then the cave would at times run in a zig-zag sort of fashion.

"The walls were of limestone and we picked up specimens of what resembles bismuth in some respects. There was a great deal of guano on the floor. Towards the last of our explorations the ground commenced to get wet and for this reason I am satisfied that there is lots of water there. We did not go as far as we might have gone for the reason that we were not equipped for exploring a cave and either one of us might have taken a sheer drop of hundreds of feet downward without warning. I should not have objected to going farther into the cave if we had been equipped with ropes. But without ropes it appeared to be taking too great a risk. However, we did get three or four hundred feet into the cave without reaching any end to the opening in the ground. The air was fairly good and from that it might be argued that there was another entrance somewhere besides that one we found.

"I have turned a piece of the black rock or bismuth which I found over to an assayer and I expect to have a report on it soon. I do not believe that that black rock will show any traces of the gold. But I do believe that Moraga found that black rock and those specimens of gold at the entrance to the cave just as he said he did. One man's guess as to where the gold came from is as good as another man's. It would be interesting to follow the cave to the end for it must cover a good lot of country and might strike into a different formation. And it is possible that Moraga stumbled onto one way that the Lost Dutchman or some other Dutchman came out with his ores. Again we might have run up against a solid stone wall a dozen feet from where we stopped. Moraga can throw no light on that situation for I went in with him farther than he had ever been alone."

## GOLDFIELD

*Of all the prospecting ventures into the weird and beautiful Superstition Mountain area, undoubtedly the largest centered on the north side of the mountain in a camp named Goldfield in 1893. Perhaps more gold has been taken from that place than any other in the area. Although the camp lasted but a short time, there was great activity for that brief period, and even to this day there is some mining activity there.*

*In a story on the Lost Dutchman mine, which appeared in the Miami Silver Belt in 1914, Dave Gibson was quoted as saying:*

He and the old Apache scout, Al Sieber, in 1876, had roamed

that country but that the Indians bothered them then. Later, about the turn of the century, he and Steve Graham went into the Superstitions trying to find the Lost Dutchman.

In the old days [says Gibson] a good many people seemed to be afraid to go into the Superstition Mountains, but I could never figure out that there was anything to be afraid of—any more than in any other mountains. But most men are sort of superstitious, anyhow, I guess, and they may have been afraid of the name.

The Superstition Mountains, taken as a whole, are apparently of volcanic formation. At least there is lots of volcanic ash there. Toward Phoenix, between Goldfield and Mesa, there is more granite and there are better chances for finding gold.

As nearly as I can figure out, the Lost Dutchman must have been Goldfield. I think there is where the gold of the Lost Dutchman that made so much excitement at the Silver King mines so many years ago, must have come from. I wasn't at Goldfield during the excitement, but I have been over the grounds a number of times since. Goldfield looks to me to be about the best place in the entire Superstition Mountains for finding that kind of metal.

To get a picture of an early-day boom mining camp, let us pull back the curtain on old Goldfield as it was presented in the Phoenix Herald and Republican in 1893. Some of the letters graphically describing the camp and activities there were written by Lewis H. Eddy, and a few were signed "Prospector":

To see the great Superstition Mountain from Phoenix you have only to step into the middle of Washington Street and look straight to the east, or as the street runs. If you will take a field glass you may see some of the rugged grandeur of that old structure of nature. No doubt a telescope would enable you to see the particles of free gold on some of the immensely rich specimens which are being dug out of the prospect holes between the shaggy top of old Superstition and the frowning shadow of Bull Dog Point.

What a pretty story might be woven out of the beauty and wonders of the new camp of Goldfield in the Superstitions and its surroundings. But the men to whom I am writing are not seeking literary effects. They want cold, honest facts. They have no eye for the mere glitter of the free gold in the quartz. They want to see the result of the horn or read the assayer's certificate. They want to know if the width of the vein and the quality of the ore will hold out as depth is gained. They want some assurances that Superstition is a paying investment. Some of them are really in earnest when they hope to make a half million dollars upon an investment of $5,000. Others are content to spend a few hundred dollars and make a few thousand.

All of them are looking toward the Superstition in the hope of turning gold-bearing rock into legal tender gold dollars. Beauty of scenery and romance of story have no attraction for them. They have been filled with scenery and have stories to give away. So instead of indulging a desire to write a story, I will for the purpose of this series of articles and the benefit of readers resort to the truth, which must not be mistaken for fiction if it should happen to have a pretty close rub.

Starting from Phoenix to visit the Superstition, I chose my own method of travel and made no plans. I traveled and talked where the notion took me. My purpose was to write the truth, be it good or ill, of the much-disputed subject of Superstition's greatness as a gold district. And this is the truth and nothing but the truth, though it would be impossible in five times the space to tell the whole truth.

The young man Stillman, who wears "Frank Miller's Stage" band on his hat, called "all aboard" as he drove up in front of the Fruit Store on Washington Street in Phoenix one pleasant morning last week, and in company with other passengers bound for the gold fields, I boarded the stage. The road to Tempe had some rough places, especially near the river, but none so bad that a carriage team cannot travel with comparative ease. This seven miles is quickly covered and then to Mesa is eight miles farther east, and from its nearness to the Superstition, is proving itself quite a rival of Phoenix as a trading point. It stands on a beautiful mesa land, some three hundred feet higher than Phoenix, stretching many miles to the north, east and south.

We reached there at 10:30 o'clock, and after enjoying an excellent dinner at the Pioneer House, owned and conducted by W. A. Kimball, I mounted a stage on the line run by Mr. Kimball between Mesa and Goldfield. The stage wasn't loaded to the guards, but the passenger seats were filled and the large and small packages, entrusted to the care of Ed Bloomer, the driver, made up a very respectable load for the two horses.

It was one o'clock on the dot when we started from Mesa and the clock in the kitchen of the Mammoth boarding house was just striking six as we pulled up on the roadway between the boarding house and Peterson Bros. store at Goldfield in the great Superstitions. Five hours over the easiest roads ever traveled, between an agricultural town and a mining camp. The broad mesa land, a large portion of which is under ditch and cultivation, reminded a fellow passenger of the prairies of Illinois. It is not a desert, but a beautiful sandy plain, sloping to the west so gradually that the 700 feet of incline between the town and the mountains was not perceptible to any but the driver and the horses, until the edge of the new camp of Goldfield was reached.

Just as we entered the camp we saw evidences of the prospector's art in the monuments built of round smooth boulders marking the corners of claims on ground which looked to be more adapted to raising sweet potatoes and chasing chipmunks than prospecting for gold.

I became interested before we had sat down to supper. But I was astonished before bed time. I was astonished at the size of the camp, the deal of work going on and at the moral atmosphere and the presence of a large number of families.

Gold is where you find it, whether it be in mountains which stand 10,000 to 14,000 feet above the sea or in the foothills of Arizona at an altitude of only that many hundred feet. The Indian legends which gave Superstition its name, and which are contradictory and unreliable, need have no importance in this writing. It is important, however, that unwritten history points to the fact that there was mining for gold done in the Superstitions a hundred years ago and more.

Over on the north side of this wonderful mountain so peculiar in shape, standing like the ruins of some great walled city with its tall spires and huge monuments, there has been discovered an ancient mining camp. Whether this mining was done by the Indians and Mexicans of the last century, or whether the operations date back to years when de Vaca and Black Stephen started from the coast of Florida to find the gold fields toward the setting sun, may never be known. It is certain, however, that there are shafts and tunnels and drifts and stopes and the clearly-defined walls of a great mine. On the dumps are found tons and tons of rock which without doubt came out of these workings.

These evidences of early mining led a party of prospectors some five years ago to follow down the trail of the hills till they found gold much richer than was found by the Indians or Spaniards, or whoever they may have been. These prospectors who risked their lives in the face of the dangerous Apaches who lurked about the hills some five years ago, were not as careful gold hunters as those of later years. They had but little time to look for gold, so sharp needs be their watchfulness for the coming Apache.

But there was quite a mining excitement created and some dozen claims were located. Among these was the Lucky Boy, which was the first location made. Its locator was J. R. Morse, and its present owner is Ed Jones. Nothing more was done then until about a year ago when Morse, C. R. Hakes and Orrin Merrill renewed the search for gold. These three prospectors, whose faith in Superstition has never wavered, located the Bee's Nest, the Old Man, the Abe Lincoln and the George Washington. Though there was at that time little to fear from Indians, their work was not extensive. They merely did enough work to hold the claims, feeling that the time was not quite ripe enough to create much interest in the new find. There was some little scare now and then on account of the notorious reputation of the Apache Kid who had proven such a terror, and whether it was he or some other wandering Apache who killed a boy near Frazer's ranch, there has been a little timidity shown on the part of persons who would probably have done more mining in any other locality.

But Indian scares or disbelief in the riches of Goldfield did not deter Morse, Hakes and Merrill from continuing their prospecting and development work. They were satisfied that there was gold there and plenty of it, and now they have the satisfaction of knowing they were right. Seeing these three men so determined in the development of the new fields, a few others stayed with them in the search. These were Buck Cosner, Mr. Case, Mr. Ridenour, Orlando

Merrill and a Mexican named Velasco. They kept steadily at work, being camped over the hill from the present center of operations. And these men together with Morse, Hakes and Merrill continued their prospecting and development work until others became interested and Morse accidentally found a claim that proved the starting point for the present prosperous camp.

Zigzagging over the hills one day with his gun on his shoulder looking for game, J. R. Morse kicked out from a ledge, with the toe of his shoe, a piece of rock which has proven to be the foundation of Goldfield and give a reputation to the great Superstition. Like many a prospector under similar circumstances, he inclined to throw it away, but each additional look at it would change his mind. This piece of rock proved to be the luckiest find that he had made in all his prospecting, but he did not know it. It was the lodestone which drew him to the discovery of the Black Queen, the Black King, the Tom Thumb, the Mother Hubbard and the Mammoth, the five claims which he and his partners sold for $20,000.

Regarding the home life at Goldfield—Goldfield and Bull Dog cover an area some three miles square, and while they are separated in the mind of the observer, they are, for the purpose of this writing, considered as one; and the name Goldfield covers both. The majority of the habitations are built of canvas and palo verde poles. There are a few very respectable looking boarding houses, compactly built to keep out rain and heat in the summer and the cool night air of fall and winter.

The boarding house owned by Mr. Kimball of Mesa and patronized by the miners and carpenters employed on the Mammoth mine and mill, is a neat wooden structure containing two rooms, one for the dining-room and the other for a kitchen. This is located close to the mine and alongside the roadway, which is the main thoroughfare of the camp. Across the road is the general store of Peterson Bros., that is also a wooden building, and the young men who conduct it deserve the large patronage they have gained for their enterprise and faith in the camp.

There's a butcher shop down on the road which is also a board building, and a saloon off in the other direction up the hill, a neat wooden structure. Here and there, scattered about the low hills, re tents and pole shacks providing comfortable semi-outdoor abodes. A favorite style of dwelling is a tent with a porch built at the opening, of palo verde poles and the branches of mesquite and other trees. The porch forms a kitchen, dining-room, sitting-room and in fact the living-room, as the women call it, or parlor as the men jocularly term it. At any rate they are pleasant and comfortable living places for a new mining camp and the housewives and daughters keep them as clean as the ground can be swept. The miners and other workmen without families, are provided with, or provide for themselves, tents and cots. Many of them during the warm weather unroll their blankets on the ground and sleep with the sky for a covering, without a notion of fear of the creeping and crawling insects and reptiles which terrify a tenderfoot. Sleeping outdoors is a common thing and there are many of these sleepers to be seen scattered over the low hills of Goldfield.

The canteen in Goldfield is as indispensable as the Bible in a camp meeting. The miner and the prospector cling to it as closely

as does the Christian to the Book. From the canteen comes that fountain of temporal life and without it the traveler is likely to suffer as much the misery of thirst as the sinner without salvation suffers the fear of damnation.

Water in Goldfield is almost as abundant as gold-bearing rock; though much of it, like the gold, is hidden deep in the earth. Here and there are springs from which family supplies are carried in barrels. For immediate use in the heart of the camp, the supply is drawn from wells on the Mammoth and other claims. Here the workmen fill their canteens and here the horses are driven to quench their thirst. Many a housekeeper draws her supply from these wells and the careful ones boil it before using it for drinking or cooking purposes. It is not good water without filtering.

Ice may be had from Mesa at four cents a pound, and there is a considerable quantity used for iced tea and other beverages. Altogether the inhabitants of Goldfield fare well in respect to water, but the tenderfoot must be careful how he drinks until his stomach has become used to the change; or he must hunt for the springs.

The food in Goldfield is as wholesome as in city or village homes; the table may not be spread so prettily; the tinware and keystone dishes may not shine so brightly as the silver and china at home; but the hungry man is as easily satisfied with food served in camp as in the palatial dining-room. Bacon and Irish potatoes and coffee are the standard edibles, while fresh beef and sweet potatoes and iced tea are by no means a rarity. Everybody lives well and they are all strong, healthy and ambitious.

There is an abundance of wood for $2.50 a cord. Most of the wood for cooking purposes is picked up about the hills, where teams are driven. The roads are a little rough in places, but there is scarcely a place where a carriage may not be driven; and in most cases wagon roads may be made directly to the mines.

This camp, like most of the mining camps, gets hilarious after pay day. The boys don't think they have any use for their money and they (that is some of them) give it over the bar to the saloon men who are always ready to take it. It would not be so bad if the drink had a more quieting effect, but it has a different effect on some and they tried to see if they could not make more noise than the whistle, to the annoyance of those who wanted to sleep. If it was possible, your correspondent would like to have same kinds of drink introduced that would quiet those thus hilarious.

One by one the Superstition camp takes on the embellishments of civilization and every day sees several new domiciles erected. Goldfield now has twenty-nine houses used either for business purposes or for residences. The mill is building and will before many weeks be in running order. A second mill is in contemplation by private parties, who will erect and run it for custom work.

While business is being pushed energetically, the morals of the camp are looked after also. Rev. Clarke, a local divine of the local Christian persuasion, preached on Sunday night in one of the leading saloons of the camp, and fifty people including several ladies listened to the eloquent sermon preached from a text which refers to Zacchaeus, a little man who climbed a sycamore tree to get a good view of the Savior as He passed by. Many old, hardened sinners who had not heard a sermon in twenty years were present, prominent among which were Tex, Tennessee and Barnum, three toughs well-known throughout Central Arizona as men of the old-time proclivities for blowing in quite suddenly after each pay day. The music for attendance services was not of the classical style; the choir consisted of the entire congregation and what was lacking in quality was made up in volume, as the sturdy prospectors took great pride in lending what feeble assistance they could in making the service impressive. While services were in progress, the bar was closed and through respect for the minister, who had been invited to occupy the improvised pulpit, it was not opened again that night. Beneath the ragged jackets of these pioneers there still lurks a feeling of respect for the religion of their mothers and the grizzled features of some of the old-timers, the moistened eye and the stained cheek, indicated the true manliness of those who vainly delve in unfrequented spots of the earth in quest of gold.

The store of Peterson Bros. was decorated with a splendidly gotten-up notice of a dance at the boarding-house. Those who were on the night shift who wished to attend were busy finding a substitute [for their night jobs], while others, who were on the day shift, were rustling around the camp hunting up suits befitting the occasion.

At last the evening arrived and you could see the young men

making the acquaintance of married ladies so that when the hour arrived they would not be entire strangers. At 7:30 the tables were removed from the dining-room and the company began to arrive. On account of the long jaunt the day before and the [lack of] comeliness of your reporter's attire, he did not participate in the pleasures of the evening, but was allowed the privilege of standing some distance from the building and gaping through the window at honored guests in the well-lighted room. The grandeur displayed was good enough to decorate the parlor of the fine polished residence of eastern cities. The gentlemen were togged up with square-cut coats and low-cut vests, Prince Albert suits and dressy sack coats. Those who had none of their own borrowed from their accommodating friends.

The ladies were well dressed as Arizona ladies know how to tog up for refined society. They are among those who come from gorgeous halls of the East and have taken up the life in Arizona to better their circumstances.

At last the hour arrived for the festivities. The guitar and violin started up while Hime Stewart, in his gorgeous attire, stepped to the center and cried out in his stentorian voice "honors to your partners," and off went the giddy partners whirling through the room like phantoms.

The party had an enjoyable time and all went off pleasantly and time passed swiftly away and the wee small hours arrived too soon for them to depart, but being laboring men it broke up and those who partook of the evening pleasures went home to dream pleasant dreams over the last enjoyable hours of their lives. May such be the case in the future. May no strife or discord exist and boys be gentlemen in ladies' society and they will be a success.

In a letter signed "A Goldbug" that appeared in the October 22, 1897, issue of the Phoenix Herald was this encouraging message titled "Among Golden Sands":

Goldfield! Here is no need of the Golden Touch, for all things now are tinged with gold from the crown of the Superstition to the curls on baby's head. There are no fields here but fields of gold. The flowers are all golden, the yellow cactus blossom and the buttercup being most common, the mountains have a golden hue, and the brooks flow golden sand, when it rains, and golden sunbeams afford the balmiest climate.

The people here did not come for the sake of all this gold that meets the eye at every glance, but for that which lies as deep in the earth as desire for gold is deep in the bosoms of those who seek it; but the world is much mistaken if it thinks that this desire for gold renders the miners penurious, ungenerous or inhospitable, for he seeks not to obtain wealth by robbing his fellow-man, but from that source from whence, if his hopes are fulfilled, he not only enriches himself but adds to the wealth of the world. Each may rejoice over his neighbor's success for no one loses, but each gains, if not materially, much in hope and anticipation.

The climate here is lovely. It is not high enough to be cold, but just high enough to be well drained and dry. The atmosphere is of the purest, being free from smoke, dust and miasma of all kinds. The only disease to which the people here are liable is the gold fever, recovery from which requires a longer or shorter time, according to the severity of the attack. It rarely proves fatal but often becomes chronic, and a few cases have been known to develop into money-mania.

For the benefit of those who will want to come, for come they will to this land of gold, if you mean to stay all winter you will need a tent, provisions and some silver. All who come are sure to go away rich in experience and vital energy.

School is in session now as in other parts of the country, and the children here are just the same as children anywhere else; it is only after they have reached the age when cupidity is developed that their true relation to the Goldbug family can be developed. And the teacher is not at all as the mining-camp schoolma'am is wont to be described. She is nothing of an adventuress; does not wear a bowie-knife, six-shooter or other visible arms, and judging from appearance, I believe she trusts more to the good will of the miners for safety than to any stiletto concealed in her bosom. She occupies, free of charge, a cottage built by the generosity of the miners for the benefit of the teachers who may come here.

Nowhere else on earth does the stream of time flow so smoothly. There is not a ripple on its bosom. At six each morn and eve the whistle blows and men pass, some to work and some to rest, Sundays not excepted. Even pay day was not celebrated with any drunken brawls, and the peaceful quiet of the evening is only broken by the puff of the engine, the cries of children at play and the voices of the mothers singing their lullabys.

*Adding to this nostalgic picture of a literal paradise is the following optimistic evaluation of the camp which was printed in the* Phoenix Herald *a few weeks later:*

There are at present fifteen or sixteen mining claims in the camp which pan out gold, and some of them, such as the Mammoth, Black Queen, Sunset, Fair Stake, Treasure Vault, Highland, Bull Dog, and others are producing sufficient ore suitable for milling to pay well for the investment. Others which will be equally as good when they are developed, are covered by mother earth, but the steady click of the hammer and the boom of the blast will show their wealth. Then the poor prospector will become the bloated bond-holder or else a whiskey bum, but either will cause him to feel rich. This is now but the starting of our camp, but long before her sun is set I hope millions of dollars worth of gold will pass out of the camp to be crowned by the majestic eagle or to decorate the tiny hand of the fair ladies of America.

*But before the end of this month of November, 1897, as suddenly as a tornado could strike, the Herald carried this startling story:*

Goldfield is dead! The camp was seemingly in perfect health, everything continued as usual; no intimation being given of the change until one of the owners of the mine returned from Mesa as usual and orders began to be given which showed unmistakable signs of a speedy dissolution.

Car-tracks in the mine began to be taken up, temporary buildings to be torn down and boards nailed over the windows of other buildings, and the quiet felicity of the little town became suddenly perturbed, and "the mine is going to close down" the dismal greeting of every one you met.

Those who thought themselves settled at least for the winter, began to contemplate finding new homes. Women sighed at the thought of having to move so soon, and many little prospective luxuries were given up, and a greater burden of work is carried in the effort to economize because of the prospect of no work for the men and consequently no income.

No one knows the intention of the company but by conjecture, but all watch with interest every indication. All know that many must go, but would not a few be kept and who would be favored? Who was laid off today and how many went to work was often the query. When and where are you going was the topic of the day. Only the steadfastness of the mountains, the beautiful calm of the sunshiny days and the merriment of the children seemed undisturbed. The fate of the school is often discussed and the children counted o'er and o'er, as the probability of this one going, that one staying, is conjectured, and the teacher receives many expressions of sympathy on the prospect of losing her situation. Truly there was not an individual whose sojourn here was not a precarious one.

Sometimes from what they heard, one might think there would not be a family in Goldfield by the end of the week, but things don't move quite so rapidly, yet as the week passes on, all realize that the end is nigh and what little hope some had of being retained, begins to wane. As the end is neared many of the boys were discharged. Some of them wished to celebrate the decease of the town with a true Irish wake, but for some reason did not succeed in getting the people together, and they prepared to depart. And as the days pass, each bringing less hope than the day before, till Saturday afternoon, their work being then completed, the last man came on top and the engine gave a last expiring sob and its soul passed away, and now the mill and hoists stand outlined against the mountains "lonely and spectral and sombre and still."

At last it is known that Mr. Meehan and Uncle Billy Moyle, two old-timers, will be left as watchmen, while to everyone else "the world is all before them where to choose their place of rest" —or toil. Men without families go as soon as discharged. Some left Saturday and Sunday, but those who have families cannot so readily leave. Most of them will remain for a week or two and some may leave their families here till they go and find new homes for them. So the fate of the school is not yet determined.

No one seems to know exactly why the mine closed, for all maintain that there is plenty of ore that would pay. It does not seem that anyone asked the superintendent if he knew and the writer certainly did not find an opportunity of doing so, but heard many probable reasons suggested. There is also talk of discontinuing the postoffice, in which event word from Goldfield will be almost as uncertain as news from André.

A mining camp. Camp is the right word, for really no one ever means to make a permanent home here. The buildings are all temporary structures, while many people live here in tents, and as one by one the inhabitants go away, so every day there is one tent or cabin less in the village, and soon there will be little trace of the once lively little town of Goldfield. Yet if the mine starts up again a new town will spring up, like a mushroom, in a night.

Near the end of December, the Herald stated that the exodus from Goldfield was almost complete, but that a few continued to come and go:

The coyotes feel sure that Goldfield will soon be their undisputed possession and one fat well-to-do fellow being impatient to

nter upon the enjoyment of his privileges went straight to headquarters and made his lair under the house of the superintendent,
but Mr. Hall, not being quite ready to turn over the premises, dealt
with him in a summary manner.

*hus, within a span of four short years there occurred the birth,
ife, and death of an Arizona mining camp, Goldfield, one of many
amps which met the same fate. Some died in less time; others
hung on" longer; some have prospered throughout many years
nd still dot the Arizona landscape to this day, and from all ap-
earances they will continue to prosper into the unforseeable
uture.*

# THE HERMIT OF THE SUPERSTITIONS

Old Man Reavis, the Hermit of the Superstitions," is dead! His
ody, half eaten by coyotes, was found near his hut in the Super-
titions. This was the startling and gruesome message carried in
ome of the Arizona newspapers in mid-May of 1896. Whether
eath was natural or violent was only a matter of conjecture, also
e time when it might have occurred, for the hunger of the
olves had not left enough evidence upon which to base an
pinion.

Word was brought into Florence by Bud Neighbors of the find-
g of the decomposed body on the trail about four or five miles
om the Reavis ranch. James Delabaugh, a prospector, was at the
eavis ranch on the 20th of April, when the hermit was about to
art out for Mesa to procure some seed potatoes. Being at Fraser's
nch on the 6th of May, and finding that Reavis had not passed
at way, as he would necessarily be compelled to do, Delabaugh
ecame alarmed and went back on the trail to learn the reason.
e found the body of the old hermit near the trail. His burros

were tied near by, half starved from their fast of several days, an
his two big mongrel dogs were hovering near the body of their dea
master, and had evidently destroyed a portion of his body. [*It seem*
*doubtful that these dogs would allow any varmint to approach th*
*body of Reavis and mutilate it as some of the stories have it. I*
*seems logical that they, sensing death, tugged at their master*
*body, causing the damaged state in which it was found.*]

Of all men so widely known there was none in Arizona of whom
so little was known as "Old Man Reavis." Much had been writte
about him by the few who had visited him in his mountain home
but what was written was generally produced by the imaginatio
of the writers. It is said that the old recluse was driven into exile b
a disappointment in love, but he never said so and nobody else ha
been found who could have said so. It is only known that he settle
in the Superstition Mountains in the early seventies, and while h
may have been hunting for the "Lost Dutchman" mine, nothin
was ever mentioned about it. He never told anybody where he cam
from, in fact he never told anybody much of anything, except a
interesting story now and then of his adventures.

The Apaches were roaming the hills in those days, but they soo
learned to shun the cabin of the hermit whose unerring rifle fir
inspired respect, and then a sort of superstitious terror. The ol
man spent the most of his time in hunting and raising vegetable
and fruit which were carried by burro train to the various minin
camps in the area, among them Silver King, Goldfield, Globe an
Pinal, as well as the towns of Florence, Mesa and Tempe.

The Reavis ranch of some fifteen acres, located in an almo
inaccessible part of the Superstitions, was about fifteen miles nortl
west of Silver King and some forty miles east of Phoenix. Ther
was always plenty of wild game in the area, and for many yea
the Apaches hunted both man and beast throughout this area.
never failing stream of pure water flowed there which was used t
irrigate the land. The elevation, about five thousand feet above se
level, provided an excellent climate where all kinds of deciduo
fruits flourished, as did most varieties of vegetables. Wild walnu
and cherries grew abundantly. Blackberries and raspberries gre
wild in plentiful quantities all around the mountains.

Reavis specialized in fresh vegetables, including some of the bi gest and best cabbages ever grown. Reavis cabbages were famous. Heads that averaged more than ten pounds in weight were solid and firm, and as tender as young lettuce. He raised parsnips, five inches in diameter, that were extremely tender, and in fact all of his vegetables possessed the most superior qualities.

There are some very interesting Indian ruins not far from the Reavis ranch and a cave in which many relics have been found. They are situated on Rogers Creek and but few white people have ever visited them and none in a scientific way. The whole neighborhood is full of interesting features, and the place, a splendid summer resort, although comparatively few were ever privileged to take advantage of this very delightful place.

Reavis was a typical frontiersman; active, restless, hardy and hospitable. He was nearly six feet in height, very straight, and strongly built; his massive head covered with a long hirsute matting of auburn hue, innocent alike of shears or comb for perhaps years. His deep-set gray eyes looked out from under shaggy brows, leaving no feature visible except his nose, which was straight and large denoting character. He wore overalls, a flannel shirt and a seedy coat, and this costume, it is said, he had never been known to vary during the time he had been in the country. He was affable and intelligent, a thorough scholar and great reader. He possessed an excellent library of standard books, and from each trip to a settlement he carried back a bagful of newspapers and it is said that his acquaintance with the affairs of the outer world was thorough and surprising. The story of his life and adventures surely would have made an interesting volume of historical value.

Reavis had many peculiar eccentricities, such as never cutting or combing his hair; at least it gave the appearance of never having been given any care. He was really more of a recluse than a hermit, and although he attracted the attention of strangers because of his odd appearance, his burro train and dogs, those acquainted with him paid no more attention to him than they did any other mountain rancher. Once while he was visiting in Phoenix a tourist took a snapshot of him with a kodak. The picture was finished, enlarged and made a part of the Arizona exhibit at the Columbian Exposition where it was said to have been recognized by a woman from California as her long lost brother, and that there was an attempt

at correspondence and a very romantic story that the old man had left a daughter in San Francisco whom he had educated and was secretly supporting. The only thing though that really resulted from the exhibition of the picture was a threat sent down the mountain side by the hermit that if he ever met the amateur artist he would send a bullet through his brain. His picture, however, had been taken some years previous to that and an enlargement of it hung in a Phoenix saloon. It represented a man whose face might have looked upon a century. The hair was long and matted and crowned by a slouched and ragged hat. A Winchester lay across his lap, the fingers of the right hand grasping the stock of the gun.

On the occasion of one of Reavis' visits to Phoenix he was entertained by a couple of gentlemen who had been at his home in the mountains. The entertainment evolved into a circuit of saloons. In one of them he was introduced to a concert-hall singer. He was a model of courtesy, a reminiscence of a former life somewhere. But when he was asked to drink a glass of champagne with the painted singer he refused laughingly, politely but firmly. He would drink with the boys, but he had never learned, wherever he had been, to drink with a woman in a saloon.

—A composite of Arizona newspaper items, 1896

*In 1890 the Phoenix* Herald *carried the following item concerning Reavis:*

Old Man Reavis, the famous hermit of the Superstition Mountains, whose long, matted beard and hair, uncut since the great Centennial, made him a well-known landmark, appeared in Florence last week, but no one recognized him. In fact he failed to remember himself. It seems that, on returning from Tempe, he met some companions of ante-bellum days, up in a canyon where mescal brewed itself and they had only to drink that soft, oily beverage. The hermit over-estimated his load-carrying capacity and fell upon some cholla [choy-ya] cactus. Thereupon his mischievous pards sheared his Samsonian locks and Aaronic whiskers. In fact they gave him a genuine Riley cut. When the old man awoke next morning he looked around in a strange dumbfounded way, and inquired if that was Hermit Reavis or not. Receiving no satisfactory answer, he went to Florence, where St. Claire & Pratt recognized him by one lock behind his left ear that had escaped the scissors. He then had himself branded "H," in the brisket, so that the enumerator would be able to find him for the census come June.

Another of his eccentricities [wrote the Tucson Star in 1891], was that he was scrupulously honest and a square-toed Democrat and would fight at the drop of the hat, and when the Phoenix Republican dubbed him "The Hermit of the Superstition Mountains," we venture a cooky that the editor of that paper will have to modify, or take back altogether, the "dub" which he has seen fit to bestow upon Mr. Reavis, provided Mr. Reavis sees the "flattering notice" or his attention is called to it. We know the gentleman well. He disdains notoriety, and particularly dislikes any newspaper mention made of him and his habits.

In commenting upon the above in 1891, the Phoenix Herald inserted an item that a friendly "scrap" with one of its fellow journals in the city was quite evidently in preparation by the Tucson Star. The Herald said:

The Phoenix Republican dubs Mr. E. M. Reavis, who arrived in Phoenix on last Friday, "The Hermit of the Superstition Mountains." Now this soubriquet won't suit the gentleman. In the first place he is not a "hermit," for he carried on farming and gardening and stock-raising, and employs a number of men on his place. He makes Florence his headquarters and goes there and mingles with the people as often as any other rancher. He has his peculiar eccentricities—one of which is that he wears his hair and beard long in an unkempt condition, and in consequence attracts the attention of strangers. Then the Pueblo [Tucson Star] proceeds as directly as it can without arrest for exciting a riot, to goad Mr. Reavis into knocking the eternal stuffing out of the editorial author of his so-called and mis-applied soubriquet.

In a letter from Florence to the Phoenix Herald in 1895, a reporter wrote that:

Mr. Reavis, the "old man of the mountain" was down with his

burros "loaded to the gunwale" with the choicest vegetables ever brought to this market. Cabbages that would make a Dutchman's mouth water, cauliflower, beets and lettuce among other things. No Delilah's shears could clip those locks and no comb or brush must touch that hirsute head. Let no Indians trespass on his hunting grounds for that rifle is a "dead shot" every time.

The man who takes Reavis for an ignoramus will soon find he has "caught a tartar." No more intelligent man can be found in Phoenix than this noted hermit and no host can treat his guests with greater affability or generosity. He is a college graduate and has not forgotten his knowledge of mathematics, languages, sciences or Belle Lettres. He is "Monarch of all he surveys" in his lonely home. He still cultivates his vegetable garden after the most approved methods and has plenty of sparkling water to irrigate at pleasure. When he wants venison he knows where to find his deer. If "bruin" trespasses on his grounds he never returns to his cave to "tell the tale." A strange life is this of Mr. Reavis. He enjoys it and we will not pry into the secret of his isolation from society. His history is veiled in mystery and sealed hermetically as the "semi seals of the Apocalypse." When he comes to town he is cordially received by his old friends but each year he finds some have gone to that bourne whence no traveler returns. How many times he has been reported as killed by the Indians deponent saith not, but one thing is certain, he is too lively a "coon" to be caught napping and as for "Mr. Lo" [Indians] he has long since given this "crack shot" a wide berth. (It is said the Indians have a dreaded fear of his strange appearance, believing him insane, and the Indians' superstition concerning the insane causes them to stay out of his sight.)

In 1890, on one of his trips to Florence, Reavis very reluctantly consented to relate a little adventure to an Enterprise representative and promised to supplement it with some of his more thrilling experiences at some future time:

It was about the 1st of November, 1888, quite late in the afternoon, when he took his gun and dog and went up in the pinery above his home to hunt for bear. He roamed about their accustomed haunts but failed to discover any evidence of their recent

presence, and finally he went towards a small stream with steep
banks, having about given up the search, and with the intention of
getting a drink of water. His dog preceded him and, upon reaching
the brow of the steep declivity, set up a loud barking, with its
gaze fixed up the opposite mountainside. Mr. Reavis concluded
the dog had sighted a deer but he could see nothing upon the
hillside to indicate the presence of any game. Just then he glanced
down the creek and, upon the opposite side, a short distance below,

sitting at the foot of a large tree, was a big black bear with two fairly grown cubs. The bear was looking at him and his movements. It was a good shot, but for a time he considered whether or not he would shoot it. The scene was such a peaceful one and the great eyes looked towards him with such an expression of confidence in his good intentions that he almost concluded to shoulder his gun and turn homewards. But the natural love of the hunter for game finally prevailed over his humane impulses and he took deliberate aim at its breast and fired.

The beast jumped forward through the brush and made up the hill towards Reavis who, not relishing a clash with it, got up in an adjacent cherry tree to watch the movement of the wounded bear. It came in sight of him, looked about and then returned. He descended from the tree and advanced towards the creek to see the bear climbing the opposite side and making towards the top of the mountain, followed by the cubs. He raised the gun and fired again this time at a cub, which he wounded, but did not stop its flight. He loosened the rope by which he held the dog and let it follow. He found the blood of the old bear and the cub by which he followed them for about a mile and then returned home, as darkness had come on.

The dog did not come home that night and the next morning he saddled a burro and went to the summit in search of the dog and bear. Striking the trail of blood he followed it a mile along the summit and there he found the dog whose rope had got fastened to the brush. He followed the trail further and cut across to head it off, by a pass in the high peaks overlooking Pinto Creek. Upon arriving at a good point of observation he heard a loud groaning, a most distressful sound, coming nearer and nearer. He waited for it to come up on the bench about thirty feet distant, in the low brush. It was the same wounded bear with her two cubs. Upon reaching the bench she smelled her enemy and put her nose up in the air and sat looking at him. Another shot was fired at the breast, but it evidently hurt without seriously wounding her. She jumped up, went back over the hill and rolled down. Reavis went out on the bench and looked down and saw both the cubs, crying pitifully. Another shot was fired, but too low, and it only cut the dirt under the bear.

The strangest scene then presented itself that he had ever witnessed. Forgetful of her own sufferings, the bear caught her cubs and drew them to her breast as if to protect them; one of them pulled itself away and she reached for it and hugged both to her breast so human like, while the great eyes appealed with strange human-like appearance, for mercy. So striking was this appeal that Reavis dropped his gun and could not shoot again. It was like murder to do so.

The bear then put her cubs down and went on through the brush. He kept on the trail to drop below her and head her off near the point where he intended to camp, as night was then near at hand. He arrived at the canyon he had selected for this purpose, which was intersected by a lateral canyon at this point, and hitched the burro to a walnut tree. He was sure the bear would come that way as he could still hear the groans, so he went a little way up the opposite hillside and lay down to sleep. The night was quite dark and all he could see from his position was the white spot on the burro's nose. He expected the animal would make some noise if the bear appeared, which would be the signal of its approach. No sleep came to his eyelids, and he could still hear occasional groans, then a rustle of the leaves not far away, and again close by and suddenly one of the cubs came over the point where he was lying, and in its flight jumped squarely upon him!

This was something more realistic than a nightmare, and he jumped down from his position to the tree where his burro was tied. In doing so he passed close to the bank of the creek and was almost paralyzed to hear an unearthly snort and to feel the hot breath of the huge bear not over a foot away! A moment later and he was up the tree where he remained for three hours.

The next morning he tracked the bear and followed it until it stopped bleeding. It had wallowed in the sand occasionally and had built several houses to lie down as is usual when the bear is about to die. It evidently did die, but he did not pursue it further to make sure of the fact.

# 9

# BEAR FIGHTS AND
# BADGER FIGHTS

BEAR FIGHTS AND BADGER FIGHTS

Although bear fights and badger fights have nothing in common, they were both quite conspicuous in Arizona's earlier days. One seldom, if ever, reads of a bear fight in this day and age, although there are still plenty of bear to be had in the great Mogollon (Mogey-own) country stretching across central Arizona. The inroads of civilization have decimated them, however, and forced them into the more remote areas.

Now badger fights, unlike bear fights, seldom resulted in injury to the human participants, except perhaps their pride, but the lust for blood was amply satisfied when a ferocious bulldog tangled with a vicious, clawing badger, both trained to "fight to the death." Accounts of these affairs were usually important enough to rate bold-type headings on the front pages of the newspapers in the towns where they were held and were often reprinted in other Arizona newspapers.

But, alas, along with bull fights, dog fights, and cock fights, the badger fight was "forbidden by law." It was a function pulled off in basements of store buildings and other out-of-the-way places and was kept secret from all but the sports of the town and their guests. Nevertheless, the police would often get wind of the event and raid the place about the time the festivities were over. The ringleaders were usually arrested, tried, and fined for breaking the law.

Accounts from the Arizona press of a few of the more interesting badger fights are presented in the second part of this chapter. There is no need to explain to the old-timers the technical details of the sport; but to the younger folks, those who have probably never heard of a badger fight, the secrets of the ritual will not be divulged here. All the facts that are permissible are contained in the stories.

But first, the bear fights.

## BEAR FIGHTS

A citizen of the Blue River country wrote the following letter to the Clifton Copper Era in 1907:

Among your many good articles we never see any bear stories. Now I can see you smile and hear you say, "Bear stories!" Reputable newspapers have long since quit "loading" their readers with bear and fish stories. I am sure this is the attitude of your worthy papers; were it not, your news gatherers could obtain facts from the Blue River ranchers showing desperate encounters with wounded bears and hairbreadth escapes as wild and thrilling as the adventures of the big game hunters in Darkest Africa.

The bear and cattlemen of the mountains are sworn enemies, and whenever and wherever they chance to meet, the crack of the unerring rifle deals death or brings on a desperate combat. There is no animal in the world more dangerous and hard to kill as an enraged and wounded grizzly bear and woe unto man or horse who permits his embrace or comes within reach of his terrible claws. Many times a bear will put up a stiff fight after being shot through the vitals.

All of the cowmen in this section have killed many bears; many have had narrow escapes and not a few wear the marks of bruin's valor. Johnson, Fritz, Cosper, Jones, Thomas, and Forest Hall are all veteran bear hunters, and there is scarcely a time when they came to town but some of them could tell of encounters with bears that are true and would be interesting reading. But they are so modest and little given to boasting of their exploits that the facts can only be obtained after a thorough cross-examination. For example, Jones could tell of crawling into a bear's den and dispatching him, while Fritz could inform you how it feels to be caressed by a wounded, enraged silvertip, and how when he was all but dead, a lucky chance shot broke the bear's jaw, and saved Fritz from a horrible death. [The Fritz story later.]

Awakening one night at the barking of his dog, Forest Hall got up and shot a bear from a tree so close to his camp that the bear fell on his bed.

But J. H. T. Cosper, better known as Toll Cosper, bears the reputation of having killed more bears than any other man in the Blue country. His ranch and range lies on and adjacent to the Blue range, a wild and rugged country, with deep canyons and high hills whose slopes are covered with dense thickets of pine and underbrush. Many bears inhabit these canyons and forests, and Cosper's work frequently brings him in contact with them. He seems to have an eye for bears. His luck at finding them is phenomenal, and rarely do the soft nose bullets from his thirty-forty fail to do deadly work. But even a thirty-forty does not kill every time, and Cosper has had many narrow escapes with enraged and wounded bears.

Some years ago when in a bear fight and while trying to protect a boy from a wounded bear that was pursuing him, Cosper rode too near the bear. The desperate animal unable to stand the fire from behind, suddenly wheeled, charged Cosper, and leaped upon his horse, and in another instant would have torn him to pieces had not a well-directed bullet broken his jaw and sent him reeling to the ground.

Last fall while riding along a lonely trail on the Blue range, a huge silvertip suddenly appeared in the path not over forty yards away, and insisted on the right-of-way. While the bear stood sizing him up, Cosper quietly dismounted, took deliberate aim and began "fogging" him. Although the first bullet dealt him a mortal wound, the bear uttered a savage roar and made for his enemy. His horse took fright and fled, and Cosper thinking discretion the better part of valor, tried to fly up a pine tree, but ere he could climb beyond his reach, the bear was almost upon him and would have caught him had not the snorting and plunging of his horse attracted bruin's attention for a moment. As the bear turned to the horse, the hunter seized the opportunity and while holding to the tree with one hand fired his gun with the other, breaking the bear's neck. When he descended and examined his gun, there was only one cartridge left in the magazine. The bear weighed about seven hundred pounds.

Unless wounded, a bear rarely shows fight, but either runs or stands curiously eyeing the hunter, but occasionally and especially when hungry, a bear will assume the offensive.

Last May, Cosper, his two sons and Charles Chapman were "riming" for cattle in Stray Horse, a deep canyon that heads on the Blue range. When they reached Rose Peak, a high mountain near the head of the canyon, they stopped to rest their horses and while seated on a log Chapman jestingly remarked that he wished seven hundred bears would charge them. The others laughed and expressed their opinions as to how quickly he could ascend a tree in case even one should happen along. Scarcely had their laughter died away when a hoarse growl told them his wish had come to pass. They scarcely had time to snatch their guns from the scabbards, when a huge silvertip appeared in the trail above them not twenty yards away, making straight for them. Four rifles spouted forth and sent death-dealing missiles into his body, but the bear was not checked until he was almost upon them and a dozen bullets had entered his body, one going down his windpipe and through his heart. Had it been one man instead of four, nothing but a lucky shot could have saved him from death. This bear weighed fully eight hundred pounds. He measured eight feet from his nose to tail and the hide when spread out measured nine feet across from the front paw to the hind paw.

Mr. Editor, if you ever want to go on a bear hunt, go with Cosper, and there will be "something doing."

Yours very truly,

J. T. MATHEWS

*Fred Fritz, a ranchman of the Blue River country, visited Clifton in 1905 and gave the Clifton Copper Era the details of a fierce fight which he had had some time since with an old silvertip bear which had been a terror to the ranchmen of that section for many years:*

While riding his range in the neighborhood of Maple Springs he cut the trail of a bear, which was nothing unusual in that section. He had four dogs with him and a pistol, hence he did not hesitate to follow the trail, feeling certain that he would have little trouble in dispatching bruin. Fritz had killed many bears previous to this time without an experience worth reporting. But this bear was different. He was not only big, old and tough, but also a fighter. He trailed the old fellow only a short distance when he was overtaken in some piñon timber. Fritz opened fire with his pistol. The dogs also took an interest in the fight, but the bear did not apparently take an interest in them, but he made a break for Fritz, and being on higher ground he jumped partly onto the horse and grabbed him with his mouth and claws. Fritz then got another shot which broke the bear's jaw, and caused him to relax his hold on the horse. He then emptied his revolver at the bear thinking he would settle him, but owing to the fact that the horse was fractious and the bear's hide tough, he was not able to land a fatal shot. He rode off a short distance and reloaded, and then discovered that he had only six cartridges. In the meantime the dogs were following bruin and worrying him greatly. He then took up the trail, and after following it about a mile overtook the bear in a narrow canyon. He dismounted from his horse and followed the bear up into some sharp rock, and just as he was surmounting one of them the bear jumped onto him and together they rolled down several feet, the bear landing on top. Fritz landed face downward. He was somewhat stunned by the fall, but was quickly brought to his senses by the bear taking the back of his head in its mouth, and had it not been for the fact that the brute's jaw had previously been broken, no doubt the battle would have ended in favor of bruin.

Fritz managed to get his gun into action and firing over his shoulder caught the bear in the mouth, the bullet coming out at the butt of his ear. Ordinarily this should have ended the fight, but not so in this case. The bear apparently realizing that he could not use his mouth effectively proceeded with his claws to tear the leather "chaps" off of the now almost helpless man. This turned him over and he was again able to use his pistol, which he did until every shot had been fired. The dogs again took an interest in the fight, and attracted bruin's attention, but every time Fritz attempted to get up the bear came back and sat upon him while slapping at the dogs. He used the pistol as a club and broke it. He then managed to get out his pocket knife, which was so small and light that it would not penetrate through the tough hide of the bear. Fritz then realized that his only show of escape was through the dogs, and he encouraged them in their attack, and in this manner more dead than alive, with his clothes almost torn off, and bloody from head to foot, he managed to reach his horse. At this time his nephew, who had heard the shooting, arrived on the scene, and the two men followed the bear who was dragging the dogs with him. When they overtook the bear they saw that he was very sick. The nephew took one shot at him, and the bear soon afterwards died. Fritz was laid up at his ranch for many days, and will carry the scars of the battle with him to his grave. When the bear was skinned seven bullets were found in his body.

*The* Copper Era *carried this story in 1907:*

Bear stories usually made their appearance in Clifton about this time of the year when hunting parties begin to return from the mountains. Jack Holman, Reese Webster, Judge Hampton, Sheriff Anderson, Dick Franz, Jack Hagerty and several others recently returned from the White Mountains. Now it had always been reported that Hagerty was the only bear hunter in the country, but it seems that he got his reputation in the level parts of Kansas, where running is good, and parties who knew him there say they know of several thrilling bear fights in which Jack actually run the bear to death. Bear hunting in the mountains was a new thing

to Hagerty and it took him several days to get next. He always
had a hobby to do his hunting alone. One day the party started
out on a hunt and it was some time before he could conveniently
separate himself from the crowd. The rest of the hunters finished
their skirmish and returned to camp with empty bags. Hagerty
sneaked through the rough places and finally came across the tracks
of a monster bear. He trailed the bear for some time and the boys
in camp decided that he was lost, when he appeared in a fit of
excitement. His flushed face, glaring eyes and short breath convinced the boys that Jack had had another fierce encounter. When
he settled down he told his story. Well, he followed the bear until
he located him. The bear was above him and the country was so
rough that he at once decided not to shoot; as running was poor.
About that time another bear appeared and Jack forgot to shoot.
Covering a rocky country with a heavy gun was the limit and that
is the reason he returned to Clifton without his gun. He says the
next time he goes bear hunting it will be in a level country.

*The Tombstone Prospector in 1890, says that from a man who
just came in from Huachuca [wa-choo'-ka], further particulars were
learned of the recent fight with a bear, wherein Sergeant Anson
nearly lost his life and from the effects of which he is still confined
to the fort hospital.*

It seems that the unfortunate man had gone out to hunt deer
and had become separated from his companions. He went to a
spring of water where he knew the deer were used to water and
waited but a minute before seeing one coming towards the spring
from the opposite direction. He kneeled down and kept his eye
on the deer, while behind him a bear was watching his movements.
She evidently had cubs near by, for as soon as getting near enough
she sprang upon the man's right leg and tore it in a horrible manner. He turned and shot the brute but where he hit her he does
not know. She rose upon her hind legs and with one blow from
her paw struck the gun away from him and planted the claws of
the other foot in his face. He realized the danger he was in and as
she neared him the second time with extended jaws, and while
he felt her hot breath, he thrust his right arm into her throat and
endeavored to reach his knife with his left which he could not.

All this time the teeth of the animal were closed through the flesh of his arm like a vice, but being a powerful man he held her paws away from him and they both went down together. In this position they rolled to the bottom of the hill, he fighting with his left hand, and many times having the best of it, in the meantime yelling at the top of his voice. His comrades heard his cries for help and went to his rescue as rapidly as possible. When the bear saw them she let go of Anson's arm and deliberately ran up the hill to where the encounter began and seizing the carbine she had struck from the hands of Anson, took it in her teeth and went off in the brush.

Anson was taken immediately to the post where his wounds were dressed. His face will be disfigured for life and his arm where the teeth lacerated, the flesh resembles a piece of raw meat. Anson is a powerful man and to this fact he owes his life; had he been less powerful the bear would have made short work of him. He is considered the best hunter stationed at Huachuca, and recently had killed fourteen deer in fifteen days, a feat which was remarkable, but a wounded bear is not a deer.

—Graham County *Bulletin*, 1890

*From the Prescott* Courier *in 1892 comes this story, "In the Jaws of a Bear":*

George Conners rode in from Pine Flat, Camp Wood district, with W. R. Monroe, a young man recently from Colorado, who had a fight with three bears and was badly chewed and scratched up. The wounded man was carried to the office of the Plaza stable where Dr. Davis dressed his wounds. The right arm was badly chewed, and the doctor said "compound fracture of the ulna," as he dressed it. A long claw scratch extended across the stomach, near the short ribs; the right shoulder was badly lacerated; several stitches were taken in an ugly gash right behind the left shoulder; there were two ugly tooth wounds in the right foot, which was swollen; the left thigh was badly bitten.

The bear had been seen in the vicinity several times. Monroe started out with a dog and a 42-82 Winchester rifle to hunt the bear. When three miles from home he looked up and saw a big cinnamon bear coming down the trail toward him, not thirty feet away. He fired and knocked the bear down. The bear sprang to her feet, when another bullet stretched her dead. Her cub next put in an appearance and a shot laid it low. Then came a great he-bear, with savage growls and grinding teeth, rushing on the young hunter, and a shot knocked this bear over only a few feet away. The bear was on his feet in an instant; rushed on Monroe and downed him, and in the rough-and-tumble fight which followed, broke Monroe's arm in his teeth and lacerated his shoulder. The gun was knocked from Monroe's hands as he fell. He had a pocket knife in one of his pockets, but could not get at it. The dog fled while the bear was chewing his master up. Monroe called the dog; the dog crept up and smelled the bear, and the bear made a dash for the dog. Monroe ran for a tree and grabbed a limb with his uninjured arm, and was pulling himself up when the bear rushed on him again and bit him in the left thigh; grabbed his right foot, and, had not Monroe's shoe come off, the bear would have pulled him down. The bear walked off with the shoe in his mouth, looking back at the same time; laid down a few feet off, behind a pile of rocks, and died. Monroe walked three miles over the rocks back to Connor's ranch.

*The following story of a man who was hunting bear but found bobcats instead appeared in the Globe Silver Belt in 1908:*

After sliding down the mountain side for six hundred feet with two bobcats with which he had been having a desperate fight, Tom Galbraith, a prospector, succeeded in dispatching one of the animals, and made his way back to civilization, badly cut and bruised, but not painfully injured. The other cat was apparently buried in the snow. At any rate, Galbraith did not wait to find out what had become of it. He had been looking for bear for a couple of days in the Mogollon Mountains. Provided with powerful field glasses, he climbed up above the snow line and stood at the edge of a cliff, but a few feet from a tree, surveying the country below in hope of locating the particular Mr. Bruin which had made off with his supply of bacon a few days before.

Suddenly there was a rush and a snarling behind the huntsman, and he turned just in time to see two huge bobcats, which seemed to have leaped at him from the tree, falling short less than a couple of yards. The beasts paused an instant as Galbraith turned, but it was only for an instant, just long enough to permit him to drop the glasses and pick up the rifle he had laid at his feet. Before he could bring the piece in anything like position, the cats were at him, tooth and claws, and he could only attempt to fight them off with the rifle in a vain endeavor for a shot at either of them.

Fiercely fighting and whirling in the heavy snow, the desperate man and his enraged assailants approached the edge of the cliff without seeing it. It was a battle royal, a battle to the death, the blood lust raging in the heart of the human as wildly as in the bounding felines.

The huntsman at bay, bitten and scratched in a score of places, still managed to deal terrific blows on the spotted forms, but these blows only fell upon the sinuous bodies, knocking this or that cat down for a moment, but only for a moment, the other clawing and ferociously endeavoring to get at the man's throat.

Galbraith was forced out upon a rock at the very edge of the cliff. From this position he endeavored to knock at least one of the cats down the steep side of the hill. Then the unexpected happened. The ground gave way beneath the feet of the man whose strength was fast waning. Shaken by the tramping and fighting, the rock was dislodged, and with it started an avalanche of snow and rocks that carried him and the madly clawing cats down with it to the bottom of the gulch. Once on the way down, Galbraith was thrown almost against one of the beasts. He strove to shoot it even as he fell; the cat snapped at the barrel; and in the next instant both were covered with snow. As he arose from the snow at the bottom of the gulch, saved by a miracle and instinctively clutching to his rifle, he heard a wicked snarl behind him. Turning, he saw a bobcat, seemingly crippled, but still endeavoring to make for him. A shot put the animal out of its misery, and Galbraith, bleeding from two dozen wounds, made his way out of the place as best he could, several times narrowly escaping being smothered in deep drifts.

## BADGER FIGHTS

Just about the time Arizona begins to think she is properly and sufficiently civilized and ready to take her place alongside the more staid and enlightened commonwealths, some forcible and deplorable reminder of frontier days bobs up to shatter fat-headed delusions.

Such an occurrence was the badger fight pulled off in the rear of the Dominion Hotel in Globe. The practice of badger fighting has been denounced from time to time, in pulpit and press, but it seems that the disgraceful practice has not yet been entirely stamped out. And to prove that Western people are not alone susceptible to the allurments of this enticing sport, is the fact that one of the leaders in the Globe affair was an Eastern man. Not only is he an Eastern man, but he hails from the staid and cultured city of Boston. He seems to be a man of refinement and position in the business world. But, away from the influences of home life and gentle surroundings, he allowed his sporting blood to get the better of his careful breeding and participated in the unlawful sport of fighting badgers. This man's name is F. C. Carter. He is a capitalist, in Globe, in the interests of a mining deal of large import which is nearing consummation.

He pulled the badger! And this is the story: It is not definitely known who the chief organizers of the fight were, but suffice to say that a party of Globe sports gathered in the rear of the Dominion Hotel for the purpose of witnessing a badger fight. The badger was concealed beneath a box on which sat a bell boy of the hotel—obviously connecting the management of the hotel with the affair. Large sums of money were bet on the encounter, the odds being two to one in favor of the badger. But trouble came when the selection of a man to pull the badger came up. In fact, insinuations of unfair dealing were freely indulged in, and a disgraceful personal encounter between Charley Clark and Judge French was only averted by the timely interference of bystanders.

But it was finally decided to allow Carter [*the sport from Back Bay in Boston*] to pull the badger. He averred that he had no money bet on the fight and nad no interest in the deal except to see fair play. Before accepting the task of the "puller" he made a short address to the assembled crowd, saying that no matter what the result of the bloody encounter, he wanted it understood that he was an entirely innocent party and would do only as instructed by the referee. He was a square shooter and wanted the crowd to know it. This declaration was greeted by cheers from the crowd and he was the popular choice of all interested for the most honored position in the game.

And he pulled the badger, all right! J. C. Gatti held Hurd's bulldog, and as the box was lifted from the badger, Carter yanked it forth from its lurking place with all his might. The encounter that ensued was terrific and would have gone on to a bloody end had not the crowd interfered and separated the infuriated animals before either had succumbed. The battle was pronounced a draw, but the badger was the hero of the hour. He was proudly led into the hotel barroom by C. E. Rule, where Carter was made more personally acquainted with the fierce animal.

But the climax of the proceedings was yet to come. The officers of the city had gotten wind of the affair, and as Carter was the leading figure in the disgraceful sport, he was arrested and quite unceremoniously bustled into Justice Thomas' court, where, at his earnest request, he was given an immediate hearing, not caring to remain in jail over night.

In the absence of Justice Thomas, George Mauk acted as judge, jury and master of ceremonies. Many witnesses were examined, and during the course of the trial many were fined for contempt of court. C. E. Rule drew a jail sentence for boisterous conduct in the presence of the court, but was released on the payment of a fine of a dollar and a half.

Attorney Weinberger as assistant district attorney, appeared to prosecute the case, and the defense was conducted by Judge French. After the examination of several witnesses and masterly pleas by the opposing counsel the defendant was fined the drinks for the crowd, which penalty he willingly paid, and was released from custody.

But it is an ill wind that brings no man good. The Santa Claus fund of the *Silver Belt* was enriched by more than seventeen dollars on account of the badger fight. No, do not ask how the money was raised. It is there, all right, properly credited, and will help to make glad the heart of many little folk on Christmas morning who would otherwise have awakened to find empty stockings. Yes, it is an ill wind that brings no man good; and children too.

—Globe *Silver Belt*, 1908

Ed Freeman, a Coney Island grain operator, was the hero at a badger fight in the cellar of the Lawler block, in which the badger was worsted by Frank Miller's dog, considered to be the most ferocious and vicious fighting canine in Prescott. Freeman's conduct in striking the badger with a brick before the fight started was denounced by those present who placed their money on the badger. Freeman was selected to hold the badger on account of his athletic build and acrobatic accomplishments. Those who lost their money on the fight declare that Freeman will not be allowed to coach any more badgers during his stay in Prescott. Freeman stated after the fight that this was his first experience in badger fighting and that he did not want any more of it.

—Prescott *Journal-Miner*, 1908

*The following night another badger fight was held in the basement of the Lawler block:*

C. T. Miller, of Prescott, proved his superiority over Ed Freeman, the Coney Island grain operator, as a badger coach, the badger easily proving his superiority over a dog belonging to Charley Burton, seconded by George Ruffner. A large amount of money changed hands after the fight, the badger and dog having a large number of enthusiastic admirers present.

Before the contest Miller announced that the fight would be called off in case anyone interfered with the badger after it was turned loose. The disgraceful performance of the night before caused this precaution. Those present sought the high places in the basement, the only man remaining on the floor being Ed Meeks, who acted as referee. Miller's pants were slightly damaged by the overturning of a vessel filled with water during the affray, which lasted only a short time as the badger soon had the canine at its mercy.

—Prescott *Journal-Miner*, 1908

*Next day the* Journal-Miner *received the following communication:*

Mr. Editor, Dear Sir:

Will you please publish the following in your valued paper:

In the *Journal-Miner* of the 29-30 I read the horrible and shocking exposure of the recent badger fights, or rather a dog, vicious in nature, pitted against a poor badger with, as I understand it, all odds against the animals. As a gentleman and a minister of the gospel I am forced to speak out; to cry out against such barbarous actions. Think, oh think of the horrible proceedings of such a fight, encouraged by real men of sound mind and ability! Are we living in advanced civilization or have we gone back to the days of Caesar? I would like to ask where is the humane society that they allow such proceedings? Have the authorities nothing to say? Oh society, where art thou! Just think of the poor dog, without human instinct, and the frail badger without mind or brain held in the arena with a long chain in deadly combat. There is no escape, ONE MUST DIE! Then thrown to the ash pile, defunct, gone, with no one to mourn, but jocular attitude and boisterous laughter follow. Is this beautiful city to be tainted in this manner? Is there no preventative? If not, then let us elect a Nero and have cruelty reign supreme.

> REV. KNOX,
> A visitor to your city

(For the information of Rev. Knox, the *Journal-Miner* is pleased to state that the badger fights of the past few days have not been accompanied by any bloodshed. Other liquids but no blood have been spilled. In case any bloodshed is reported in these combats and the sports present do not promptly stop it, the whole power of the *Journal-Miner* will be brought to bear to stop badger fighting in this city. No bulldog jowl shall snap the badger neck without a wow from this newspaper which shall make the teeth of the humane officers chatter and the knees of the sheriff shake as he rushes to duty.)

Jealous at the reputation of C. T. Miller, achieved in the basement of the Lawler block as coach to the badger in the fight with Charley Burton's dog, seconded by George Ruffner, Bert Davis, an attache of the Linn Hotel volunteered to coach the victorious badger in a fight with one of George Ruffner's bloodhounds, last night, only to desert his post and leave the badger to the mercy of its antagonist when the ferocious fight started.

Davis first mounted a stepladder which was overturned by the badger and dog immediately after the start of the combat. He immediately escaped through the back door and when last seen was running across the plaza in the direction of the new jail. After Davis' exit from the place, the fight was stopped by the referee who recognized that the badger was at the decided disadvantage without a coach against Ruffner's bloodhound, backed by its experienced master, who is considered among the best badger and dog coaches in the Territory.

The bloodhound, which has treed lions and bayed bear, did not make the showing against the badger expected by the sports present during the short fight. Another fight will be arranged in the near future as Ruffner announced that he was ready to back his famous canine with a good amount in coin of the realm that it can vanquish any badger, that can be badgered into a fight catch weights, the badger to start with a jerk from a barrel and no bricks.

—Prescott Journal-Miner, 1908

In the meantime, Tombstone was having a series of more or less important badger fights, among which were the following battles reported in the Prospector:

Several members of the Society for the Prevention of Cruelty to Animals have importuned Mayor Wentworth and Chief of Police Bravin to abolish badger fighting in Tombstone. Chief Bravin fails to find an ordinance that would warrant him in complying with the request of the sober-minded who would deprive the public of a sport that is rapidly becoming popular throughout Arizona.

Mayor Wentworth, who owns a ferocious badger, and who is arranging a fight between that animal and Ollie Simpson's bulldog, utterly refuses to lend his municipal authority to the abridgement of innocent pastime that a few pikers might be satisfied to the sorrow of the multitude. So it may be stated positively that badger fighting will be continued in Tombstone, the one about to be pulled off promising to be of greater interest than any similar event for some time past.

The time for the battle royal has not as yet been agreed upon, Mayor Wentworth preferring to wait for Gene Larrieu, who last handled the badger and is an adept at getting all the fun out of a fight that science is capable of conceiving. Only a few invitations will be given, and those delivered by mental telepathy. Considerable gold will change hands on the result of the coming fight.

—Tombstone *Prospector*, 1907

Editor E. P. White, of the Cochise County *Press*, who is quite a naturalist and has made a study of badgers and their habits, does not see any brutality in the badger and dog fights, which is a prevalent sport in Arizona at this season of the year. He devotes considerable space in his interesting paper to badger items, from among which the following is taken:

> Eugene Larrieu stated to a Cochise County *Press* reporter that there was no truth in the report that he will have charge of Mayor Wentworth's badger in the coming tournament, as announced in the Tombstone *Prospector*. Larrieu stated that when he arrived here, he was told that the animals were overfed and were not properly exercised, consequently becoming so strong and vicious that they had to be kept muzzled all the time. The *Prospector's* big badger "Dreadnaught," slipped his muzzle last week and drove all the typos from the job room of the printing office before he was finally downed by Pedro, the press engineer.
>
> Badgers, according to Larrieu, should be fed sparingly, and exercised every morning. They should be kept in a dark place during the day time and not taken out until night. He stated that Colonel Puss Gray would make a good trainer of badgers,

the only objection being he is too fond of pets, and humors them too much.

Chief Bravin and Attorney W. G. Gilmore have been named on the committee to draw up a new set of rules to govern the game, and which will no doubt meet with the approval of the Society for the Prevention of Cruelty to Animals. If unsuccessful, an appeal will be made to the next territorial legislature to legalize badger fighting in Arizona. —Tombstone *Prospector*, 1907.

*The next badger fight of note took place in Tombstone two years later, according to a Prospector account in 1909:*

The Revenue Saloon was to be the site of this encounter, on Thursday night about an hour after the Murray and Mack show is out, as several of the male members of that company are to be especial guests on this eventful night. The badger is now being starved to get him into an ugly mood—it is said that forty-eight hours of starving always puts a badger into the best of fighting trim. The dog that will do the honors in this fight is that thoroughbred bull terrior, "Mike Walker," who is owned by John Walker and A. H. Gardner. A great deal of interest has already been manifested in the coming fight and money is being bet quite freely with the badger as the favorite. The Society for the Prevention of Cruelty to Animals stopped a badger fight up in Globe one night last week, but it is hardly thought that the feeling against badger fights is so strong in Tombstone as to call for interference on the part of our citizens or the police officers.

*The night of the fight at hand, the event proved to be one of the fiercest badger fights ever pulled off in Tombstone. The Prospector noted:*

It was intended that the bull terrior "Mike Walker" would be the champion in this fight, but as he could not be found at the seasonable hour, Mr. Gains consented to lend his dog "Doc" instead. "Doc" is a veteran in the ring and has killed more badgers than any other canine in Arizona. The badger was as fine a specimen of its kind as was ever captured in Arizona wilds, and had his fighting clothes on. E. W. Topping was master of ceremonies and was kept busy getting his bets placed. Those most eagerly backing the fight were George O. Wales, Al Stumpf, O. D. Walker, J. N. Gaines and several others in whose veins runs the blood of the true sport. About the time the betting began the entire male membership of the Murray and Mack show appeared on the scene and for a while excitement was at white heat. Chief of Police Bravin stepped in about this time and said that if bull fights could be pulled off in Old Mexico, that was no reason why badger fights might be baited in Arizona. Topping, the chief promoter, was put under arrest but was promptly bailed out by his friends, and it was then agreed upon that if the badger would be given a fair chance there would be no more trouble.

The badger was kept in the pen until this decision had been rendered and then was turned loose. George Stokes, of the Murray and Mack Company, was chosen as the man to do the honors and he fulfilled his part in a masterful manner. It was a good exhibition, and Tombstone will long remember it.

*The Prescott Journal-Miner reported this interesting skirmish in 1915:*

To the longest day of his life will Theodore Kleiner, a Prescott barber, remember the night he pulled a badger in Prescott before an assemblage of sports numbering fifty or more, and how narrowly he averted being thrown in jail for the pains he took as the central figure in one of the most vicious and dangerous undertakings connected with this most exciting sport of the Southwest.

The affair took place in the basement of the Dillon & Jones cigar store. "Mutt," the famous badger fighter of this section was again on hand, and notwithstanding his previous victories, Mr. Badger came within an ace of doing him up in this particular instance. In fact, so close was the contest that the dog had to be withdrawn and the fight called a draw, much to the discomfiture of the jolly bunch of sports who had wagered considerable amounts pro and con.

Kleiner made sure that he could not be bitten. He was aware of the fact that a badger of the vicious nature of the one which had been engaged in a number of the recent fights here was dangerous, and believed the well-known fact that badgers of this type are likely to be infected with hydrophobia because of constant harassing and many wounds received from the teeth of vicious canines. He stipulated that his limbs, hands and face, as much as possible, should be protected against danger, and to this end took his position well bandaged with towels, practically from head to foot. His courage served him well up to the propitious moment, when he fairly shook with tremors of fear, much as a man suffering from ague. It was thought for a few moments that he would be unable to compose himself after this ordeal, but much to his credit, he drew manfully on every inch of his latent courage, and by the time the word "go" was said he was in fairly good condition. It is a well-known fact that badgers of the kind kept for contests of this kind in Prescott jump at the first object they see after they emerge from the darkened barrel, hence the necessity of such great care in protecting the person who pulls the animal. It is also necessary to have someone pull the animal who has never performed such a feat before, because there is usually a large sum of money wagered on the fight and the "puller," if experienced, can perform the duty to the advantage of either side he may desire. Kleiner was familiar with all these facts, and had faithfully promised that he would do his level best to be impartial to all parties concerned. With all the precautions taken, however, he came within an ace of being wounded, and but for his dexterity when "Mutt" made his first lunge he would have been caught.

The hilarity of the occasion enabled the officers to lay for the crowd, and it was their intention to arrest those at the bottom of the fight. Patrolmen Baker and Rybon had been informed that Kleiner was mixed up in the deal and determined to arrest him as soon as he came out of the basement and "sweat" him in the jail for information that would lead to the arrest of others. They grabbed him as planned, and it was with great difficulty he escaped, declaring to his honor "as a barber and a man," that he was not the instigator of the affair and had only participated at the request of others who wanted a fair run for their money, and he promised never to pull another badger. All evidence of the fight had been smothered by the time the officers were able to gain admittance to the cellar and the matter was dropped.

One of the most cruel badger fights that has ever been pulled off in Prescott was that in which two Chinese were engaged, to the amusement and excitement of a large delegation of sports. In the absence of "Mutt," the champion badger-fighting dog in the country, and for the purpose of giving his opponents a run for their money, George C. Ruffner had two Chinese walk all the way from Williamson Valley to Prescott leading a dog they owned which they felt sure would best the vicious badger Ruffner had caged at his garage. And one of them pulled the badger while the other held the dog, while a number of their fellow-countrymen stood about with the crowd in excitement, wonderment and amazement. The outcome of the fight was anything but pleasing to the Chinese, and on the way back home one of them swore backwards for a number of miles, as a prelude to saying, "me no likee badger flight. Badger no good—dog velly better. Ruffner damn bad."

—Prescott *Journal-Miner*, 1915

# 10

## BLACK RIVER COUNTRY

In the Clifton Copper Era over the span of three years, 1902-05, there appeared periodically some very interesting letters written by C. H. Farnsworth, who was with the outfit of the Chiricahua Cattle Company (the CCC) in the Black River country. The writer tells of the country, the trials and tribulations of the cattle companies, good years and bad, expresses his concern over the welfare and treatment of the Apache Indians, upon whose reservations the white man's cattle grazed, and sets down many other notes of common interest on the facets of life in one of the most beautiful sections of Arizona.

January 23, 1902. Black River, "the home of the outlaw," and desire of the sportsman, is now enjoying peace and quiet that is unusual. The report of the outlaw's Winchester is no longer heard. Only the cry of the live eagle as he flies away in search of food, disturbs the ceaseless roar of the noted stream as it dashes on its way to join Salt River below.

Thanks to the Sheriff of Graham County, a man fearless in pur-

suit of duty. The too frequent visits of business-like-looking officers, carrying a Winchester in one hand and a frying pan in the
other, has caused the Smith boys to hunt more congenial climate.

[The Smith band of outlaws, according to an item in the Copper
Era in 1907, who often went into hiding in the Black River country
after their frequent forays across the line in New Mexico, had a
desperate fight here about the year 1901 with a posse from New
Mexico. Also, Bill Smith, the gang's leader, was wanted for being
implicated in the Holbrook train robbery in Arizona. He and his
two brothers were in retirement on the Blue when the New Mexico officers surprised them. A ranger named Defoya and a deputy
sheriff named Maxwell were killed, and George Smith, the young-
ster of the gang, was shot through the body and terribly wounded.
The outlaws escaped and were not apprehended. George finally
went into Morenci and voluntarily surrendered to the officers there.
No specific charge being found against him, he was released. He
told of the battle on the Blue and how his brother Bill did all the
fighting and repulsed the officers alone, and how, although he himself was badly wounded, he had wandered for weeks in the hills and
finally recovered without medical attention.]

The country is more free from would-be "bad men" and unde-
sirable persons than for years. No one is more glad to see a state of
affairs such as this, than the law-abiding men who have chosen this
section for their work. The last two officers that left our camp, left
in disgust, denouncing the fates that brought them up here on a
"wild goose chase."

The fact that one of them was painfully if not seriously wounded
while here, is a matter to be regretted. Not wounded by the bullet
of an evil, hunted "outlaw." But while in the stinging cold of
early morning opening the necessary negotiation for packing an
unruly mule, he had his favorite foot innocently, but nevertheless
heavily, walked upon and came limping painfully to the fire reciting
Sunday School lessons learned in boyhood and with an emphasis
that would have astonished his teacher.

Verily, "the way of the transgressor is hard," and in welcoming
the passing of the "bad man," let us all join in wishing a future
peace-harmony and a good will towards all men.

The recent capture of the renegade Apache from Fort Grant, surely relieves us from a feeling of uneasiness. We are now more free to stand our Winchesters against a tree, while we prepare our simple meal without fear of an Indian with a "bad heart" and a rifle, rising from behind some nearby rock and taking a shot that might give him free access to the camp. As he crossed the Gila, the Indian agent at San Carlos sent out warning that the renegade Indian was headed this way. But tired and foot-sore, he at last turned his steps to the San Carlos River and the camp of some of his "friends." Thinking himself among such he was induced to leave his rifle and partake of some food and whiskey set before him. A squaw was put on a swift pony and sent into San Carlos for the Indian police. When the latter arrived, said Indian had the good fortune to be feeling very happy and his heart was good from drink until the police were upon him in force. One more Apache with a bad heart and a thirst for blood out of the way for the time being at least.

Our range is very good; best for several years, notwithstanding the dry winter. The CCC ranch that has the government contract for beef at Fort Apache and San Carlos, is breaking records for fat cattle and weights.

*February 20, 1902.* Black River is the dividing line between the San Carlos and Fort Apache Indian reservations. For years the former has been opened for grazing purposes, but the latter has been closed to stockmen. But it is a matter of interest to many that, according to report, the Fort Apache reservation has been opened for leasing to cattlemen, thus furnishing a vast tract of grazing land that is hardly equalled in the Territory. . . .

While true that companies were unable to entirely suppress and must contend with more or less stealing and eating of beef by the Indians, the agent is ruling the Apaches with a firm hand, bringing them strictly to account for any and all depredations committed.

The CCC boys have in the last year caught several Indians stealing beef cattle, and have been the direct cause of a number of them paying a much longer visit to Yuma prison than would have been otherwise necessary. It seems that they are not overly pleased with the climate in that section, consequently, the San Carlos Apaches have a bitter hatred for the CCC cowboys.

The new agent at San Carlos is making progress in civilizing the Indians, that causes the half-clad old bucks to stare in wild-eyed astonishment. It will be only a short time until they will be a self-supporting tribe instead of the heavy drain on the government purse that they are now. It is reported that the time is near at hand, when the weekly issue of rations will be stopped. As it is they are issued rations, beef and clothing. The latter is worn by many, but some continue the old custom of selling, trading or giving the articles away at the first opportunity for much or little and remain satisfied with their attire that a more refined class would consider both insufficient and far from modest.

Comfortable houses are being built for them. They gaze at them in a natural disapproval and continue to live in their wickiups of grass and poles. They consider a house "bad medicine," "heap sick," and, surely, it is taking a great step when we try to tame their wild nature to the extent of putting them in a house, which deprives them of so much born freedom.

Farms are being laid out, neatly kept and worked along the San Carlos River, and a stranger passing through the country noting the neat improvements, the newly dug wells along the public road that are so refreshing to the dusty traveler, would hardly realize that he was in an Indian country, were it not for the fact that the work is all done by Indian labor with white superintendents.

The wild and blood-thirsty Apaches of old will soon be converted into law-abiding men, that must necessarily earn their bread by the sweat of the brow and equally take their chances in meeting the world unaided. The opportunity they have for an education at both San Carlos and Rice are such that many young people of the farther East would be glad to enjoy.

At the present writing we are experiencing a snow storm that many persons in Arizona might consider a novelty. We have eighteen inches of snow and still snowing. We are schooled to be thankful for small favors, and consider ourselves to be fortunate to be permitted to sit in our tent at night by a cheerful fire without interruption. Those of the boys who are with the outfit, and are now gathering beef for delivery in the forepart of February, are not so fortunate, and are experiencing hardships that will remind them of the home "fireside." . . .

Owing to the heavy snows higher up in the mountains, we expect to soon see Black River in a badly swollen condition and when so, with the boulders rolling along in the stream and the swift current, it is as dangerous a mountain stream as is usually encountered.

The last rise previous to this storm, will long be remembered by two of our men, Bascom and Snider. They were taking a small bunch of beef steers into Fort Apache, and on reaching the river, there was no choice but to swim the stream, steers, pack mule, bedding and all. All went nicely until Snider jumped the mule into the icy waters and attempted to spur his horse after. The stubborn animal would not swim, but sank under the water. Upon coming up he struck a large boulder with his fore feet, tried to gain the tip of the rock, slipped, and the swift current catching him, he was carried off down stream, rolling over like a log.

His rider more dead than alive with his heavy clothing and the horse rolling over him in the water, was barely able to keep his head above water. But Bascom at this period came to the rescue. With a skill that only practice and experience will obtain, he threw his rope at full length. Snider caught the noose and was drawn ashore, just as his horse struggled up the opposite bank farther down the river. This caused Bascom to again swim the cold waters, and after some difficulty in the gathering darkness, succeeded in cutting and forcing the animals this time to swim the stream. They had but a short distance to go to reach Pine corral and penned the steers for the night.

After building up a hot fire and drying themselves, they crawled supperless in between their half-wet blankets, thanking their stars that circumstances were no worse. But on crawling out in the cold of early dawn next morning their disgust could hardly be described when they discovered that the horse that caused so much trouble the night before had broken his stake rope and gone. We are still looking for the horse.

The remaining twelve miles were made next day by Bascom driving the steers and Snider following leading the discouraged pack-mule with his saddle tied to the top of the pack. Snider is very bitter in denouncing a man that would "punch cows" during the winter. We partly agree with him, that perhaps one's sanity is a little questionable when they might do otherwise. These cold mornings with feet wrapped up in sacks, overcoats on and other incumbrances that the custom of the country demands, we do not feel enthusiastic in mounting our cold horses that have been standing all night on a stake rope and in snow up to their knees. It not infrequently happens that they have an uncontrollable desire to test our horsemanship.

We are not in the least discouraged if thrown, but round up a little more courage not unmixed with a certain amount of confidence and mount again. While we make no pretentions of such, it is an established fact that we are not all riders in the true sense of the word. At one time I was an employee of the Arizona Copper Company store in Clifton, and remember hearing some of my friends confidently expressing their opinion as to successfully riding as they called a "bucking horse." Should they still have a desire for the experience in reality, we cordially invite them to pay us a visit at our camp, and we will unselfishly permit them the first saddle of several of our horses.

March 27, 1902. A considerable stir has been created in this section of the country by the effort of the department to raise the grazing tax on the San Carlos reservation to a dollar a head. Considering the losses, this is an exorbitant price compared to the former. It is reported that the Double Circle outfit is making preparations to move their cattle providing the tax is raised. But it is merely an unauthorized report and may not be true.

The CCC ranch has leased a considerable tract of grazing land north of Black River; have thrown one herd on that side and will put more over as soon as convenient. The company intends making quite a large shipment this spring, and if the government stops the issue of beef to the Indians, as are the intentions now, it will be only a very short time until the cowboys will find it necessary to seek other parts in order to follow their favorite but hard and trying occupation. The cowpuncher, even in Arizona, is fast becoming but a memory and should the CCC and the Double Circle both close out, it will deprive many an excitement-seeking young man of work.

Stockmen now are looking forward to the stopping of the Indians' beef with uneasiness. It is utterly impossible with the present means at hand, for the Apaches to support themselves on the reservation. There is but little grain to be had and even the Gila River is now being taxed to its utmost to furnish sufficient water to water the land already in cultivation, and should there fail to be a rise of the river, it will be impossible to grow the crops. Even the Apache Indian cannot be expected to permit starvation to enter his wickiup when there are thousands of cattle running at will over the mountains of the reservation. . . .

We start in a few days to San Carlos to work in that vicinity. Most of us agree with one of our best and noted riders (Smokey Bill) that Carlos is a favorite starting point for many persons desiring a trip to a climate that the men of the pulpit warn us to avoid. At any rate, it is a land of perpetual sunshine and dust storms and is a place dreaded by those that have enjoyed its advantages.

The government saw-mill erected thirty-five miles north of Carlos is again in operation. The whistle breaking the morning stillness and echoing through the pines has an unnatural sound when heard forty miles from the railroad. The able superintendent's wife, Mrs. J. H. Harris, is the only lady on the range and enjoys the distinction of being the first white woman to ride over the Apache Trail. This ride in itself gains her the respect of all the men on the range. A tired, hungry and dirty cowboy cannot be more welcome at home than he is at the home of this man and his wife. The CCC roundup will commence the middle of April. Owing to the lack of rain in the lower country known as Ash Flat, it will be hard work. Cattle are very poor on parts of the range and with the great scarcity of water and feed, a trying time will be experienced. But with about forty half-broken horses, we expect the monotony to be occasionally broken by a pitching horse.

*April 24, 1902.* The CCC roundup is well under way. Bronco riding has arrived with all its terrors. The boys are having an experience that will cause them to remember this work for a long time to come. Your correspondent in a spirit of "bronco busting" this morning offered to ride a horse of a very questionable character and name. Anyone that is in any way acquainted with my riding could easily guess the natural result. I was thrown and trampled upon.

The range under the mountain is very poor. Grass and water are both very short. The result will be quite a loss. The company intends throwing a great many cattle on Black River in May, where grass is abundant.

We are enjoying a great deal of night guard now and but little sleep. We consider ourselves fortunate to secure five hours of sleep out of the twenty-four. Our cook (Banjo Joe) is one that we look to as our only salvation. His cooking causes the boys to locate camp at a distance of a half mile and spur their tired horses into a gallop as they smilingly head away from the roundup. We expect to have a herd of steers of about three or four thousand head.

The San Carlos beef contract expires on July 1st. The result will be watched with great anxiety. As circumstances exist this year, it will be an injustice to the Apaches. They will not be able to make their usual crops on their few farms and with the stopping of both beef and rations, there is but one alternative. Some have a few cattle, but they sell and eat them faster than they increase. Quite a number of years ago the government placed a good stock of cattle on the Apache reservation, but the Indians knew nothing of running them and the government permitted them to handle them after their own fashion, with the result that they have hardly anything left.

[*The leases to white cattlemen on the Apache reservation were cancelled starting in 1924, and in 1937 the government re-established tribal cattle herds which have developed into the present registered herd. Through the purchase of high-quality registered bulls, the Apache project has been highly successful. Now the Apache reservation is one of the finest cattle ranges in Arizona, and, surprisingly, the Apaches have, through expert guidance, become expert cattlemen and maintain a handsome income from their herds.*]

*June 19, 1902.* As hot weather approaches our hearts go out to our less fortunate friends in Clifton. The cold spring water and the cool shade of the tall pines are a pleasant contrast to the glistening heat of the busy camp.

We believe that young turkey will be plentiful this year, as everything has been favorable for them. On May 20th we were blessed with quite a good rain in this vicinity, but the inch of snow that followed that night was hardly considered much. While the roundup was still in progress, a fire was started along the border of Black River (presumably by Indians). As it was damaging the range extensively, the Double Circle and the CCC boys joined forced and fought fires several days before it was put out.

The CCC ranch only got here and shipped two thousand head of steers. We were glad to see the work stop. Cattle were poor, horses poor, and the range in bad condition. The recent rain has made a vast improvement, however.

It was a tired and weary lot of cowboys that drove into Geronimo, amid a great cloud of alkali dust. The herd had been running all night and we had been unable to obtain scarcely any sleep, but the next night after the long freight train had taken out the last steer, the boys rounded up all the girls in the settlement and had a dance that discounted anything Graham County ever witnessed.

We were very glad to learn that Sheriff Jim Parks is again in the field for office and all in this vicinity are wishing him a successful campaign. That he has made as good, if not the best sheriff Graham County has ever had, is an admitted fact. Had this section of the country had such a man a few years back, the result would have been different. A man that will mount a horse and with his few followers ride unhesitatingly into the heart of the mountains to the retreat of a band of outlaws, such is the man we want and have at present. A man that comes in, takes his man, and is out before we know he has been in the locality and he comes without sending a messenger in advance or without the blare of trumpets. Such a man is Jim Parks, brave and considerate, but determined to do his duty as an officer. When we hear him praised by men whose hair has grown white with years in Arizona, we know that such praise is deserved and just.

*December 25, 1902.* After one of the driest and most discouraging years in a long time, we are experiencing a snow and rain storm

hat causes the stockmen to have a more hopeful view of the comng year. The fact that the Apache reservation was opened to lease
ast spring, thus permitting grazing on both reservations, and that
eed is excellent in the vicinity, has saved the Double Circle and
he CCC outfits heavy loss. The range bordering the Gila River
s in a very poor condition and stock in poor shape for the coming
vinter, and unless it be a most favorable one, the loss will be heavy.
3en Parks from Bonita has thrown two herds on Black River on
he line between the Double Circle and the CCC ranges, and
1opes by so doing to save many cattle, consequently Black River
vill be well populated this winter with cow camps.

A companion and I are stationed in a line camp north of the
iver. Recently we have been puzzled by some unknown person
1iding in the vicinity and coming into camp as soon as we leave
1nd helping himself to everything in the edible line. While we are
villing to share with anyone that may happen this way, it would
)e, to say the least, more companionable for them to call while we
re at home.

The Apaches are being treated in a manner this winter that
hould be most satisfactory to those who wish to see them put on
heir own resources. Twelve thousand dollars has been appropriated
)y the government to construct a wagon road from the sawmill
hirty-five miles north of San Carlos, on across Black River into
'ort Apache—a distance of forty miles. It is expected that two or
hree hundred Indians will be employed on this work. Besides this
oad work ditches are being made on both reservations, thus em
)loying a large number of Indians. . . .

As we sit in our small tent by a comfortable fire, and see the
arge white snowflakes falling outside, we experience a feeling of
)ity for the less fortunate boys who must pass the cold, wet day
n the saddle, and almost wish myself back in Clifton. By the beauiful advertising of the Bazaar Department store, we are reminded
hat Christmas is at hand again. We cannot enjoy our Christmas
n Clifton this year, but we extend a hearty invitation to any who
eel like passing Christmas on Black River to take dinner with us in
)ur comfortable little camp.

*April 22, 1903.* The warm days of spring have at last arrived.

The nights here in the mountains are still cold—ice freezing on the water during the night, but the days are warm and pleasant. We experienced a very cold but a wet, favorable winter, a winter that was the means of saving thousands of dollars in stock. The cattle are the fattest the writer has ever seen on the range at this season of the year. The range—with the green feed and flowers in bloom—has the appearance of a vast clover meadow. It is impossible to realize that a few months ago this same country was nothing but a barren waste, fit for only the coyote and buzzard.

The CCC will have an abundance of as good beef steers as the country affords. No better can be placed on the market. The roundup has been in progress a number of days. We will probably ship the herd from Geronimo about or near the 5th of May. As soon as the last train-load of cattle disappears around the hill up the Gila, the true, worn-out, but ever-ready, cowboys will commence the roundup of the settlement in the vicinity of Ft. Thomas and Geronimo, and if a sufficient number of young ladies can be secured, the last night in town will be celebrated with a dance at Geronimo, where the many cowboys are always so royally treated, instead of being wondered at and treated as though they were a fit specimen for the up-to-date scientist, or at least, a peculiar specimen of humanity.

The Indians tell me that the agent at Fort Apache is as far as possible disarming the Indians, and also intends prohibiting them killing any game for one year. As a sole means for a livelihood he hopes to provide them sufficient work to permit them to be able to buy all necessities—even giving them credit for the work done on their own farms. In this manner, they are encouraged to work, and dispense with the old system of issuing them free rations. The past winter they have been very troublesome; have killed much beef owned by cattlemen on the reservation. It is thought they will now be less bold on the range, and furnished sufficient employment, they will not be forced by hunger to steal and kill beef at large.

With game fast disappearing from the country on and off the reservation, the agent's effort to protect what remains of the game on the Indians' land is a move that should be approved and aided by the game wardens on the borders. It is an evident fact and plain to an observer that game is becoming less and less every passing year, and unless an awakening is made and the game laws of the Territory enforced, the deer and other game animals will soon be but a past sport in Arizona.

During my stay in Clifton two years ago last winter, I saw several wagon-loads of deer brought down the 'Frisco and sold unmolested, over the town. I think there was a law in effect at the time making this a penalty. But if there was a local game warden in the country, he took no notice of what was going on. I am speaking of the conditions that existed at that time to my personal knowledge. Since then I only know what transpires here on the borders and on the two reservations. I enjoy the sport with the Winchester as much as any man in Arizona, but could I but see an effort made on all sides to preserve the game, I would be among the first to lay down my rifle and aid such a movement. And I think I am expressing the sentiments of many men living in the country and surrounded by game, for I have heard good hunters and reliable men of the country complaining of the useless slaughter of deer and turkey.

In this part many have held the opinion that the Indians, the cowmen and the hunting parties were fast killing off the game and they were entitled to their share while it was going. This is a very practical and material view of the matter, but if the Indian is not allowed to kill game on his own land then it would be an injustice to permit white men to come in and do so. Consequently we hope to see the laws enforced here this year, at least more rigidly than usual. And if all the game wardens would enforce them in their localities, making it very expensive for all violations, something would be accomplished. . . .

*April 9, 1905.* We have not noticed items from our section in our Clifton paper for a number of months, and as we are desirous that our friends should know that Black River is still hurrying down towards Salt River, and that if the season continues as it has for three months past, we will in time have water enough in our vicinity to justify a man slipping a line in his pocket when he heads this way later in the season. So much rain and snow has not been experienced in the history of the country. Cattle and horses have not wintered as well as might have been expected on account of so much bad weather and the ground being so boggy, but if we can

only have nice weather now, stock will soon fatten on the fast growing feed.

On the first of this month the country known as Ash Flat, was
visited by a hard rain, followed by ten inches of snow. The CCC
outfit was compelled to gather the government beef issue for San
Carlos. The general makeup of the Apache necessitates beef, rain
or shine, consequently we went plowing over the flat gathering
steers, while our horses went most to their knees at every step and
the glare of the sun on the white snow was enough to make the
angels weep. It was no unusual sight to see a cowboy start to head
off a bunch of cattle; his horse would bog down and then the
good-humored puncher would head the steers on foot. Everything
passed off as a joke and the air was often blue with brimstone,
caused from much carefully chosen language. But this was merely
because it was considered that the occasion demanded something
in this line, not that any harm was intended at all. There are times
when the most up-to-date language will hardly suit the occasion,
and while, unlike the cowboys, the CCC men usually keep a copy
of the ten commandments hanging in their tent and all effort is
made to abide by them. We should be excused of a spring like
this as we sometimes wander from their teachings.

Hundreds of San Carlos Apaches have been furnished work by
washouts on the Globe railroad this winter, six hundred of them
being employed at one time. Doubtless this fact would look discouraging to those that insist that the Indian will not work. A
close observer cannot fail to see that the Apache is usually glad
to accept work, thereby earning money to buy the luxuries so dear
to even an Indian's heart.

*From the letters quoted above we get a quite different and a truer
picture of the working cowboy and his way of life. This real cowboy is in sharp contrast to the characters that have been referred to
as "cowboys" in many of the stories in this volume. In the old,
turbulent days it became customary to lump men of very various
occupations together in one category—fellows engaged in the
respectible business of herding and driving cattle were classed with
cattle thieves, horse thieves, stagecoach robbers, and suchlike lawless elements.*

Some of the early newspapers even included cattlemen and ranchmen in this all-inclusive classification. This careless nomenclature did a lot of damage, giving a false impression to the general public and even leading to fearsome consequences.

## LAY OF THE COWBOY

Oh, I am a cowboy, of legend and story,
Whom the back eastern youngsters so admire.
The slaughter of pilgrims is ever my glory,
And few have escaped when they drew out my fire.

On the deck of my bronco, I skim o'er the prairie,
A terror to all who my daring behold.
I defy any civilized constabulary,
And all vigilantes the country can hold.

As proud as the proud soaring bird of the ocean,
I speed on my way over valley and plain,
And no man dare make the least treacherous motion,
That he lives for a minute to do it again.

The joys of existence I don't claim forever;
Some day I must missle, like other galoots,
But the Old Boy will have to be devilish clever,
If he gets me laid out while I stand in my boots.

When I'm roped, at the roundup of judgement eternal,
And corraled in a furnace, forever to dwell,
I'll be able to teach them some capers infernal;
I won't be a tenderfoot, even in h——l.

Written for the Prescott *Journal-Miner*, 1888

# 11

## INDIAN WAYS

### THE MYSTERY OF THE MOQUIS

*The Moqui, in latter years called Hopi [Hoe-pee], meaning "peaceful ones," are a most fascinating tribe of Arizona Indians, numbering more than four thousand. They live in several villages perched on the tops and slopes of three high mesas in northern Arizona, where their ancestors before them have lived for many generations.*

*The noted ethnologist, Dr. J. Walter Fewkes, who died in 1930 after spending a great deal of his life among the various Indian tribes, furnished the information for the following account of the Moquis which appeared in the San Francisco Call and was reprinted in the Phoenix Republican in 1899:*

A white man has at last witnessed the secret rites of the fire worshippers of America. He accomplished this after years of unremitting effort to convince these people of his friendliness. It was not, however, until he entered the Moqui priesthood that he was successful. The fortunate man is J. Walter Fewkes, who has done more toward supplying the connecting links between ancient and modern Indians than any other man. His work along these lines has made him famous the world over.

The Moqui Indians are the sole representatives of what their sort of Indian was in past centuries. They are almost the same today as when Coronado's men found them early in the sixteenth century. In the village where Fewkes lived, Walpi [Wal-pee], the houses are centuries old, located on the brow of the cliff hundreds of feet above a great plain, and are not one jot different from the dwellings that have occupied that site for perhaps a thousand years. The scientist lived among the Indians as one of them, and in this isolation from the white folks has been alone, except during the latter years of his investigation when Mrs. Fewkes accompanied him, the first white woman ever looked on with favor by the Moqui race.

The customs of their neighbors, the Apaches, as well as those of the other Indian tribes with whom people are familiar, are utterly unlike the ways and habits of the Moqui. In the '80s when the white men of science first visited them, they were still using stone implements, and, in fact, living in just the way that we are taught the Indians lived when Columbus made his entrance on the scene.

While history is unable to give any information of the Moquis before the advent of Coronado's men, investigation of the graves made by Dr. Fewkes furnishes conclusive proofs that the symbols of the tribes were as ancient in the sixteenth century as they are regarded by the Moquis of today.

While Dr. Fewkes had no difficulty in witnessing a number of the Moqui ceremonies, he was well aware that there were very interesting secrets in connection with the religious rites of the Indians of which he was entirely ignorant. Every effort he made to learn was checkmated, and he found that as an outsider he was at the end of his invesigation.

"I saw," he said, when telling me the result of his investigations, "that it was through the priesthood I must get at the facts. The Moquis were distinctly fire worshippers, though unlike any other of the fire worshipping sect of which I ever heard. They created their sacred fire—this I knew—but how it was all done was beyond me. It took a very long time, and the utmost care, to convince the Indians that I meant only good and that I did not want to use the information I gained to their disadvantage. At last I brought them to a frame of mind where they agreed that I should enter their priesthood and be initiated into the secrets of their underground temples, for the more important features of the Moqui ritual are performed in these caves.

"It was in one of these temples that I witnessed what to me was as interesting a thing as could be seen, of all the more interest because I knew that I was the first white man whom the Moquis had ever permitted to be present on such an occasion. To the Moqui, fire is a living breathing thing. Its creation is to him exactly the same as the birth of a child. It is a sacred creation, however, and the Indian pays to the flame as great a tribute as he can conceive of—no one is permitted to light either pipe or cigarette from it. And when you stop to think that with the Indian all things begin and end with a smoke you see the significance of his action.

"The ritual observed in the creation of the fire is so simple that it is impressive. The members of the priesthood present gather in a semicircle in front of the altar, and the priest upon whom falls the duty of bringing the fire into being takes a notched piece of wood and in that notch places a stick which nearly fills it. This stick he rapidly rotates. Directly beneath the earth has been covered with shredded cedar. A hush that is impressive follows, nothing being heard except the grinding noise made by the two pieces of wood. The friction of the wood is continued for not more than a minute when a spark falls upon the cedar, and then another. The blaze is instantly nursed and presently is of sufficient size to permit a torch to be lighted from it. The sacred fire has come into being.

"Then one of the priests is selected to carry the fire and the news from house to house. In every dwelling the squaws are waiting for him, the pile of fuel is ready and he lights it with his torch. The proceeding is the same in every dwelling, and after a while every house in the village has its flame, which will not be allowed to die out until summer comes. That is all that happens the day of the fire's creation, but the day following is celebrated with processions and incantations of various sorts, of a nature which does not permit of description. It is all along the line of the Indians' idea of the resemblance of the birth of fire to that of a human being.

"The ceremonies do not, I think, have the same weight with the younger generation of Indians that they do with the elders. In fact, I am inclined to believe that the younger element would willingly break away from this sort of thing if it could. This ceremony of the fire creation seemed all the more interesting to me because it is an undeniable fact that the rites I saw in the caves have never before been witnessed by a white man.

"The Moqui priesthood is made up of a number of different degrees and I succeeded in being admitted to four of the priesthoods. Further progress was refused me by the older priests on the ground that they did not think I could stand the ordeal. I rather doubt the truth of that statement, because I do not think the ordeal was very severe, judging from what I had already endured. As it is, however, I was enabled through my membership of the priesthood to gain a knowledge of the aboriginal rites that has hitherto been unknown to history. I know of no more interesting than that of the creation of fire. . . .

"By nature the Moquis are a peaceful people. They are short of stature and slight. At first they clung very closely to the customs of their ancestors and resented the first attempt made to introduce the white man's among them. I remember when I first visited them years ago, just after it had been decided to try to educate them, a young lieutenant of cavalry with six men rode over to my camp from the railroad to get some information about the Moquis. He was on his way to another village, a larger one, where he proposed to enforce the government order that some of the Indian children be sent to an Indian school, a building for which had been erected fifteen miles distant. The lieutenant wanted me to go with him, but I refused, because it would have been fatal to my plan to learn the Indian rites.

"The cavalrymen camped with me that night, and the next morning rode over to the other village. That afternoon they returned, but without any children. The lieutenant said that when he reached the village he found every inhabitant armed and saw that if he attempted any force he and his soldiers would be wiped out. He said he was going back to the railroad and telegraph for four companies of cavalry to come to his assistance. The Indians, he said, would be made to give up their children.

"The day went by and all sorts of rumors began to circulate as to what was going to happen. I had learned the Indian language fairly well, and the old chiefs told me that over at the other village they believed the whole United States army, whatever that was, was coming. A few days later I noticed a commotion among the Indians and saw away out on the prairie a long line of blue marching in our direction. It proved to be the four companies of regulars, headed by Major, now Adjutant-General, Corbin. The troops went into camp on the mesa below the cliff where the obstinate villagers lived. I camped with them, and the next morning Major Corbin sent a message up to the Indians to send down six of their chiefs for a parley.

"After a while the chiefs came down and were very meek indeed. After a bit the colonel ordered an advance, and we marched up to the village. What was our amazement but to find the village deserted. There was not an Indian in sight. But at last one of our prisoners told us that they were out on the point—that is, a point of land stretching out north away from the village and out of sight of the dwellings. We followed this up and found it to be true. There they were, huddled together, 800 men, women and children, expecting to be killed, I suppose. They had no idea there were so many white men in the world, and were simply terrified at the thought that Washington—for to the Indian every government official and the government is Washington—had come out in such array against them.

"Major Corbin talked to them and explained how impossible it was for them to resist Washington and how their children were going to be educated whether they wanted them to be or not. Just to emphasize his words about the power of the soldiers, the major ordered one of the two mountain howitzers discharged. Now those howitzers carried a very ugly little shell about a mile out on the mesa, where it tore the sand up and dug a big hole. The Indians were almost paralyzed with fright, except one of the chiefs whom the troops were holding as hostage. At the report of the gun he went over the side of the cliff, which must have been at least twenty feet high, as if he had been shot, and though the troops fired in the direction he had gone and hunted for him, we never saw him again.

"After parleying a while longer, Major Corbin induced the chiefs to select a number of children to be sent to the school, smoked the pipe of peace with the head men, and led his troops back to the railroad, taking the young Indians with him. That was the end of the Moqui attempt to resist 'Washington's' idea of education."

*Regarding the names Hopi and Moqui, the Tucson Star reprinted the following from the* Craftsman *in 1906:*

To those few in the outer world who ever heard of them at all they are mostly known as Moquis—this through the publicity gained by their annual Snake Dance. But Moqui or Moki is a misnomer. Hopi is how they would have us know them—because it is right and because it means something to them and it is justly symbolical of their racial characteristics. Peaceful—gentle is its significance—and the worst word they know to apply to an offender is ka-hopi—negative of Hopi—or pas-ka-hopi, the superlative of this; and any one as bad as this is hopeless.

Moki in their language means dead, and the accepted theory of its first application to them as a tribal name is that the Navajo, their long time enemy, in a spirit of derision so called them on account of their distaste for warfare and love of quiet, stay at home life. According to the Navajo code, they were "dead ones." From the Navajo whose country entirely surrounds the Hopi, the early traders and settlers acquired the word Moki before ever seeing the Hopi; and from the trader it easily passed without question to the government representatives, so it now stands as the official appellation in the Indian department. But ask a Hopi if he is a Moqui— his quick resentment will be convincing enough.

## NAVAJO SWEAT BATHS

*The vast Navajo nation in northern Arizona completely surrounds the reservation of the Hopi. This largest of all tribes, whose lands* extend into New Mexico and Utah, has a population of more than seventy thousand.

The Navajo, or Navaho, call themselves diné, "the people," and are among Arizona's more colorful Indians. The following article, written by Cosmos Mindeleff for the Commercial Advertiser, appeared in the Phoenix Republican in 1899. Considering the great scarcity of water in that region, parts of the following article which may sound a bit facetious were perhaps more to the point than otherwise:

The American Indian, be his tribe what it may, has no great fondness for water taken internally, and no use at all for it as an external application. One or two quarts of water will carry a family through a day, and even in the arid regions of Arizona and New Mexico, where the atmosphere takes up moisture from the body before it reaches the surface of the skin, the per capita of water used is small. Perhaps the scarcity of that fluid has something to do with the wonderful economy in its use which prevails, for it is almost never applied to the body, with the single exception that no Indian will lose an opportunity to wash his long, glossy black hair. Of their hair they are as proud as any woman, and devote much time and attention to its proper care, even sacrificing a small quantity of the precious water now and then for that purpose. Two quarts, with the bruised roots of the yucca, or soap weed, are all that is necessary for this purpose.

As might be expected under these conditions the tribes are periodically visited by dreadful epidemics of smallpox, which often decimate them. Although the Indian population of the southwest increases steadily from year to year, once in a decade or so this plague cuts down so many that taken over any considerable period of time each tribe shows a decrease in numbers. This is the burden which the Indian has taken from the white man, although the latter did not free himself from it when he passed it over. But aside from the great epidemics which carry off hundreds and even thousands there is much illness prevalent among the Indians, and oddly enough the great and universal remedy in the Indian mind for all ills of the flesh and many of the spirit is a bath. Not a water bath as we use the word, but an operation something on the order of a Turkish bath, with the water omitted.

It should be said in the first place that cause and effect, as we use the term and apply it to natural phenomena, are absolutely incomprehensible to the Indian mind. He can form no conception of medicine, for example, which even remotely resembles ours. To his mind all diseases and disorders are the work of evil spirits, and the remedy is to exorcise those spirits and, if possible, induce them to pass into some substance, such as a magic stone, where they will be under the control of the medicine man, who is, in fact, the priest, for he merely sings over his patient and never thinks of giving him anything but prayers. Even in the case of a person bitten by a rattlesnake the palpable cause of injury is entirely over-looked, and resort is had to songs and prayers, until the patient dies. In that case, death is attributed to his own evil spirit or to the lack of skill on the part of the priest singers, never to the poison of the serpent.

While this aspect of the Indian mind is universal, nowhere is it better exhibited than on the Navajo reservation. Many parts of that region in northern Arizona have never been visited by a white man and, indeed, the children of some of the older chiefs, who stay away from the agency, as a matter of principle, have never seen an "American," and their families have little intercourse with each other, each living by itself and, as it were, on its own ground. Thus many of the ancient customs and rites can still be found in their aboriginal forms, not at all modified by the influence of the white man. Among these rites none is of greater importance than the bath, which is in effect a religious ceremony, undertaken for the purpose of driving away some evil spirit which has taken posses-sion of the patient and produced the phenomena we call disease.

The Navajos live in rude, earth-covered huts scattered widely throughout the reservation and never grouped into villages. Rude as the huts appear, however, they are always built strictly according to rule and the building is followed by an elaborate religious cere-mony by which the house is dedicated. Each timber in it must be laid in a certain way and in a prescribed order, and finally a door-way is added not unlike the dormer windows of our houses. This is the home proper, but all over the reservation there are hundreds of little structures which are miniature models, as it were, of the houses, except that they lack the projecting doorway. These miniature huts, scarcely as high as a man's hip, look like children's play houses, but they occupy an important place in the Navajo system, for they are the sweat houses or bath houses and are the main reliance of those people against sorcery and disease. Each of these structures is designed to hold but one person at a time, and he must crawl in and squat upon his heels, with his knees drawn up to his chin.

In the construction of the sweat houses the same procedure is followed as in the building of a home hut, each timber in the latter having its counterpart in shape and function in the miniature structure, and, like the home hut, the doorway is invariably placed to face the east. When the framework is in place enough bark and earth is laid to make the structure practically air tight when the entrance is closed. When the place is to be used, a fire is made close beside it, and in this fire numerous stones are heated. The subject to be treated is then stripped naked and placed inside. The hot stones are rolled in beside him and the entrance is closed with several blankets, forming, in fact, a hot air bath. In a short time the patient sweats profusely, and he is then removed to rub himself dry with sand, or if he is too ill and weak to do this himself, his friends do it for him.

During the Yebichai dance, perhaps the most important of all the Navajo's religious ceremonies, four bath houses are set around a large structure known as the song house, about forty yards distant from it, one at each cardinal point. The chief medicine man sweats the patient, who may be physically well but bewitched, in these houses on four successive mornings just at dawn, beginning with the one on east. That one is merely an uncovered frame and after the patient has entered and hot stones have been rolled in, it is covered with many blankets and a large bucksin is spread over all. On this skin the medicine man sprinkles iron ochres and other colored sands in many-colored bands, symbolical of the rainbow and sunbeams which covered an early mythical structure. He and his assistants stand near the hut shaking rattles and singing a song to the god of the under world, at the conclusion of which the patient is released, to be subjected to the same ordeal in the other huts on successive days.

The initial spark of the fire used in these ceremonies and for all religious purposes is obtained by friction, and is regarded as essentially different from fire produced by flint and steel, or otherwise. . . . Smoke is produced in less than a minute, and finally, in perhaps two minutes, little sparks drop on the pile of dry powder, which takes fire from them. By careful fostering and feeding with bits of bark and grass, with much blowing a blaze is produced. This procedure must be followed each time a bath house is used, for the fire must be perfectly pure and straight from the under world. After a while the hut becomes impregnated with the evil influences which have been extracted from those who used it, and thereafter becomes taboo, or bad medicine, a thing to be shunned on peril of death.

The Navajos, like the other Indian tribes, have an elaborate mythological system which explains everything, past, present and to come, for to the Indian mind there is no such thing as an unknown. According to the legend two famous brothers, the great heroes in all the Navajo folk tales, were sent to the Sun by the goddess of the East, the beneficent deity from whom most of the good things in this world emanate. It is in order to be open to her influence that the huts of these people are always faced to the rising sun. When the twins reached the house of the Sun they called him father, as they had been instructed to do; but the Sun disowned them and subjected them to many ordeals and even thrust at them with a spear; but the goddess had given each of the youths a magic feather mantle impervious to any weapon. The night-bearer —the moon—also scoffed at them and filled the mind of the Sun with doubts, so he determined to subject the brothers to a further test.

He made four bath houses, but instead of using wood in their construction he made them of a metallic substance like iron, and placing them at the cardinal points he sent the moon to make a fire in each of them. This fire was obtained from the "burning stars," the comets, and the huts were made exceedingly hot. The brothers were placed in them successively, but so far from being harmed they came out of the last one stronger and more vigorous than ever. Then the Sun acknowledged them as his sons and gave the elder one some magic weapons with which he destroyed the evil genii who infested the Navajo land. This is the reason, the

Navajos say, why the bath huts drive out evil spirits and give a man renewed strength.

# HOW A GOOD INDIAN WENT

*The Colorado River Indians consist of several tribes, one of which is the Yuma, who live on a reservation just west of the town that bears their name, although some of them live on the Arizona side of the river. They call themselves Kwichán, or as roughly pronounced by the whites, Cuchans, and by this name they were often referred to in the early newspapers. The following story appeared in the Yuma Sun in 1898:*

Great was the mourning in the tribe of the Cuchans, for fearless and handsome Aih-Kune, the beloved of his mother and second son of Spah-go-tear, the Eagle, was no more.

Not alone was the grief of the dusky tribesmen and tribeswomen so great because of the fact that Aih-Kune was bold and favored in face and form, but Spah-go-tear, his father, was an ex-chief of the Cuchans, and still the recognized leader of the powerful element which has little regard for the teachings of the noble Sisters of Mercy and the patient, plodding "padre." Besides, Aih-Kune had traveled and seen strange sights, the describing of which, embellished as only a Cuchan can, had filled his less favored friends and relatives with wonderment approaching to awe, and in the eyes of old and young, male and female, Aih-Kune was a hero indeed.

True, Aih-Kune's travels were not the conception of his own mind, for the year before he had slain a medicine man, in accordance with the olden-time custom of his tribe, for losing too many patients, and the pale-face authorities, probably out of jealousy for the originators of this wise provision, had taken Aih-Kune, in company with a companion—companion in the chase and the sports of the people as well as in the alleged offense—to San Quentin, California's penitentiary. But this punishment, which, in the eyes of the white men, is deemed a disgrace, rendered these men no less than martyrs in the eyes of their people. They were not kept in close confinement, for the white man still has some humanity in his soul, and the keepers of the institution realized that, deprived entirely of their liberty, these dusky sons of the desert would soon have pined and fretted their lives away, even as a bird will beat its life out flapping against the bars of its cage. So Aih-Kune and his companion were moved from place to place, working everywhere, for they were sentenced to hard labor. This is how they came to see the sights they saw, to them wonderfully magnified by their limited knowledge of such things, and again multiplied in the telling when they were released and returned to the tribe from which they were taken.

So it came about that when Aih-Kune died, not alone the heartbroken father and mother—for Indian fathers and mothers can love as well as others—and brothers and sisters mourned his departure, but the patriarchs who heard from his lips such tales as all their hundred years had never before brought them, the companions who gained from his reports of the wonderful lands he had visited a great and unquenchable desire to see something of the wide world for themselves, the children who hung on every word that fell from the lips of this great man of their own kind whom they had never seen before, and the black-eyed maidens who courted his glances, found consolation in unrestrained grief.

Hence it was that the whole of the long night through the Cuchans near at hand their watchful vigils kept, over all that remained of brave Aih-Kune.

Embalmed in mud, robed in a winding sheet of flaming red, his cold, stiff form measured its length in front of Spah-go-tear's pretentious Indian cabin, while hundreds of mourners surrounded the corpse and the vaunted stoicism of the red man was swallowed up in the most unearthly and most heart-rendering lamentations that can be conceived. The Cuchans have many orators, and while one well acquainted with the dead hero, stationed at the head of the lifeless form which occasioned this solemn ceremony, was relating, in impressive tones, incidents of Aih-Kune's courage, and exhorting the young men of the tribe to do likewise, Hi-pah-pan-yah, Aih-Kune's mother, was pouring out her grief at her dead son's feet, as if her heartstrings would break.

By the dim light of a few flickering fires, ghostly forms might be seen flitting to and fro. The funeral pyre, in the flames of which Aih-Kune's spirit was to ascend to the heights from which he might view the world and go where he listeth, according to the Cuchan belief, was being built. Up and down the valley in which the Cuchans dwell fleet couriers carried the sad news of Aih-Kune's death, that all who cared might hasten to do his memory honor.

And thus, at the break of dawn, as a faint breeze wafted the sound of a mighty grieving through the woodland and over the river, Unya-mem-sah-kia, high in the tribe, and bosom friend of the dead man's father, exhorted his hearers to imitate and emulate the virtues of the dead.

"As yonder sun climbs the hills and floods the valleys, and none may stay it, so will Aih-Kune, in the spirit, sit enthroned on the highest peak, and his eyes will pierce to your very soul, and the coward will be abashed."

For an hour the orator continued, and strong men wept, while the comely matron dried her infant's eyes with strands of long, black, glistening hair. Then, of a sudden, all was silent, and as the mourners surrounding the body gave way, twenty stalwart braves with dejected miens and sorrowful countenances, came forth from —where! the pale-faced witness could not tell—and grouped around their dead comrade, cried aloud in their grief, while old women in the rear, chanting Cuchan requiems to the departed, passed from one to another of the friends and relatives of Aih-Kune, touching each other on the head or shoulder and muttering a blessing.

Then began the funeral procession, Aih-Kune's last journey on earth. Strong arms lifted the body, and with measured tread these desert people turned toward the funeral pyre, while shrill and still shriller shrieks rent the air.

On the pile of wood, built hollow in the middle, the Indian who had seen strange lands was placed face downward, while more wood was placed upon him. The torch was applied, and as the flames shot up into the air the circle around the pile widened and widened, and the cries of the mourners grew louder and louder.

Then came forth Hi-pah-pan-yah, the mother, and Ah-koy-pan-yah, the aged aunt of Aih-Kune, and with loud cries to the Great Spirit, the dead man's clothing was consigned to the flames. It was the signal for a sacrifice, and the doffing of articles of attire by men, women and children speedily developed into an epidemic which bade fair to render nude the multitude assembled.

Within the circle, near the head of the pile wafting into nothingness the mortal remains of Aih-Kune, an orator stationed himself, and eloquent pleading fell from his bronzed lips. Another and another took his place and each had something new to tell of the excellence of Aih-Kune. Again and again is the pile replenished, but fainter and fainter grow the moanings and mournings of those composing the circle.

The sun is high in the heavens. Under the shade of a mesquite bush a young squaw is regaling her wretchedly dirty infant with a half-ripe watermelon; a patriarch of the tribe, flat on his back, is drowned in slumber under a near-by pole shade, while a solitary pale-face sits on a woefully uncertain fence gazing without seeing at a small pile of ashes that marks the last resting place of a true son of the desert.

The name of Aih-Kune will be heard among the Cuchans no more.

The Wallapai, or Hualpai, another tribe of the Yuman family, live on a reservation south of the Grand Canyon. They are a small tribe, numbering about four hundred, and like the other Colorado River Indians, they practiced cremation of the dead.

In 1891 the Phoenix Herald carried the following item, which had been reprinted from the Mohave County Miner, published at Kingman, a few miles southwest of the reservation:

The first funeral rite ever performed by the Wallapais after the American fashion took place Friday. One of the several squaws of Wallapai Charley's harem passed over the silent river Tuesday night, and couriers were sent out to notify all the relatives of the deceased, and active preparations were at once made for the funeral. Horses were gathered and the funeral pyre prepared. But Charley had been converted to the usage and custom of his white brethren and concluded he had other uses for his ponies and blankets than offering them as a sacrifice and ordered a grave dug and the body consigned to the silent tomb on the hillside, where the cactus blows and the coyote will howl a requiem over the grave of the first of the tribe to be placed in the sod.

*The Tucson Star printed this item concerning the Yuman crema-tion rites in 1910:*

Religious rites of the Yuma Indians which have been in force for many generations will be broken up within a few weeks by govern-ment agents. One of the particularly weird rites to which the gov-ernment strongly objects is that observed at midnight after the death of a member of the tribe. This rite is considered most essen-tial by the Indians, and it is believed that it will be abolished only after a struggle. It consists of the burning of the deceased's hut, his barn and all personal property. The belief of the tribe that the property so destroyed by fire again takes shape in the happy hunt-ing grounds to be enjoyed there by the departed while he awaits the coming of loved ones. The Indians believe also that such fires insure the speedy progress of deceased towards attainment of peace of soul.

The order to abolish these rites was received from the Indian office of the Department of the Interior. Should the Indians refuse to recognize the order of the department at Washington and per-sist in observing the weird ceremony they will be prosecuted under the federal statute for the crime of arson.

Settlers in the vicinity of the Yuma Indian reservation, accord-ing to government officials there, fear an outbreak among the tribes, which are perhaps the most uncivilized and warlike Indians occupy-ing government reservations. This fear arises from the fact that the religious rites objected to by the government have been estab-lished and observed by the tribes for so long that they believe that the Indians will not relinquish their ancient customs without a struggle.

*In commenting editorially on the recent government edict to the Yuma Indians, the Star made these remarks in a later edition in 1910:*

True, both the Roman Catholic and Methodist denominations maintain missions on the reservation, but they are carried on in a desultory sort of a way that probably does not mean a genuine conversion in a decade. That the Indians should be allowed to continue to burn their dead goes without saying. It is a clean, healthful way of disposing of them. But that in 1910 they should use the same pagan rites they were using when they first saw the cross about forty-five years after the discovery of America, is an enigma to the average layman. These said rites include the destruction by fire of all the property of which the deceased dies possessed. Often times this is a wanton waste of useful material, and entails poverty on the immediate family. This the government should sternly forbid; the rest of it is up to the church. But as one form is apparently as effective as the other, the present generation and probably the next will be found worshiping the God of their forefathers.

They have an abiding faith in a Supreme Being, in a life apart from the present. This is demonstrated not only around the funeral pyre, but at the corn festival. This festival is a great religious ceremony and involves enormous destruction of property. Occasionally circumstances will not permit the festival to be held, but when it is, all the intervening time is cared for, and those that have died in the interim receive due recognition. Figures representing the dead are made of inflammable material and these figures are dressed according to the means of their living relatives. Everything that money can buy or fancy dictate is placed upon them and at a given signal the great ramada or brush house in which they are placed is burned to ashes. It is this destruction of property the government should interdict.

At funerals when bodies are being burned the same waste of material takes place. Trunks filled with clothing and all the finery they can buy are heaped on the burning corpse. Blankets and silks go the common way. This is done in the belief of a future life, and friends and relatives of other dead take this means of sending food, clothing and ornaments to their dear departed. In the same spirit houses are burned and stock killed. Among the Yuma Mohaves the latter custom is believed to be in vogue today. A few years ago a stallion was invariably killed over the grave, and the flesh roasted and eaten. The word grave may be taken literally. A hole is dug about two feet wide and four feet long and over this grave the funeral pyre is built. This consists of dry poles about eight feet long and from six to ten inches thick, placed about three deep, and on these the corpse is laid, face down. Two green stakes are planted near the head of the grave, and two on each side for the purpose of keeping the wood in place. Dry logs, about three to four deep, are then placed on the body and the fires started. This is done by a line of inflammable material placed entirely around the pile. It is fired with a torch in several places as the man with the brand walks round it. As the flames shoot up wailings and lamentations are heard on every side. All the old people gather about the fire, usually the women on one side, the men on the other. Old people, smoke-dried and blear-eyed, keep up a crooning, monotonous wail, but, oddly enough, the men do the crying. The orator, and at night one is always present, is generally a loud, clear-toned man. In a voice that can be heard far he tells of the virtues of the deceased and of future expectations.

With each statement the crying men burst out afresh with supposed grief. To be selected as a mourner is an honor that is much sought. These and similar ceremonies are sometimes kept up for two or three days, according to the rank and standing of the deceased. When the funeral pyre has been consumed the ashes and all that remain of the decedent fall into the pit and are covered over. In the destruction of small bodies everything is consumed by the excessively hot fire, but when the dead is large the extremities burn off first and the heavy trunk frequently needs an extra supply of fuel. As Indians are frequently subject to contagious disease this burning of their dead should be encouraged and continued, but the destruction of uncontaminated property should be prevented by the government.

*Most of the Mohave tribe, another Yuman group, live on the Colorado River reservation near Parker, although some of them live on the other side of the river near Needles. The* Mohave County Miner *reported this incident in 1897:*

While driving about a mile north of Needles last Monday the *Miner* editor and party witnessed a rather novel sight. Two Mohave squaws stood in the road holding an excited conversation. The cause of the excitement was a big rattler. One of the party jumped from the wagon and killed the snake with a long-handled shovel. As soon as the reptile was dead the squaws began to disrobe and with many incantations would throw each article of apparel to the snake. When they had got to a point where there was little else for them to offer his snakeship they would raise their beaded necklace, let it slip through their fingers and go through the motions of throwing it with the balance of their togs. When the weird incantation was gone through with the squaws donned the discarded clothing and went on their way rejoicing.

Mohaves believe that if a rattlesnake is killed it portends the death of a big chief and the squaws worked a spell to propitiate the gods and keep the avenger away from their immediate relations. Two squaws clothed in a bead necklace and sandals making offering to the big snake god is a sight that would make even the editor of our contemporary blush.

# INDEX